Contents

Map of the units

Unit title	Reading and Use of English	Writing	Listening
1 A family affair	Part 6: 'Surviving teenagers' Part 2: 'Doing the chores'	Part 1 An essay: Teenagers and young people should share housework equally with their parents. Do you agree? Expressing opinions Using *although, however, on the other hand* and *whereas*	Part 1: Young people talking about their families and activities
2 Leisure and pleasure	Part 5: 'My first bike' Part 4: Key word transformation	Part 2 An article: A leisure-time activity you really enjoy Writing compound and complex sentences	Part 2: A talk from a games developer
Vocabulary and grammar reviews Units 1 and 2			
3 Happy holidays?	Part 3: 'A bus journey' Part 7: 'My nightmare holiday!'	Part 2 A report: A one-day excursion	Part 3: Five young people talking about their holidays
4 Food, glorious food	Part 6: 'Learning about food' Part 1: 'Moso Moso' – a restaurant review	Part 2 A review: A local restaurant, café or snack bar	Part 4: A radio interview with the owner of a popular café
Vocabulary and grammar reviews Units 3 and 4			
5 Study time	Part 7: 'At school abroad' Part 3: 'Culture shock for international students'	Part 1 An essay: All young people who have the opportunity should study in a foreign school or college for a year. Do you agree? Writing opening paragraphs Using linking words and phrases	Part 1: People talking about studying and school
6 My first job	Part 5: 'Lucy's first job' Part 2: 'A new summer programme'	Part 2 A letter or email: Describe the jobs students do in your country Commonly misspelled words	Part 3: Five people talking about their first job
Vocabulary and grammar reviews Units 5 and 6			
7 High adventure	Part 6: 'Are you ready for an adventure race?' Part 4: Key word transformation	Part 2 An article: A great way to keep fit	Part 2: A talk about adventure racing Part 4: A radio interview with a paraglider
8 Dream of the stars	Part 7: 'Five young actors' Part 1: 'YouTube millionaire celebrities'	Part 1 An essay: There are both advantages and disadvantages to a career as a musician or an actor. Writing a balanced essay	Part 2: A talk about a television quiz show
Vocabulary and grammar reviews Units 7 and 8			
9 Secrets of the mind	Part 5: 'The secrets of happiness' Part 4: Key word transformation	Part 2 A report: The benefits of improving classrooms and students' social activities Making suggestions and recommendations	Part 1: People talking about different aspects of psychology
10 Spend, spend, spend?	Part 2: 'Shopping online versus shopping locally' Part 5: 'My greatest influence'	Part 2 A review: A place where people have a good time Words/Phrases to build up more complex sentences	Part 4: A student interview about a new shopping centre
Vocabulary and grammar reviews Units 9 and 10			
11 Medical matters	Part 6: 'What's it like to study medicine?' Part 3: 'Is there a doctor on board?'	Part 1 An essay: Modern lifestyles can seriously endanger our health. Do you agree? Writing concluding paragraphs An essay: Young people generally don't pay enough attention to their health and fitness. Do you agree?	Part 3: Five people talking about visits to the doctor
12 Animal kingdom	Part 1: 'My sister's circus' Part 7: 'Surviving an animal attack'	Part 2 A letter or email: Advice to a visitor to your country Giving advice	Part 1: People talking about animals in different situations
Vocabulary and grammar reviews Units 11 and 12			
13 House space	Part 5: 'My new home in Venice, 1733' Part 2: 'Living on a houseboat'	Part 2 An article: My ideal home	Part 2: A talk about a haunted house
14 Fiesta!	Part 6: 'The world's highest festival?' Part 3: 'My local festival'	Part 1 An essay: Is it better to watch films at the cinema or at home? *it, this, that* and *they* for reference	Part 4: A radio interview with a street performer
Vocabulary and grammar reviews Units 13 and 14			

Speaking	Pronunciation	Vocabulary	Grammar
Part 1: Talking about yourself, your home and your family Giving extended answers	Word stress (1): Stress in words with two or more syllables	Phrasal verbs: *get on with, do up*, etc. Collocations with *make* and *do*	Present perfect simple and continuous
Part 2: Comparing photos of free-time activities Using discourse markers to structure the answer	Sentence stress (1): Stress on words carrying the most meaning	Phrasal verbs and expressions: *take up, sum up*, etc.	Making comparisons Adjectives with *-ed* and *-ing*
Part 3: Discussing the benefits of different kinds of trip Phrases to involve partners in discussion Strategies for dealing with the second section of Part 3	Intonation (1): Indicating when you have/haven't finished speaking	*travel, journey, trip* and *way* Adjective suffixes	Past simple, past continuous and *used to* *at, in* or *on* in time phrases Past perfect simple and continuous
Part 4: Discussing diet, food and health Supporting opinions with reasons and examples	Grouping words and pausing (1)	*food, dish* and *meal* Adjectives to describe restaurants	*so* and *such* *too* and *enough*
Part 1: Talking about your studies Giving reasons, offering several possible ideas	Word stress (2): Shifting word stress	Phrasal verbs: *get over, live up to*, etc. *find out, get to know, know, learn, teach* and *study; attend, join, take part* and *assist* Forming nouns from verbs	Zero, first and second conditionals
Part 2: Comparing photos of different kinds of work Describing similarities and differences when comparing	Sentence stress (2): Contrastive sentence stress	*work/job; possibility/occasion/ opportunity; fun/funny* Collocations with *work* and *job*	Countable and uncountable nouns Articles
Part 3: Discussing ways of encouraging people to do more sport Suggesting ideas, asking opinion, agreeing and disagreeing	Intonation (2): Showing attitude	Verb collocations with sporting activities *look, see, watch, listen* and *hear*	Infinitive and verb + *-ing*
Part 4: Discussing different aspects of media and celebrity Giving balanced, general answers Expressing agreement/disagreement	Grouping words and pausing (2)	Verb collocations with *ambition, career, experience* and *job* *play, performance* and *acting; audience, (the) public* and *spectators; scene* and *stage*	*at, in* and *on* in phrases expressing location Reported speech
Part 2: Comparing photos of different kinds of feeling and emotion Speculating about photos using *look, seem* and *appear*	Sentence stress (3): Using sentence stress for emphasis	*achieve, carry out* and *devote* *stay, spend* and *pass; make, cause* and *have*	Modal verbs to express certainty and possibility
Part 1: Talking about how you spend your money Strategies for answering Part 1 questions	Linking (1): Linking to increase fluency	*arrive, get* and *reach* Phrasal verbs: *come up with, pull in*, etc.	*as* and *like* Modals expressing ability
Part 2: Comparing photos of situations related to health Strategies for dealing with difficulties: finding the right word	Intonation (3): Showing certainty/uncertainty	Idiomatic expressions: *taken aback*, etc. Health vocabulary: *illness, infection*, etc.	Relative pronouns and relative clauses
Parts 3 and 4: Discussing topics related to animals Commenting on the question Expressing other people's opinions Expressing agreement/disagreement	Word stress (3): Strong and weak forms	*avoid, prevent* and *protect; check, control, keep an eye on* and *supervise* Negative prefixes	Third conditional and mixed conditionals *wish, if only* and *hope*
Part 2: Comparing photos of people in different locations	Linking (2): Linking with consonant sounds	*space, place, room, area, location* and *square*	Causative *have* and *get* Expressing obligation and permission
Parts 3 and 4: Discussing different topics related to festivals and celebrations	Improving fluency	Vocabulary for festivals: *celebrate, commemorate*, etc. Suffixes to form personal nouns	The passive

Introduction

Who this book is for

Complete First Second Edition is a stimulating and thorough preparation course for students wishing to take the revised **Cambridge English: First** exam from 2015. It teaches you the reading, writing, listening and speaking skills which are necessary for the exam, how to approach each exam task, as well as essential grammar and vocabulary. The book also teaches you the language knowledge and develops the skills you need to reach an upper-intermediate B2 level in the Common European Framework of Reference. *Complete First Second Edition* is official Cambridge English preparation material for the exam.

What the book contains

In the **Student's Book** there are:

- 14 units for classroom study. Each unit contains:
  - at least one part of each of the Writing, Speaking and Listening papers and two parts of the Reading and Use of English Paper in the Cambridge English: First exam. The units provide language input, skills practice and exam technique to help you to deal successfully with each of the tasks in the exam.
  - essential information and advice on what each part of the exam involves and the best way to approach each task.
  - a wide range of enjoyable and stimulating speaking activities designed to increase your fluency and your ability to express yourself.
  - detailed advice and practice of strategies to perfect your performance in the Speaking paper.
  - a pronunciation section working on stress, intonation, pausing, linking and fluency.
  - a step-by-step approach to doing Cambridge English: First writing tasks.
  - grammar activities and exercises with the grammar you need to know for the exam. When you are doing grammar exercises you will sometimes see this symbol: . These are exercises which are based on research from the Cambridge English Corpus and they deal with areas which cause problems for many candidates in the exam.
  - vocabulary input needed for success at Cambridge English: First based on the English Vocabulary Profile (EVP) at B2 level. When you see this symbol: EP, the exercise is based on EVP research. When you see this symbol next to a vocabulary exercise, the exercise is based on research from the Cambridge English Corpus and focuses on words which candidates often confuse or use wrongly in the exam.
- 14 Vocabulary and Grammar reviews. These contain exercises which revise the grammar and vocabulary that you have studied during the unit.
- A **Language reference section** which clearly explains all the main areas of language, including grammar, word formation, spelling and punctuation, which you need to know for the Cambridge English: First exam.
- **Writing and Speaking reference sections**. These explain the possible tasks you may have to do in the Speaking and Writing papers, and they give you examples, language and advice on how best to approach them.
- A **CD-ROM** provides extra practice, with all activities linked to the topics in the Student's Book.

Also available are:

- **two audio CDs** containing listening material for the 14 units. The listening material is indicated by different-coloured icons in the Student's Book as follows: 02. 02.
- a **Workbook** to accompany the Student's Book, with four pages of exercises for each unit. The Workbook is also accompanied by an **audio CD**.

Cambridge English: First content and overview

Part / timing	Content	Test focus
Reading and Use of English 1 hour 15 minutes	**Part 1** A modified cloze text containing eight gaps and followed by eight multiple-choice items **Part 2** A modified open cloze text containing eight gaps **Part 3** A text containing eight gaps. Each gap corresponds to a word. The stems of the missing words are given beside the text and must be changed to form the missing word. **Part 4** Six separate questions, each with a lead-in sentence and a gapped second sentence to be completed in two to five words, one of which is given as a 'key word' **Part 5** A text followed by six multiple-choice questions **Part 6** A text from which six sentences have been removed and placed in a jumbled order after the text. A seventh sentence, which does not need to be used, is also included. **Part 7** A text, or several short texts preceded by ten multiple-matching questions	Candidates are expected to demonstrate the ability to apply their knowledge of the language system by completing the first four tasks; candidates are also expected to show understanding of specific information, text organisation features, tone and text structure.
Writing 1 hour 20 minutes	**Part 1** One compulsory essay question presented through a rubric and short notes **Part 2** Candidates choose one task from a choice of three task types. The tasks are situationally based and presented through a rubric and possibly a short input text. The task types are: • an article • a letter or email • a review • a report	Candidates are expected to be able to write using different degrees of formailty and diffferent functions: advising, comparing, describing, explaining, expressing opinions, justifying, persuading, recommending and suggesting.
Listening Approximately 40 minutes	**Part 1** A series of eight short unrelated extracts from monologues or exchanges between interacting speakers. There is one three-option multiple-choice question per extract. **Part 2** A short talk or lecture on a topic, with a sentence-completion task which has ten items **Part 3** Five short related monologues, with five multiple-matching questions **Part 4** An interview or conversation, with seven multiple-choice questions	Candidates are expected to be able to show understanding of attitude, detail, function, genre, gist, main idea, opinion, place, purpose, situation, specific information, relationship, topic, agreement, etc.
Speaking 14 minutes	**Part 1** A conversation between the examiner (the 'interlocutor') and each candidate (spoken questions) **Part 2** An individual 'long turn' for each candidate, with a brief response from the second candidate (visual and written stimuli, with spoken instructions) **Part 3** A discussion question with five written prompts **Part 4** A discussion on topics related to Part 3 (spoken questions)	

1 A family affair

Starting off

Work in pairs.

- What aspects of family life does each of the photos show?
- Which of these activities do you most enjoy doing with members of your family? Which do you prefer to do with friends? Why?
- What other activities do you enjoy doing with members of your family? Why?
- How important is it for families to spend time together? Why?

Listening | Part 1

Exam information

In Listening Part 1, you:

- listen to people talking in eight different situations which may be either a conversation between two or more people, or just one person speaking;
- answer one question for each situation by choosing A, B or C;
- hear each piece twice.

This part tests your ability to understand a variety of things, including the general idea being expressed, a detail, a reason or a purpose.

1 Work in pairs. You will hear people talking in eight different situations. Before you listen, read questions 1–8 and underline the main idea in each. An example has been done for you.

1 You hear part of a conversation with a boy called Patrick. He thinks his mother helps him because
A she enjoys it.
B she worries about him.
C she has plenty of time.

2 You hear a girl called Tracey talking to a friend. What is her family doing to the house at the moment?
A extending it
B painting it
C cleaning it

3 You hear a girl called Vicky taking part in a class discussion. How often does she do sporting activities with her father?
A more often than before
B the same as before
C less often than before

4 You hear a boy called Kostas talking about family celebrations. How does he feel about them?
A bored
B embarrassed
C amused

5 You hear a boy called Rajiv talking to his sister on the phone. He is annoyed with her because
A she has taken something without permission.
B she has gone out without telling him.
C she has lost something he needs.

6 You hear a boy called Marco talking to a friend. He is tired because he has done too much
A studying.
B exercise.
C travelling.

7 You hear a girl called Samin leaving a telephone message for her mother. She is phoning to
A explain something.
B complain about something.
C ask permission for something.

8 You hear an interview with a young musician called Pau. Why does he say he chose to play the trumpet?
A It was the only instrument available.
B It was his favourite instrument.
C It was a family tradition.

2 ▶ **02** Listen and choose the best answer (A, B or C).

3 Work in pairs. Correct the mistakes in questions 1–6 on the tablet.

1 How much you help around the house?
How much do you help around the house?
2 How often you all doing things together as a family?
3 You ever do sports with other people in your family?
4 Are you enjoy family celebrations?
5 How other members of the family annoy you?
6 You have any family traditions?

4 Now take turns to ask and answer questions 1–6 in Exercise 3.

Vocabulary

Phrasal verbs

1 EP Match these phrasal verbs from Listening Part 1 with their definitions.

1 get on with
2 do up
3 clear up
4 go on
5 wear out
6 pick up

a collect (or go and get) someone or something
b continue
c continue doing something, especially work
d make a place tidy by removing things from it or putting them where they should be
e make someone extremely tired
f repair or decorate a building so that it looks attractive

2 Complete these sentences by writing a phrasal verb from Exercise 1 in the correct form in each of the gaps.

1 I need to *get on with* my homework project, otherwise I won't finish it for tomorrow.
2 Mati had a little sleep because she felt .... after spending all morning .... the mess in her room.

3 I got bored with the film because it .... for too long.
4 We'll need to .... some more pots of paint if we're going to .... your room this weekend.

Reading and Use of English | Part 6

1 EP Work in pairs. You are going to read an article giving advice to parents. Before you read, write these adjectives in the most appropriate column below.

~~aggressive~~ anxious bad-tempered concerned critical enthusiastic hard-working impatient impolite mature organised reasonable responsible self-confident sensitive strict understanding unreliable

usually positive	usually negative	could be either
	aggressive	

2 Add one of these prefixes *dis-*, *un-*, *im-*, *ir-*, *in-* to each of these words to make opposites.

critical *uncritical* concerned enthusiastic mature organised reasonable responsible sensitive

➡ **page 181 Language reference:** Word formation – adding prefixes

3 Work in pairs. Which of the adjectives in Exercise 2 describe typical attitudes of parents to teenagers? Why? Which describe typical attitudes of teenagers to parents? Why?

4 Work in groups.

- Make a list of things that parents sometimes say about their teenage children.
  He's so bad-tempered! He gets angry whenever I ask him to tidy his room!
  She's very hard-working. She spends hours studying in her room.
- What do you think parents can do to live happily with their teenage children?
  Listen to what their children say.

5 Read the article carefully, ignoring the gaps, and make a note of the main idea of each paragraph. An example has been done for you.

SURVIVING TEENAGERS

It might be difficult to accept, but a new approach to living happily with teenagers is for parents to look at their own behaviour.

treat teenagers differently from before

"The key to getting teenagers to respect you is to respect them first," says Penny Palmano, who has written a best-selling book on teenagers. "You can't continue to treat them the same way that you have been treating them for the previous 12 years: they have opinions that count. **1** ____ You'd be very upset. You'd never say that to an adult, because it shows a total lack of respect."

Palmano, who has a daughter aged 19 and a 16-year-old stepdaughter, has even allowed the children to hold several teenage parties at her home. They passed without problems. "I've found that if you have brought them up to do the right thing, and then trust them to do it, usually they'll behave well," she says. "I make them sandwiches and leave them alone. But I make it clear that they have to clear up any mess. **2** ____ "

She agrees that teenagers can be irritating: enjoying a world that is free of responsibility, yet desperate for independence. She doesn't think, however, that they are trying to annoy you. Until recently, scientists assumed that the brain finished growing at about the age of 13 and that teenage problems were a result of rising hormones and a desire for independence. **3** ____

"This would explain why many teenagers can't make good decisions, control their emotions, prioritise or concentrate on several different things at the same time. **4** ___ It means that they do not intentionally do the wrong thing just to annoy their parents," says Palmano.

The key to happiness for all, Palmano believes, is calm negotiation and compromise. If you want your teenagers to be home by 11 pm, explain why, but listen to their counter-arguments. If it's a Saturday, you might consider agreeing to midnight (rather than 1 am, which is what they had in mind). **5** ___ Instead, ask if they've had a problem with public transport and let it pass; they've almost managed what you asked. She urges a bit of perspective about other things, too. "There have been times when my daughter's room has not been as tidy as I expected, but as she said once, 'I'm a teenager – what do you expect? I'm not turning into a criminal, it's just clothes on the floor.'"

"It's vital to choose your battles carefully: don't criticise teenagers for having an untidy room, then suddenly criticise them for other things. **6** ___ One minute, it's about an untidy room and the next, you're saying, 'And another thing ...' and criticising them for everything."

Adapted from *The Daily Telegraph*

6 Six sentences have been removed from the article. Choose the correct sentence from A–G which fits each gap (1–6). There is one extra sentence which you do not need. Use the underlined words and phrases in the sentences and in the text to help you.

A But it turns out that the region of the brain that controls common sense and emotions is not fully mature until the early twenties.

B If they are up to 20 minutes late, don't react angrily.

C For example, they may find it difficult to make the right decision between watching television, ringing a friend, or finishing their homework.

D Parents often complain that teenagers can be charming to people outside the home but irritating to their family.

E I've never had a problem; in fact, the kitchen was sometimes cleaner than I'd left it.

F On these occasions, parents tend to mention all the other things that they may or may not have done wrong.

G Imagine if you'd spent two hours getting ready to go out for the evening and someone said, 'You're not going out looking like that, are you?'

Exam information

In Reading and Use of English Part 6, you read a text of 500–600 words with six gaps where sentences have been removed. You choose one sentence from a list of seven sentences A–G for each gap; there is one sentence you will not need.

This part tests your ability to understand the structure of the text, how the argument develops and how ideas in the sentences A–G refer and link to ideas in the text.

7 Work in groups of four. Two students should take the role of parents and two students should take the role of teenagers.

- Work with the student who has the same role as you. Read your role and prepare what you are going to say.
- When you are ready, change partners and have your conversations.

Parents
It is Saturday night and your teenage son/daughter has gone out with friends. You are annoyed because
- you asked them to be back by midnight and they came home half an hour late
- you phoned their mobile but they did not answer
- this has already happened once before this month.

Have a conversation with your teenage son/daughter. Find out what happened and decide how to avoid this situation in the future.

Teenage son/daughter
It is Saturday night. You went out with your friends, but you promised your parent(s) you would be back by midnight. However, you got home half an hour late.

Have a conversation with your parents. Explain what happened and discuss how to avoid this situation in the future.

Grammar
Present perfect simple and continuous

1 Look at each of the pairs of sentences in *italics* and answer the questions that follow.

1 a *Penny Palmano has written a best-selling book on teenagers.*
b *She's been writing books for more than 20 years.*

Which sentence (a or b) talks about ...
1 the result of an activity?
2 the length of an activity?

2 a *I've been learning how to do things like carpentry and so on.*
b *I've phoned her more than six times, but she never answers the phone.*

Which sentence (a or b) talks about ...
1 how many times something has been repeated?
2 changes or developments which are not finished?

3 a *I've been helping my mum while her assistant is on holiday.*
b *We've lived in this house since I was a small child.*

Which sentence (a or b) talks about something which is ...
1 temporary?
2 permanent?

➔ **page 178 Language reference:** Verb tenses – present perfect simple and continuous

2 Complete these sentences by writing the verbs in brackets in the correct form (present perfect simple or continuous) in the gaps.

1 I ....*'ve been visiting*..... (*visit*) friends, so I haven't spoken to my parents yet today.
2 I .... (*ask*) him to tidy his room several times.
3 I .... (*clean*) the kitchen, so what would you like me to do next?
4 My neighbour .... (*play*) the violin for the last three hours and it's driving me mad!
5 Congratulations! You .... (*pass*) the exam with really high marks!
6 We can't leave Adrianna to run the shop. She .... (*only work*) here for a few days.
7 We .... (*spend*) every summer in Crete since I was a child, so it'll be sad if we don't go there this year.
8 I'm really tired because I .... (*cook*) all day!

3 Candidates often make mistakes with the present perfect simple and continuous. Correct one mistake with a verb tense in each of these sentences.

1 I ~~was~~ interested in it since I was a child. have been
2 In the last three weeks, I learned so many interesting things which I didn't know how to do before.
3 This isn't the first time I work at a camp.
4 My name is Sarah Beauland, I'm 25 years old and I play tennis since 1996.
5 Since I started the project, I had been doing research on someone famous from my country.
6 Vicky and Kostas are friends for many years. They actually met at primary school.
7 They had been talking about it for years, but nothing has been done up to now.
8 I dance since I was very young and now I'm working very hard to fulfil my dream of becoming a famous dancer.

Reading and Use of English | Part 2

1 Work in pairs. You will read an article about housework. Before you read, match the verbs (1–8) with the nouns (a–h) to make phrases for common household chores.

1 do	a the beds
2 do	b the dinner ready
3 dust	c the floor
4 get	d the furniture
5 hang	e the ironing
6 lay	f the table
7 make	g the washing out to dry
8 sweep	h the washing-up

2 Work in groups.

- Who does each of the chores in Exercise 1 in your family, and why?
  We all do our own ironing because we're all very busy. My dad gets the dinner ready because he says it helps him relax.
- Which of the chores do you not mind doing? Which would you prefer to avoid?

3 Read the text quickly. Why do teenagers do housework?

4 Complete the text by writing one word in each gap. Make sure that you spell the word correctly.

Doing the chores

According to a recent study of teenagers, most of them do not do housework just **(0)** ....for........ pocket money. While many do household chores because they see it **(1)** .... a way of getting ready for adult life, others feel they have a duty to help their parents because it is fair, especially if their parents work.

More than two-thirds of the young people who were surveyed clean floors **(2)** .... least once a week and more than 80% regularly set the table for meals or **(3)** .... the washing-up. Girls are more likely than boys to wash **(4)** .... own clothes.

(5) .... are, however, a few teens who only do the housework because they are made **(6)** .... by their parents. They argue that they should **(7)** .... be expected to help out at home because in their view, their teenage years are a period which should be enjoyed **(8)** .... than interrupted with household responsibilities.

5 Now check or complete your answers by using these clues.

1 This preposition is used with *see* to mean *believe it is (that thing)*. Other verbs which are followed by this preposition are *consider* and *regard*.
2 In other words, they clean floors a minimum of once a week.
3 Which verb do we use with *washing-up*?
4 Whose clothes do they wash?
5 This word is often used to introduce a sentence before the verb *be*.
6 *Their parents make them do the housework* = They are made .... do the housework by their parents.
7 Do you understand that a *minority of teens* mentioned in this paragraph believe they should help?
8 This word is part of a two-word phrase which means *instead of*.

Exam information

In Reading and Use of English Part 2, you read a text of 150–160 words with eight gaps where words have been removed. You write one word in each gap. You are given an example (0).

This part tests your knowledge of grammar, e.g. articles (*a*, *the*, *an*), prepositions (*to*, *with*, *by*, etc.), modal verbs (*can*, *must*, *should*, etc.) auxiliary verbs (*do*, *did*, *have*, etc.), pronouns (*it*, *them*, *which*, etc.), conjunctions (*and*, *although*, *but*, etc.), quantifiers (*much*, *few*, *a little*, etc.).

6 Work in pairs. Do you think what the text says about teenagers and household chores is true in your country as well?

Vocabulary

Collocations with *make* and *do*

1 EP Complete the third column of the table below by writing these words and phrases in the correct row.

~~an activity~~ ~~an appointment~~ an arrangement the bed business a change a choice the cleaning a course a decision an effort an excuse (an) exercise a favour friends homework housework an impression a job a mistake money a noise a phone call a plan progress a promise the shopping (a) sport work

verb	definition	common collocation
make	to create or produce something	make an appointment
do	to perform an activity or job	do an activity

2 Candidates often confuse *make* and *do*. Complete these sentences by writing *make* or *do* in the correct form in the gaps.

1 According to a recent study of teenagers, most of them .... not do housework just for pocket money.
2 I always .... my own bed in the morning, but I don't .... any cleaning.
3 He had to .... a phone call in order to .... the arrangements.
4 Essential changes should be .... so that we avoid .... the same mistake in the future.
5 People who .... language courses tend to .... a lot of friends at the same time.
6 This weekend, as well as .... the shopping, I'm hoping to .... some outdoor activities as well.

3 Work in pairs. Each choose five words/phrases from the box in Exercise 1 and think about when you did or made each of these things. Then take turns to tell your partner about each of them.

I had to make a choice between going away with my family, or doing a language course during the summer. Although it was a difficult choice to make, I decided to do the language course and miss my holiday.

Speaking | Part 1

Exam information

In Speaking Part 1, the examiner asks you questions about yourself. These may include questions about your life, your work or studies, your plans for the future, your family and your interests, etc.

This part is intended to break the ice and tests your ability to interact with the examiner and use general social language.

1 Look at these two questions, which the examiner may ask you in Speaking Part 1.

- Where are you from?
- What do you like about the place where you live?

1 Which question asks you to give your personal opinion? Which asks you for personal information?
2 Which question can be answered with quite a short phrase? Which question needs a longer answer?

2 ▶**03** Listen to two candidates, Irene and Peter, answering the questions above. Who do you think gives the best answers? Why?

3 In the exam, you will get higher marks if you use a range of appropriate vocabulary. Work in pairs. Which of these phrases can you use to describe the place where you live?

a a large industrial city
b a relaxed atmosphere
c a busy tourist resort
d in the middle of some great countryside
e a pleasant residential district
f an important business centre
g some impressive architecture
h a lot of historic buildings
i a lot of attractive buildings
j some pretty good shopping
k a busy city centre
l wonderful beaches nearby

4 Which of the phrases (a–l) can you use with … ?

It is … a large industrial city
It has …

(In some cases, both are correct.)

5 Pronunciation: word stress

In the Speaking paper, you will get higher marks if your pronunciation is clear. In words of more than one syllable, one syllable is stressed more than the others. If you stress the wrong syllable, the word becomes difficult to understand. In dictionaries the stressed syllable is marked like this: in'dustrial.

1 Underline the stressed syllable in each of these words and phrases.

industrial relaxed atmosphere wonderful
important business impressive historic
attractive residential

2 ▶**04** Listen and check your answers. Then work in pairs and take turns to read the words aloud.

6 How can you extend your answers to these two questions? Think about Irene's extended answers you heard in (Speaking) Exercise 2, and use the frameworks given to help you.

> Examiner: Where are you from?
> Student: I'm from … It's a … which …

> Examiner: What do you like about the place where you live?
> Student: Well, it's … , so … , but … and … Also …

7 Work in pairs. Take turns to ask and answer the questions in Exercise 6. Use some of the vocabulary from (Speaking) Exercise 3.

8 Read questions 1–8.

- Spend a little time thinking about how you can give extended answers.
- Work in pairs and take turns to ask and answer the questions.

1 Do you come from a large family?
2 What do you like about being part of a large/small family?
3 Who does the housework in your family?
4 What things do you enjoy doing with your family?
5 Tell me about your friends.
6 What things do you enjoy doing with your friends?
7 Which are more important to you: your family or your friends?
8 Do you have similar interests to your parents?

→ page 194 Speaking reference: Speaking Part 1

Writing | Part 1 An essay

Exam information

In Writing Part 1, you:

- write an essay in which you discuss a question or topic. After the essay title, there are some notes which you must use.
- must also include your own ideas.
- must write between 140 and 190 words.

This part tests your ability to develop an argument or discussion on a topic, express your opinion on the topic clearly and support your ideas with reasons and examples.

1 Read this writing task and underline the points you must deal with.

> In your English class, you have been talking about how much teenagers and young people should help with the housework.
>
> Now your English teacher has asked you to write an essay.
>
> Write an essay using **all** the notes and give reasons for your point of view.
>
> **Essay question**
> Teenagers and young people should share housework equally with their parents. Do you agree?
>
> **Notes**
> Write about:
>
> *1. who has more time for housework*
> *2. who does housework better*
> *3. .... (your own idea)*
>
> Write your **essay**.

2 Work in groups. Discuss the task and try to find two or three things you can say about each of the notes 1–3.

3 Read Violetta's answer to the task, ignoring the gaps. Which of her ideas do you agree with and which do you disagree with?

> **(1)** .... it is fashionable to say that everyone should share the housework equally, in many homes parents do most of it. **(2)** .... , I believe people of all ages should do their fair share.
>
> It is true that young people spend most of the day at school or college and they also have large amounts of homework to do when they come home. **(3)** .... , parents go out to work and come home tired. In my view, family life is more pleasant when everyone shares the responsibility for cleaning and tidying because it takes less time.
>
> People often argue that parents do the cooking and ironing better. **(4)** .... in my opinion, young people should learn to do them as preparation for the future.
>
> Finally, housework is boring if you do it alone **(5)** .... when families do it together, it gives parents and children a chance to talk to each other about the things that matter to them. This greatly improves family life and makes young people more cooperative and responsible.
>
> For all these reasons, I think that family life is more pleasant when everyone shares the chores.

4 Complete this plan for Violetta's essay by matching the notes (a–e) with the paragraphs (1–5).

> Para. 1: intro: ....
> Para. 2: ....
> Para. 3: ....
> Para. 4: ....
> Para. 5: conclusion: ....

a life more enjoyable doing things together
b time: young people studying, parents working, chores finished more quickly
c get practice – you improve
d sharing work together – better family life
e parents do most of it + my opinion

5 It is important to express your opinions in an essay. Find four phrases which Violetta uses to introduce her personal opinions.

6 When you write an essay, you should try to present contrasting points of view. Complete Violetta's essay by writing *although, however, on the other hand* or *whereas* in each of the gaps 1–5. Then check your answers by reading the Language reference.

➔ **page 168 Language reference:** Linking words for contrast

7 Complete these sentences by writing *although, however, on the other hand* or *whereas* in the gaps. In some cases, more than one answer may be possible.

1 Adults tend to worry more about their health, ... young people are more concerned about money.
2 .... I am happy to do some of the cooking, I don't want to do it all.
3 My mum and dad have similar tastes. .... , mine are completely different.
4 .... my parents give me a lot of freedom, I would prefer to have even more independence.
5 Young people often spend many hours a week on their social life. .... , older people are often too busy.
6 I enjoy making beds. .... , I'm not at all keen on doing the ironing.

8 Write your own answer to the writing task in Exercise 1. Before you write, use the notes you made in Exercise 2 to write a plan. Write between 140 and 190 words.

- Use Violetta's answer in Exercise 3 as a model, but express your own ideas and the ideas which came up during your discussion.

➔ **page 186 Writing reference:** Part 1 Essays

2 Leisure and pleasure

Starting off

Work in pairs.

1 Which of the activities in the photos have you done?
2 Which do you think is ...
  A the most enjoyable?
  B the cheapest?
  C the healthiest?
  D the most relaxing?
  E the least active?
  F the best one to do with friends?
  G the most popular among young people?
3 Which would you like to try? Why?

Listening | Part 2

1 Work in groups. You are going to hear a games developer talking about his life and work. Before you listen, complete the advantages and disadvantages of video or computer games by writing a word from the box in the gaps.

concentrate	contribute	develop	distract
encourage	make	require	solve
waste			

Advantages
1 They .... people to be more creative.
2 They can .... you from your problems.
3 People learn to .... on complicated tasks.
4 They .... many skills, such as hand and eye coordination.
5 They teach people how to .... problems.

Disadvantages
6 People .... little imagination to play them.
7 They .... people less sociable.
8 They .... to violence in society.
9 People .... time doing something which is not very useful.

2 Which sentences do you agree with? Why?

Exam information

In Listening Part 2, you hear a talk or lecture by one speaker. You:

- listen and complete ten sentences with between one and three words.
- write words you actually hear and try to spell them correctly.
- hear the recording twice.

This part tests your ability to pick out and write down details, specific information and opinions.

3 Work in pairs. Read this text. What type of information do you need to complete each sentence?

Games Developer

As a child, Mike's main interests were playing video games and reading **(1)** ....

His original ambition was to become a **(2)** ...., not a games developer.

When he was at school he formed a games **(3)** .... with other students.

He worked in his summer holidays in order to get **(4)** ....

One thing he enjoys is doing **(5)** .... to find solutions for games.

He likes working with people who have both **(6)** .... that are unlike his.

He thinks games developing is a **(7)** ...., not something to do alone.

He has worked on many successful games and one is now a **(8)** ....

Large games need **(9)** .... to develop, so he prefers working on smaller ones.

In the future, he intends to start a **(10)** ....

4 05 Now listen to the talk and complete the sentences in Exercise 3 with a word or short phrase.

5 Work in groups.

1 Which video games do you find …
- most entertaining?
- best for passing the time or taking a break?
- most educational or informative?

2 Are there any video games you would recommend?
3 Mike talked about how he made his hobby into his career. Is this something you would like to do? If so, what hobby would you like to make into a career?

Grammar

Making comparisons

1 Circle the correct phrase in *italics* in these extracts from Listening Part 2. Then listen again to check your answers.

1 My aims when I was at school were *a bit more / some more* realistic I think.
2 I thought that would be a *more safer / much safer* career where I'd make *far more / much* money than developing games.
3 At the time, it was the *most / more* exciting thing in my life.
4 And then I had this opportunity which was even *best / better.*
5 I worked *much harder / more hardly* than I ever worked at school.
6 Games development is the *more / most* creative thing you can imagine.
7 One of the *very big / biggest* thrills for me was when one of my games, The Snake Quest, was made into a film.
8 I don't want to spend *as many / so much time* on things.

page 169 Language reference: Making comparisons

2 Candidates often make mistakes with comparisons. Correct the mistakes in these sentences.

1 There are lots of ways to keep fit, but I think the healthier of all is zumba.
2 Playing chess is more cheaper than playing video games.
3 Team games are more sociable that biking because you meet and speak to a lot of people.
4 When you play chess, you have to think more hardly than when you're playing video games.
5 I don't go window shopping as often than I used to.
6 For me, parachute jumping is the more risky of all sports.
7 Speaking for myself, I find team sports the less interesting.
8 Mountain biking is more good for getting exercise than most sports.

3 Complete these sentences with your own ideas.

1 It's becoming more and more …
2 Learning to ride a bicycle is not as …
3 In team games, the most …
4 I'm much better at …
5 My friends are far …
6 Computer games are not nearly …

Reading and Use of English | Part 5

1 You are going to read an extract from a book in which actor Ewan McGregor explains how he first became interested in motorbikes. Before you read, work in pairs. What do you think people most enjoy about riding motorbikes?

2 Read the extract quickly to find out how Ewan McGregor became interested in motorbikes.

Exam information

In Reading and Use of English Part 5, you:

- read a text of 550–650 words
- answer six questions about it by choosing A, B, C or D.

This part tests your ability to understand main ideas and details, the writer's opinion and purpose and your ability to work out what something means from the context.

My first bike

Film star, Ewan McGregor, recently rode round the world on a motorbike. He talks about how he first took up riding motorbikes.

My biking beginnings can be summed up in two words: teenage love. My first girlfriend was small with short, mousy blonde hair, and I was mad about her. Our romance came to an abrupt end, however, when she started going out with another guy in my hometown, Crieff. He rode a 50cc road bike first and then a 125. And whereas I had always walked my girlfriend home, suddenly she was going back with this guy.

I was nearly sixteen by then and already heartbroken. Then one day, on the way back from a shopping trip to Perth with my mum, we passed Buchan's, the local bike shop. I urged my mother to stop the car. I got out, walked up the short hill to the shop and pressed my nose to the window. There was a light-blue 50cc bike on display right at the front of the shop. I didn't know what make it was, or if it was any good. <u>Such trivialities</u> were irrelevant to me. All I knew was that I could get it in three or four months' time when I was sixteen and allowed to ride it. Maybe I could even get my girlfriend back.

I'd ridden my first bike when I was about six. My father got hold of a tiny red Honda 50 cc and we headed off to a field that belonged to a family friend. I clambered on and shot off. I went all over the field. I thought it was just the best thing. I loved the smell of it, the sound of it, the look of it, the rush of it, the high-pitched screaming of the engine. Best of all, there was a Land Rover parked next to two large piles of straw with about a metre and a half between them. I knew that from where the adults were standing it looked as if there was no distance between them. Just one large heap of straw. I thought I would have a go. I came racing towards the adults, and shot right through the gap in the straw. I was thrilled to hear the adults scream and elated that it had frightened them. It was my first time on a motorbike. It was exciting and I wanted more.

So when I looked through Buchan's window in Perth that day, it suddenly all made sense to me. It was what had to happen. I can't remember whether it was to win back my ex-girlfriend's heart or not, but more than anything else it meant that, instead of having to walk everywhere, I could ride my motorbike to school and the games fields at the bottom of Crieff and when I went out at weekends.

I started to fantasise about it. I spent all my waking hours thinking about getting on and starting up the bike, putting on the helmet and riding around Crieff.
I couldn't sleep. Driven to desperation by my desire for a bike, I made a series of promises to my mum: I won't leave town. I'll be very safe. I won't take any risks. I won't do anything stupid. But, in fact I was making the promises up – I never thought about keeping them.

At the time that I was begging for a bike, I'd already had an accident with a bike belonging to George Carson, the school laboratory technician. When I asked him if I could borrow it, he agreed, not knowing that I didn't have a clue how to ride it. The bike was in an alleyway up the side of the school hall. I managed to start it and zoomed down the alleyway until I crashed smack into a wall, bending the wheel and snapping the handlebars. Mr Carson came out to find me looking very red-faced. The bill for the damage came to more than £80, a fortune to a fifteen-year-old in those days and one that took me months of working as a dish washer and waiter at the Murray Park Hotel to pay back.

Adapted from *Long Way Round* by Ewan McGregor and Charley Boorman

3 Read and underline the main idea in questions 1–6, but not in the options A–D.

1 What does 'Such trivialities' refer to in line 22?
A his mother's attitude to the bike
B the bike's size and colour
C the bike's price
D the bike's quality and its manufacturer

2 Ewan did not buy the bike straightaway because
A he did not have enough money.
B he was too young to ride it.
C he was uncertain about its quality.
D he had to ask his girlfriend first.

3 The adults were frightened the first time Ewan rode a motorbike because
A the bike was making too much noise.
B he disappeared from view.
C they thought he was going to have an accident.
D he seemed too small for the bike.

4 What was Ewan's main reason for buying the motorbike?
A It would be exciting to ride.
B It would improve a friendship.
C It was good for his image.
D It was a useful means of transport.

5 In paragraph 5, Ewan's desire for the bike meant he
A thought about nothing else.
B spent more time with his mother.
C invented reasons for buying the bike.
D started behaving more carefully.

6 One result of Ewan's accident was that he
A was injured.
B was punished.
C had to get a job.
D lost interest in bikes.

4 For questions 1–6, choose the answer (A, B, C or D) which you think fits best according to the text.

5 Work in pairs.

Student A
You are a teenager. You want to buy a motorbike, but you need your parents to lend you the money. Think of reasons why you want a motorbike and then try to persuade your father/mother to lend you the money you need.

Student B
You are one of Student A's parents. You don't want him/her to buy a motorbike. Think of reasons why he/she shouldn't buy a motorbike and try to persuade him/her not to do so.

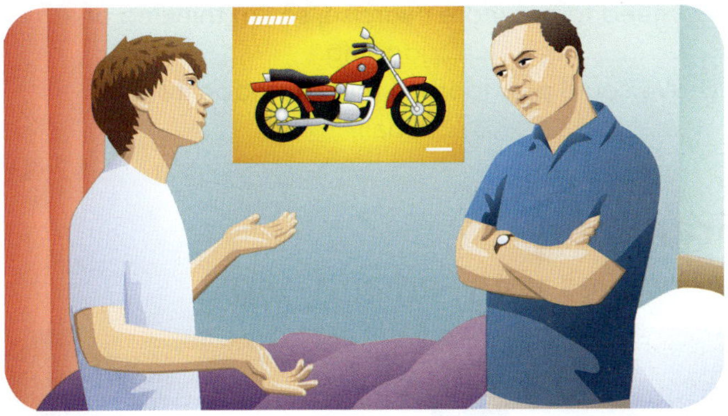

Vocabulary
Phrasal verbs and expressions

1 EP Match these phrasal verbs and expressions from the extract (1–8) with their definitions (a–h).

1 take up (line 4)
2 sum up (line 6)
3 get hold of (line 27)
4 have a go (lines 36–37)
5 take risks (line 54)
6 make up (lines 55-56)
7 keep a promise (line 56)
8 not have a clue (line 60)

a describe the important facts or characteristics about something or someone
b do what you said you would do
c say or write something which is not true
d start doing a particular job or activity
e be completely unable to guess, understand, or deal with something
f try to do something
g do something even though something bad might happen because of it
h obtain something

2 Complete these sentences by writing a phrasal verb or expression from Exercise 1 in the correct form in the gaps.

1 I'd never do something like sky-diving because I don't enjoy ....
2 How would you .... her personality in just a few words?
3 Hans let me .... on his new bike, and now I want to get one myself!
4 Sometimes when I arrive home late, I .... an excuse to tell my parents why I am late.
5 Diego .... how to answer the questions in yesterday's exam because he simply hadn't studied.
6 People won't trust you unless you can .... and do what you say you're going to do.
7 I need to get more exercise, so I'm thinking of .... jogging.
8 We could play football this afternoon if I can .... a ball.

Grammar

Adjectives with *-ed* and *-ing*

1 Look at these sentences from the extract and answer the questions below.

> I was thrilled to hear the adults scream and elated that it had frightened them. It was my first time on a motorbike. It was exciting and I wanted more.

1 Which of the underlined words refer to how Ewan felt?
2 Which of the underlined words refers to what made him feel like that?

page 163 Language reference: Adjectives with *-ed* and *-ing*

2 Candidates often confuse adjectives with *-ed* and adjectives with *-ing*. Circle the correct adjective in *italics* in these sentences.

1 When we went to Disneyland, I think we found it more *amused / amusing* than our parents.
2 It can be very *irritated / irritating* when friends arrive late for a film.
3 You will never get *bored / boring* at night in Berlin because the nightlife is wonderful.
4 I am very *confused / confusing* about what you are offering in your advertisement.
5 The situation was very *embarrassed / embarrassing* for me and I felt uncomfortable.
6 I was really *excited / exciting* and wanted to see as much of the city as possible.

3 EP Use the word given in capitals at the end of these sentences to form a word with *-ed* or *-ing* that fits the gap.

1 Everyone watches Pietro at parties because he's just an .... dancer. ASTONISH
2 We were quite .... by the attitude of the other students. PUZZLE
3 It's very .... to be able to apply things we learn in the classroom to our free-time activities. MOTIVATE
4 Anita looked quite .... when she left the police station. WORRY
5 The film was not particularly .... AMUSE
6 We were pretty .... by the time we got to the top of the mountain. EXHAUST

4 ▶ **06** You will hear a girl talking about one of these experiences (a–g). Listen and decide which experience she is talking about.

a She rode a motorbike for the first time.
b She was punished for something she didn't do.
c She had to study all weekend for an exam.
d She broke a bone.
e She was trapped in a lift.
f She won a competition.
g She did a parachute jump.

5 Listen again. Which adjectives did she use to describe how she felt …

1 about the whole experience: ...amazing....
2 after studying: .... and ....
3 about her boyfriend's suggestion: ....
4 about the thought of breaking a bone: ....
5 in the plane: .... and ....
6 about the jump itself: ....

6 Work in pairs. Look at the experiences a–g in Exercise 4. Have you done any of these or have any of them happened to you? How did you feel about them? Take turns to describe your experience.

Reading and Use of English | Part 4

Exam information

In Reading and Use of English Part 4, you:

- complete six sentences with between two and five words so that they mean the same as the sentences printed before them
- use a word given in CAPITALS without changing it in any way.

This part tests your ability to manage different grammar, vocabulary and collocations.

For questions 1–6, complete the second sentence so that it has a similar meaning to the first sentence, using the word given. Do not change the word given. You must use between two and five words, including the word given.

0 He doesn't enjoy running as much as cycling.
MORE
He likes ..cycling more than.. **running.**

1 It is easier to learn the guitar than most other musical instruments.
ONE
The guitar is .... musical instruments to learn.

2 Olivia finds watching TV more boring than reading.
NOT
For Olivia, watching TV is .... reading.

3 Maria's brothers are better tennis players than her.
AS
Maria doesn't .... her brothers.

4 No one in the class makes as much noise as Peter.
PERSON
Peter .... the class.

5 In general, cars are more expensive than motorbikes.
NOT
In general, cars are .... motorbikes.

6 It took Janusz longer to finish the game than Sarah.
MORE
Sarah finished the game .... Janusz.

Speaking | Part 2

Exam information

In Speaking Part 2, you and the other candidate take turns to speak on your own for a minute during which you:

- compare two photos which the examiner gives you.
- answer a question connected with both photos.
- answer a question quite briefly about your partner's photos.

This part tests your ability to speak at length, organise your ideas, compare, describe and express opinions.

1 Work in pairs. Look at the examiner's instructions and the question and photos below. Then discuss what you can say to compare them.

"Here are your photographs. They show people doing different activities in their free time. I'd like you to compare the photographs, and say how you think the people can benefit from spending their free time doing these different activities."

How can the people benefit from spending their free time doing these different activities?

2 ▶07 Listen to an examiner giving this task to a candidate called Martyna. According to Martyna, how can people benefit from each activity?

3 Listen again and tick ✓ this checklist.

Martyna	Yes	No
1 introduces her talk.		✓
2 describes each photo in detail.		
3 deals with each photo in turn.		
4 spends most of the time answering the printed question.		
5 refers to the first photo when talking about the second photo.		
6 talks about things not connected with the question.		
7 speaks until the examiner says 'Thank you'.		

4 Work in pairs. Complete the sentences from Martyna's answer which begin with these words and phrases.

1 I think they benefit from …
2 Firstly …
3 At the same time …
4 Also …
5 I think they also benefit because …

5 Which word(s)/phrase(s) (1–5) in Exercise 4 does Martyna use to:

a introduce her answer to the examiner's question?
b introduce the first point she wants to make?
c add additional points?

6 Which of these words/phrases could also be used for b and c in Exercise 5?

Besides First of all In addition
To start with What is more

7 Pronunciation: sentence stress (1)

We stress the words in sentences that we particularly want our listeners to hear, the words which carry the most meaning. These are usually nouns, verbs or adjectives, not small grammar words like articles or prepositions.

1 **08** Underline the words you think are stressed in these sentences. Then listen to check your answer.

1. Firstly, they're getting some exercise, which is always good for you.
2. It's great for your health and helps you to relax.
3. At the same time, they're having fun together…
4. … which is important because it builds up their social relationships and their friendships.
5. Also, it's good to see boys and girls doing a bit of sport together instead of separately.
6. I think it helps break down social boundaries between boys and girls.

2 Work in pairs. Take turns to read the sentences aloud using the same sentence stress.

3 Work in pairs. Take turns to read these extracts.

- Firstly, they're getting some exercise, which is always good for you because it's great for your health and helps you to relax.
- At the same time, they're having fun together, which is important because it builds up their social relationships and their friendships. Also, it's good to see boys and girls doing a bit of sport together instead of separately because I think it helps to break down social boundaries between boys and girls.

8 Change partners and take turns to do the Speaking Part 2 task in (Speaking) Exercise 1.

- Try to speak for a minute.
- Try to use some of the words and phrases from (Speaking) Exercise 4.
- Use your own ideas and Martyna's ideas.
- While you are listening to your partner, use the checklist in (Speaking) Exercise 3 and give feedback when your partner has finished.

9 Work in pairs and take turns to do this Speaking Part 2 task.

The photographs show people doing different free-time activities.
Compare the photographs, and say what you think the people enjoy about doing these different activities.

What do the people enjoy about doing these different activities?

page 195 Speaking reference: Speaking Part 2

Writing | Part 2 An article

1 Look at this writing task and underline the points you must write about.

You see this announcement in an English-language magazine for teenagers.

A great way to spend your free time!

Tell us about a leisure-time activity you really enjoy.

- How did you get started?
- Why do you enjoy it so much?

We will publish the most interesting articles in next month's issue.

Write your **article**.

2 Work in pairs. Tell your partner about one of your free-time activities. While speaking, answer the questions in the writing task above.

3 Work in pairs. The article in the next column would lose marks in the exam because it is not divided into paragraphs.

1 Divide it into four paragraphs.
2 Say what the main idea is in each paragraph.

Cooking – it's creative and fun!

I first got interested in cookery one summer holiday when I was about 12. I was staying with my aunt, who is a keen cook, and I wanted to try cooking for myself. She started by teaching me how to do fairly simple dishes at first. I found I really enjoyed cooking and I was soon doing things which were more complicated. Not everything I cooked was as successful as my aunt's cooking. My younger brother and sister complained about some of my dishes, but they usually ate the food quite happily. When I went back to school after the summer, I decided to do cookery lessons and now I think I'm quite a competent cook. When friends come round to my house, I often cook them something because I find it really satisfying and relaxing. I find creating new dishes fascinating and it's wonderful to see my family and friends enjoying a meal I've cooked. I'd recommend it as a hobby because for me it's one of the most creative and useful free time activities that anyone can do.

→ page 193 Writing reference: Writing Part 2 Articles

4 You can write compound sentences by joining two sentences with *and, but* and *because*. Which two sentences are joined in these compound sentences?

1 I found I really enjoyed cooking and I was soon doing things which were more complicated.
2 My younger brother and sister complained about some of my dishes, but they usually ate the food quite happily.
3 When friends come round to my house, I often cook them something because I find it really satisfying and relaxing.
4 I'd recommend it as a hobby because for me it's one of the most creative and useful free-time activities that anyone can do.
5 When I went back to school after the summer, I decided to do cookery lessons and now I think I'm quite a competent cook.

5 Write compound sentences by joining these sentences with *and, but* and *because*. Use pronouns (*he, she, it*, etc.) to avoid repetition.

1 I'd like to learn to fly. I think learning to fly is too expensive. *I'd like to learn to fly, but I think it's too expensive.*
2 I got interested in flying when I was about 14. My father took me to an airshow.
3 My parents don't want me to fly. They think flying is dangerous.
4 One of my friends is learning to fly. My friend has asked me to come with him. My friend thinks I'd like flying.

6 You can write complex sentences by joining two sentences with words such as *when, who, which* and *that*. Write these complex sentences as two separate sentences.

1 I first got interested in cookery one summer holiday when I was about 12.
I first got interested in cookery one summer holiday. I was about 12.
2 I was staying with my aunt, who is a keen cook.
3 I was soon doing things which were more complicated.
4 When I went back to school after the summer, I decided to do cookery lessons.
5 When friends come round to my house, I often cook them something.
6 For me, cooking is one of the most creative and useful free-time activities that anyone can do.

7 Join these sentences using *when, who, which* and *that*.

1 I was 13. I started running seriously.
2 My aunt encouraged me. My aunt's a keen athlete.
3 I go running most days. I've finished school and done my homework.
4 Running is a sport. Running gets you really fit.

8 Join these sentences using *and, because, but, when, which* and *who*. Use pronouns (*he, she, it*, etc.) to avoid repetition.

1 I started windsurfing. I was 13. I was staying with friends by the sea.
2 One of my friends is a keen windsurfer. She encouraged me to start. She thought I would enjoy it.
3 I kept falling into the sea to start with. It was a fairly windy day. There were a lot of waves.
4 I didn't enjoy it at first. I had to concentrate quite hard. I carried on trying.
5 I started to windsurf quite fast. It was exciting. I started to find it quite enjoyable.

9 Find adjectives in the article which describe the following.

1 the writer's feelings about cooking:
.... , ... , ... , ...
2 cooking as a leisure-time activity:
.... , ...
3 the writer's ability to cook: ....

10 EP Complete the table below by writing these words and phrases in the correct column.

astonishing competitive delightful demanding depressing dreadful economical entertaining exhausting incredible irritating popular superb time-consuming tremendous unbelievable

feelings about an activity	the type of activity

11 You are going to write your own article to answer the writing task in Exercise 1. Before you write,

- decide on a title for your article which will encourage people to read it.
- decide how many paragraphs you need, the subject of each paragraph and write a short plan.
- think about some of the vocabulary you can use.

12 When you are ready, write your article using between 140 and 190 words.

Exam information

In Writing Part 2:

- you do one writing task from a choice of three.
- the possible tasks are an article, a letter or email, a review or a report.
- you must write between 140 and 190 words.

This part tests your ability to write effectively for a range of different purposes.

Vocabulary and grammar review Unit 1

Vocabulary

1 EP Complete each of these sentences by writing an adjective in the gap. Choose from the adjectives or their opposites in the exercises in Reading and Use of English Part 6 on page 10. In some cases, more than one answer may be possible.

1 Juan's parents are very ...strict... and don't allow him to do everything he wants.
2 You need to be careful what you say to my brother, as he can be rather .... in the morning.
3 Pascale is very .... , so she's bound to finish her part of the project on time.
4 David is so .... that you can never trust him to do what he says he's going to do.
5 Melanie tries to act confidently even when she's feeling very .... about things.
6 I wouldn't have criticised you if I had known how .... you were!
7 Helen is very young, but she behaves in a .... and responsible way.
8 We're all feeling rather .... about Luis, because he's been looking rather depressed recently.

2 Complete these sentences with a phrasal verb in the correct form.

1 Your room is such a mess! Could you .... it .... before you go out?
2 Dad will .... you .... from the station when you arrive.
3 I must .... the housework, otherwise I'll never finish it.
4 I need a rest – all this shopping has .... me ....
5 We'll need to .... the flat before we move in – the paintwork is very old.
6 The game .... for about two hours, but I won in the end.

3 Complete these sentences with the correct form of *make* or *do*.

1 Could you .... me a favour and let me copy your notes from the last class?
2 Do you mind if I use your phone? I've got to .... an urgent phone call.
3 I'll .... the shopping on my way home this evening.
4 I'm .... this English course because I'm hoping to study in the USA next year.
5 I've got so much homework to .... that I can't come out with you tonight.
6 Marco has .... a big effort with his students, so I'm afraid he's a bit disappointed with their results.
7 Sarah wasn't enjoying the party, so she .... an excuse and left.
8 We phoned the police because our neighbours were .... too much noise.

Grammar

4 Complete these sentences by writing the verbs in brackets in the correct form (present perfect simple or continuous). In some cases, both forms are possible.

1 I'm celebrating because my team has .... (*win*) the league!
2 At last you .... (*arrive*) – we .... (*expect*) you for ages.
3 Of course I'm annoyed. I .... (*spend*) ages preparing for this party and no one .... (*turn up*) yet.
4 We .... (*have*) a really interesting time. Gavin .... (*tell*) us about his trip round the world. There are a few countries he still .... (*not tell*) us about, but I get the impression he .... (*see*) almost everything!
5 Kate .... (*lose*) weight recently because she .... (*get*) more exercise.
6 I wonder if Irina .... (*finish*) reading that book yet. I .... (*wait*) to read it for ages.
7 Tatiana is so greedy! She .... (*eat*) all the cakes and she .... (*not leave*) any for us.
8 Paolo .... (*look*) very tired recently. I think it's because he .... (*study*) too hard.

Vocabulary and grammar review Unit 2

Vocabulary

1 Complete these sentences by writing a phrasal verb or expression from the Vocabulary section on page 21 in the correct form in the gaps.

1 If you can't .... , no one will ever trust you.
2 I just don't like .... , so I'd never get a motorbike.
3 Mario is thinking of .... jogging, as he doesn't feel he's getting enough exercise.
4 Instead of reading to the children, I think I'll just .... a story for their bedtime.
5 I'll .... all our ideas in just a few words to save time.
6 I .... how to solve this maths problem; would you like to .... and see if you can do it?

Grammar

2 Join these sentences to form compound and complex sentences. More than one answer may be possible.

1 Katya took up karate. She was seven years old. She was interested in karate.
2 Her father is a professional karate instructor. He taught her karate. She progressed quickly. She soon became junior regional champion.
3 She did karate with other children. The other children were the same age as her. None of them was as good as her. She felt dissatisfied.
4 Last year, she participated in the national championship. She did not win. She was injured during one of the matches.
5 She hopes to become a professional karate instructor. She hopes to work in the same sports centre as her father. Her father has too many students.
6 Some of her father's students have been studying karate for several years. Her father thinks they would benefit from a different teacher. They are too familiar with his style of karate.

3 For questions 1–6, complete the second sentence so that it has a similar meaning to the first sentence, using the word given in capitals. Do not change the word given. You must use between two and five words, including the word given.

1 This motorbike is not as noisy as my previous one.
MADE
My previous .... this one.

2 Small towns are safer than large cities.
NOT
Small towns .... as large cities.

3 No one in the team plays better than Gemma.
PLAYER
Gemma .... in the team.

4 She looks more relaxed than she did before the exam.
STRESSED
She does not look .... she did before the exam.

5 Tatiana does not speak nearly as clearly as Irina.
MUCH
Irina speaks .... Tatiana.

6 None of the other sofas in the shop are as comfortable as this one.
ANY
This sofa is .... the others in the shop.

Word formation

4 EP Use the word given in capitals at the end of each sentence to form a word that fits in the gap.

1 What an .... band! I never expected they'd be that good. **AMAZE**
2 They found the journey so .... that they fell asleep as soon as they arrived. **EXHAUST**
3 It's a .... problem – I don't really know what to do about it. **PUZZLE**
4 Jake felt .... with his exam results. He had hoped to do better. **DISAPPOINT**
5 You can't expect children to work hard if they don't feel .... **MOTIVATE**
6 We were .... by the way they shouted at us. **ASTONISH**

3 Happy holidays?

Starting off

1 Work in pairs. Complete the table below by writing the words and phrases from the box in the most appropriate column.

camping holiday   at a campsite   walking and climbing
at a luxury hotel   a beach holiday   on a cruise ship
meeting new people   sunbathing   a sightseeing tour
relaxing   a cruise   at a youth hostel   backpacking
visiting monuments   in the city centre   at the seaside
seeing new places

types of holiday	holiday locations and places to stay	holiday activities

2 Now look at the photos and answer these questions using words and phrases from the table.

1 What type of holiday does each photo show?
2 What do people do on these types of holiday?
3 Why do people choose these types of holiday?
4 Which types of holiday would you enjoy most? Which would you enjoy least? Why?

Listening | Part 3

Exam information

In Listening Part 3, you:

- listen to five different speakers talking about a related subject. You must match each speaker with one of eight statements A–H. There are three extra statements you don't need.
- hear each speaker twice.

This part tests your ability to understand a variety of things, including the general idea being expressed, details, attitudes, opinions or purpose.

1 You are going to hear five people talking about the holiday they took last year. Before you listen, underline the main idea in each statement A–H.

A I didn't enjoy it much at first.
B I didn't mind the discomfort.
C I got to know lots of people.
D I'd done something similar before.
E I wanted a low-cost holiday.
F I didn't do much during the day.
G I wasn't in as much danger as some people imagined.
H I went on the trip as a break from my parents.

2 09 Now listen and, for questions 1–5, choose from the list (A–H) in Exercise 1 what each speaker says about their holiday. Use the letters only once. There are three extra letters which you do not need to use.

Francesca		1
Mike		2
Sally		3
Paul		4
Katie		5

3 Work in groups.

What do you like about holidays with your:

- family?
- friends?

Grammar

Past simple, past continuous and *used to*

1 09 Complete these extracts from Listening Part 3 by writing the verbs in brackets in the correct form in the gaps. Then listen again to check your answers.

- ... on family holidays we always **(1)** .... (*go*) to the same campsite and lie on the same beach ...
- My dad **(2)** .... (*be*) a climber when he **(3)** .... (*be*) younger ...
- Still, there was an upside because while we **(4)** .... (*go*) round yet another museum, I **(5)** .... (*get*) to meet this Polish girl called Jolanta.
- ... so we just **(6)** .... (*dump*) our parents and **(7)** .... (*go*) off for the day together. We **(8)** .... (*have*) a really great time ...
- ... we **(9)** .... (*stay*) in youth hostels, which saved us a bit of money. There were lots of other people like us from all over the world who **(10)** .... (*do*) the same sort of thing.

➜ **page 179 Language reference:** Verb tenses – past simple, past continuous and *used to*

2 Circle the correct form of the verb in *italics* in each of these sentences.

1 When he *walked / was walking* home, he found a wallet with a huge amount of money in it!
2 When I was at primary school, I *was doing / used to do* about one hour's homework a day.
3 As soon as Mandy *was getting / got* Simon's text, she *was jumping / jumped* on her bike and *was riding / rode* round to his house to speak to him.
4 When I was younger, we *used to spend / were spending* our holidays in my grandparents' village.
5 Luckily, we *walked / were walking* past a shopping centre when the storm *began / was beginning*.
6 My mum *used to visit / was visiting* lots of exotic places when she *was / was being* a tour guide.

3 Candidates often make spelling mistakes when adding *-ed* to past tense verbs. Add *-ed* to each of these words.

develop enjoy happen mention occur open plan prefer stop study travel try

➜ **page 176 Language reference:** Spelling

Vocabulary

travel, journey, trip and *way*

1 Candidates often confuse the following nouns: *travel, journey, trip* and *way*. Look at these sentences from the recording script in Listening Part 3 and complete the extract below by writing *travel, journey, trip* or *way* in the gaps.

- I went on one of those **journeys** overland to Kenya ...
- ... we made a **trip** to the beach, which was only about 20 minutes away by bus.
- We were on our **way** back down the mountain when we got caught in this really big storm.
- I really like that sort of mixing of cultures – it's one of the best things about foreign **travel** …

travel, journey, trip or *way*?

› A **(1)** .... is a journey in which you visit a place for a short time and come back again.

› '**(2)** ....' refers only to the route that you take to get from one place to another.

› The noun '**(3)** ....' is a general word which means the activity of travelling.

› Use '**(4)** ....' to talk about when you travel from one place to another.

2 Circle the correct word in *italics* in each of these sentences.

1 She met plenty of interesting people during her weekend *travel / trip* to Montreal.
2 We stopped at the supermarket on the *way / trip* to the beach to pick up some cold drinks.
3 My mum and dad have booked a *journey / trip* to Greece for our holidays this August.
4 My mum is away on a business *journey / trip*, so the house is really quiet at the moment.
5 People spend far more on foreign *travel / journeys* than they did 50 years ago.
6 The *travel / journey* to my village will take about three hours.
7 'Have a good *travel / trip* to Budapest!' 'Thanks! See you next week when I get back!'
8 You can't get to school by bicycle if the *journey / way* is too long – over 30 kilometres, for example.
9 Excuse me, I'm a bit lost. Can you tell me the best *journey / way* to the bus station?

3 Complete each of the sentences by writing an adjective from the box. In some cases, more than one answer may be possible.

a(n) homeward/outward/hard/dangerous **journey**
a business/sightseeing/shopping/day/forthcoming/ round **trip**
a(n) outward/pleasant/successful/safe/extended/ overnight **journey/trip**

1 I hope you have a(n) .... journey.
2 I'm going on a(n) .... trip to Zurich, so I won't be back till tomorrow.
3 The .... journey wasn't nearly as hard as the homeward one.
4 They've gone on a(n) .... trip, so I guess they'll come home with lots of new clothes.
5 What are you going to do on your .... trip to New York? Is it for business or pleasure?
6 Have a(n) .... journey and don't drive too fast!

4 Work in groups. Imagine you are planning a trip together this weekend. Decide:

- where to go
- how to get there
- what to do when you arrive.

Reading and Use of English | Part 3

1 EP Form adjectives from these nouns and verbs by adding a suffix.

	noun (n) or verb (v)	adjective
1	nature (n)	natural
2	adventure (n)	
3	friend (n)	
4	memory (n)	
5	mystery (n)	
6	risk (n + v)	
7	crowd (n + v)	
8	thrill (n + v)	
9	doubt (n + v)	
10	success (n)	
11	remark (n + v)	
12	access (n + v)	

➜ **page 181 Language reference:** Word formation – adding suffixes

2 EP Form adjectives from the nouns and verbs in the box. In some cases, more than one answer may be possible. When you have finished, use your dictionary to check your answers.

artist caution colour educate emotion energy mass predict reason respond storm thought wealth

Exam information

In Reading and Use of English Part 3, you read a text of 150–160 words with eight gaps and one example (0). You write the correct form of the word given in CAPITALS at the end of the line in each gap.

This part tests your knowledge of vocabulary and your ability to form words by adding prefixes and suffixes and making other changes.

In the test, the words will be a mix of nouns, adjectives, adverbs and verbs.

3 EP Read the text on the right. Use the word given in capitals at the end of some of the lines to form a word that fits in the gap in the same line. When you have finished, use your dictionary to check your answers.

A bus journey

Tasha climbed onto a **(0)** ......crowded...... CROWD
bus which was going to take her to
a nearby village. The wooden seats
looked quite **(1)** .... , so COMFORT
she decided to stand, even though a
(2) .... passenger offered THOUGHT
her a seat. As the bus moved through the
countryside, it filled with women dressed
in bright, **(3)** .... clothes COLOUR
on their way to market to do their weekly
shopping. 'This is an **(4)** .... FORGET
experience,' thought Tasha, who was
beginning to feel **(5)** .... OPTIMIST
about her journey.
More passengers climbed aboard laughing
and chatting, and the noise became
(6) .... Gradually, the bus CONSIDER
grew hotter and Tasha began to feel a little
(7) .... that she might not get ANXIETY
to the door when the bus reached her stop.
Fortunately, though, a **(8)** .... SYMPATHY
passenger saw her problem and shouted
to the other passengers to let her pass and
suddenly everyone made room for her to
get off.

4 Work in groups. What things make you nervous or anxious when you're travelling?

Grammar

at, in or *on* in time phrases

1 Complete these sentences from Listening Part 3 by writing *at, in* or *on* in the gaps.

1 We got up late .... the morning or even .... the afternoon …
2 Except of course .... days when it was cloudy.
3 But .... night, we were down at the clubs, partying to the small hours, getting back to the hotel .... two or three in the morning.
4 I went off with a couple of my friends .... March.

➔ **page 172 Language reference:** Prepositions – *at, in* and *on* in time expressions

2 Candidates often make mistakes with *at, in* and *on* in time phrases. Some of these sentences are correct. Find and correct the mistakes.

1 I would like to travel on July because it is the perfect time to go to the camp.
2 In the weekends, he only stays at home on Sunday on the afternoon, because in the mornings he goes to see football games.
3 At weekends, everything opens in 11.00 a.m.
4 I would advise you to come in summer because the weather is great and there are many islands with great beaches.
5 She graduated from Cambridge University at 2008.
6 So I prefer shopping on weekdays unless I am busy or have an appointment.
7 The traffic makes us nervous, particularly in certain times of the day when the roads are busy.
8 We used to go to the beach at the morning in a normal day, and clubbing every night.

Reading and Use of English | Part 7

Exam information

In Reading and Use of English Part 7, you will read either one long text divided into four to six sections, or four to six separate short texts. The total length will be 500–600 words. There are ten questions which you must match with the different texts or sections.

This part tests your ability to understand specific information, detail and opinion.

1 Work in groups. You are going to read about four people's nightmare holidays. Before you read, discuss what things sometimes spoil people's holidays.

2 Read questions 1–10 carefully and underline the key words in each question.

Which person

had to hide from danger?	1
found an employee intimidating?	2
was not pleased to spend so long somewhere?	3
had visited the country on a previous occasion?	4
worried about how strong something was?	5
missed speaking to people?	6
had a painful experience?	7
travelled with an ex-criminal?	8
was unaware of the danger in what they were doing?	9
realised the holiday might be a mistake before arriving?	10

3 For questions 1–10, choose from the people (A–D). Each person may be chosen more than once.

4 Work in groups. Which of the holidays sounds the worst to you? Take turns to tell each other about a memorable holiday you have had. Then decide which of you had the most interesting holiday.

My nightmare holiday!

A Pauline Vernon – Malaysia

My dad was teaching in Kota Bharu, Malaysia. When my mum and I flew out to visit him for three weeks, he had already organised our stay in great detail. On our first evening we had a party on the beach. It was an idyllic scene: a beautiful empty beach, palm trees, white sand, the warm gentle waters of the South China Sea. I swam in the shallow water thinking "this is the life", when a jellyfish swam between my legs. The sting, on both legs, was agony, and it was only then I discovered that two people had died from jellyfish stings that year and until that point, no one had bothered to mention the sea-snakes, for whose bite there is no cure. I now understood why the beach was deserted.

B Sandy Henderson – the USA

I was on a camping holiday in Yosemite National Park in California with a friend, when I awoke to the sound of screaming. I looked out of my tent and saw my friend trying to get out of his sleeping bag, with a giant black bear rearing up behind him. Quite possibly the quickest I've ever got out of bed, I scrambled up and we both sprinted in no particular direction. By pure chance, we'd passed a small cabin a little way back on the trail and we made a dash for that, jumped inside and locked the door. Seconds later, the bear was scraping at the door as we cowered inside, afraid that the whole thing might fall off. After quite a long time, the bear lost interest and we were able to leave the shelter.

C Cat O'Donovan – the USA

Twenty-three hours into an epic bus trip across the States, I began to wonder what I had let myself in for. I was at Denver bus station, sitting on my backpack, drinking coffee. Before boarding the first bus in LA, I had been filled with romantic ideas of friendship among the passengers and fascinating stops, as well as spectacular scenery. After the guy next to me had finished talking about his time in jail, I realised my expectations were a bit off. After all, I was 17 and travelling alone.

I had no idea when the next bus was, so I went up to the counter to ask. One unfriendly staff member was so large I feared she had eaten several passengers, so I waited until her colleague was free.

"Three-and-a-half hours," she said. I groaned. Would I ever reach New York? I sat back down to drink my coffee.

D Graham Whitely – Nepal

It was not my first walking holiday to Nepal, but for some reason I no longer remember, I decided to go several weeks before the walking season actually began. There were no other walkers on the flight to Kathmandu, which suggested I might not have made the best decision. Walking to my empty hotel through rainy streets on the first night, I tried not to think what conditions would be like at higher altitudes.

Next day I flew to Tumlingtar to start walking up the remote, rarely visited Arun valley. As I climbed, the bushes on either side of the path were covered in ice and the weather was constantly cloudy. The lodges where I stayed were run by people who spoke no English, and the only meal available was boiled rice with lentil soup.

Each day required at least eight hours of unpleasant solitary walking, longing for a conversation with someone. During all the long walk towards Kathmandu, it continued cloudy and I never even saw a mountain.

Grammar

Past perfect simple and continuous

1 Look at this sentence from Reading and Use of English Part 7 (A Pauline Vernon) and answer the questions below.

> When my mum and I flew out to visit him for three weeks, he had already organised our stay in great detail.

1 Which of these actions happened first?
   A He had organised their stay.
   B They flew out to visit him.
2 Which verb form is used to indicate that something happened before something else in the past?
3 Compare the sentence above with the one below. What does the sentence below suggest about when the stay was organised?
   When my mother and I flew out to visit him for three weeks, he organised our stay in great detail.

➔ **page 179 Language reference:** Verb tenses – past perfect simple

2 Work in pairs. Find six other examples of the past perfect (*had been / had done*) in Reading and Use of English Part 7. Why is the past perfect used in each case, i.e. what is the event or situation in the past simple? e.g. A Pauline Vernon: I discovered that two people had died from jellyfish stings that year – i.e. I discovered (this).

3 Complete these sentences by writing the verb in brackets in the correct form (past simple or past perfect) in the gaps.

1 We were feeling hungry although we .... (*eat*) lunch only an hour before.
2 I didn't know my way around the city because I .... (*never be*) there before.
3 The party, which our hosts .... (*organise*) before we arrived, was one of the most enjoyable parts of our trip.
4 When I .... (*arrive*) in Nairobi, I wasn't allowed into the country because I .... (*lose*) my passport.
5 I .... (*recognise*) her from the photograph, although I .... (*never speak*) to her before.
6 He helped to raise money to repair homes which the hurricane .... (*damage*).

4 Look at sentences A and B below.

1 Which sentence focuses on the length of time spent travelling?
2 Is the underlined verb in the past perfect simple or past perfect continuous?

A Paul was tired because he'd been travelling all day.
B Paul went to the information office because he'd never travelled in the region before.

➔ **page 179 Language reference:** Verb tenses – past perfect continuous

5 Complete these sentences by writing the verb in brackets in the correct form (past perfect simple or continuous) in the gaps.

1 The storm damaged the house where she .... (*live*) since she left school.
2 We .... (*walk*) up the mountain for about three hours when suddenly it .... (*begin*) to rain.
3 I .... (*already finish*) the work when she .... (*offer*) to help me.
4 I .... (*only speak*) for 30 seconds when he interrupted me with a question.
5 I was tired and dirty when I .... (*get*) home because I .... (*walk*) in the country all afternoon.

6 Candidates often make mistakes with the past perfect simple and continuous. Correct the mistakes in these sentences.

1 I couldn't believe he have done such a thing.
2 I was hungry when I arrived because I didn't have anything to eat all day.
3 He didn't go to London before and he found it really exciting.
4 On one of my birthdays, my father had bought me a bicycle because I always wanted one.
5 She was 19 years old and she just finished school two weeks earlier.
6 I was tired because I have been cleaning the house the whole day.

Speaking | Part 3

Exam information

In Speaking Part 3:

- you and the other candidate must discuss a situation or problem together and reach a decision.
- the examiner gives you a page with a task consisting of a question and five different word prompts.
- you have 15 seconds to read and think about the task and then you have two minutes to discuss your ideas.
- the examiner then asks you another question (which is not written down) so that you can summarise your thoughts. You will have one minute to do this.

This part tests your ability to interact by exchanging ideas, discussing opinions, suggesting, agreeing, disagreeing, etc.

1 Work in pairs. Read the examiner's instructions and look at the task. Which phrases in the box below could you use to talk about each option?

"I'd like you to imagine that your college has won first prize in a competition – a trip for all the students. Here are some ideas for trips that students could do and a question for you to discuss. Talk to each other about how these different trips could benefit the students."

How could each of these trips benefit students?

- A city sightseeing tour
- A visit to a museum or art gallery
- A weekend camping trip in the mountains
- A visit to a theme park
- A beach activity day

become more self-confident | become more independent | learn to work in a team | cope in another language | be educational | make a change from their everyday lives | get a real thrill | have new experiences | appreciate other cultures | learn teamwork | tough conditions | get away from their daily routine

2 10 Listen to two candidates, Miguel and Antonia, beginning this task. What benefits do they mention for three of the options?

3 In Speaking Part 3, it's important for candidates to react to each other's ideas and suggestions. You can do this by asking each other questions. Complete the students' questions below by writing a word or phrase from the box in the gaps. Then listen again to check your answers.

about that | don't you | shall | think | this one | what about

1 .... we start with .... ?
2 How do you .... a sightseeing tour of a city might be good for students?
3 .... this sort of activity holiday in the mountains?
4 Yes, and they learn to be more independent because they're away from home and their families, ... think?
5 And the beach activity day: what .... ?

4 Pronunciation: intonation (1)

You can indicate that you have finished speaking, or that you have more to say by making your voice rise or fall. This is called **intonation**. A **falling intonation** shows that you have finished speaking, while a **rising intonation** often indicates that you still have more to say.

The speaker's voice falls or rises most on words which are stressed.

1 **11** Listen to these extracts from the conversation. Decide if the speaker's voice rises or falls on the underlined words.

1 How do you think a sightseeing tour might be good for students?
2 I think you can learn a lot about architecture and history and things like that.
3 Yes, and also you can visit somewhere very different and learn about other cultures.
4 What about this sort of activity holiday in the mountains?
5 I think it can give young people exciting experiences and adventures, things they don't get in their everyday lives.

2 Work in pairs. Take turns to read sentences 1–5 aloud.

3 Write two sentences of your own, explaining the benefits of two of the options in the speaking task. Decide which words you should stress and whether your voice should rise or fall on the stressed words. When you are ready, work in pairs and

- take turns to read your sentences aloud
- react to what your partner says with your own ideas.

5 Work in pairs. Do the first part of the task yourselves.

- Ask each other the questions from (Speaking) Exercise 3.
- Talk about each of the options from the speaking task in turn. Take two minutes to do this.
- Try to use the words and phrases from the box in (Speaking) Exercise 1.

6 Work in pairs. Look at the examiner's instruction for the second part of the task and the list of strategies (1–6) which follow. Then:

- decide together which strategies would be good for this part of the task. Write Y (yes) or N (no) next to each strategy
- give reasons for your answers.

> Now you have a minute to decide which trip the school should choose.

1 Talk about each of the options in turn again.
2 Suggest which option you would choose, say why, and ask your partner if he/she agrees.
3 Agree with the first option your partner suggests.
4 Disagree with the first option your partner suggests, say why you disagree, then suggest another option and say why.
5 Agree with the first option your partner suggests, but then suggest an alternative and say why.
6 Disagree with everything your partner says in order to make the discussion longer.

7 **12** Listen to two pairs of candidates, Miguel and Antonia, and Irene and Nikolai, doing this part of the task. Which of the strategies from Exercise 6 (1–6) does each speaker use?

- Miguel: .... Antonia: ....
- Irene: .... Nikolai: ....

8 Match each of these phrases (1–7) with their function (a–e). Some functions can be matched with more than one phrase.

1 In my opinion, the best choice is … because …
2 I think we should choose … because …
3 What do you think?
4 Yes, I think you're right, but … because …
5 You might be right, but I think we should also consider … because …
6 I think … is a better option because …
7 I think your suggestion would be fine if … , but …

a suggest an option and say why
b ask your partner if they agree
c disagree with a suggestion and say why
d suggest a different option
e agree with a suggestion, but suggest a different option and say why

9 Now work in pairs and do the second part of the task using phrases from Exercise 8.

→ **page 197 Speaking reference:** Speaking Part 3

Writing | Part 2 A report

1 A report is a factual description of events or a situation. Read this writing task and underline the things you must deal with in your report.

> You recently made a one-day excursion with your class to a local place of interest. Now the director of your college has asked you to write a report about it for senior teachers to read. You should explain what you did **and** say why you think the day was a success.
>
> Write your **report**.

2 Work in pairs. Discuss these questions about the writing task above, then decide which ideas you would like to include in your answer.

- Where did you go, and what was the purpose of the excursion? (You may have to invent these details. These could be a visit to a theatre, museum, a day in the country, a visit to a sporting event, or something else.)
- When did you go, and what did you do and/or see?
- What reasons can you think of to explain why the day was a success?

3 Sandra is studying English near London. Read the report she wrote on the right and circle the correct form of the verb in *italics*.

4 Read the report again and answer these questions.

1 Does the report have a title?
2 How many sections does the report have? How do we know what each section is about?
3 How many purposes of the excursion does Sandra mention?
4 What reasons does Sandra give for the day being a success?

5 Work in pairs. Write a plan for the writing task in Exercise 1. Decide:

- what title you will give the report
- how many sections you need
- what section headings you want to use
- what each section will contain.

6 Write your report using the report in Exercise 3 as a model. You should write between 140 and 190 words.

Excursion to London

Purposes of trip
On 2nd April, our class **(1)** *took / was taking* a break from normal lessons and **(2)** *has gone / went* on a day trip to London. The purpose of our visit **(3)** *was / had been* to ride on the London Eye in the morning and then do a tour of the Globe Theatre, which **(4)** *was being / had been* Shakespeare's theatre, in the afternoon.

What we did
We **(5)** *rode / were riding* for about half an hour on the London Eye, which is a giant wheel. Fortunately, the weather was good, so we **(6)** *were / have been* able to see views across the whole of London. After lunch and a walk along the South Bank, we **(7)** *took / have taken* a guided tour of Shakespeare's Globe Theatre, where the guide explained how the theatre **(8)** *was operating / had operated* in Shakespeare's time and how the theatre works nowadays.

Comments
The excursion **(9)** *was / has been* excellent because the two activities **(10)** *were / had been* extremely interesting and very different, so everyone **(11)** *enjoyed / had enjoyed* something. Also, we **(12)** *learned / have learned* a lot. The day was well planned, and we **(13)** *had / have had* plenty of opportunities to practise our English outside the classroom, which I think the class **(14)** *found / was finding* very motivating.

Exam information

When writing a report for Writing Part 2:

- you should give it a title.
- you can divide it into sections and give each section a heading (the first and last sections could be Introduction and Conclusion).
- make suggestions and recommendations (if required by the task).
- make sure that you answer all parts of the task.

This writing question tests your ability to organise and express information and make recommendations or suggestions.

➡ **page 191 Writing reference:** Writing Part 2 Reports

4 Food, glorious food

Starting off

1 Work in groups. Complete the predictions below (1–5) about food in the future by writing a word or phrase from the box in the gaps. Then check your answers on page 42.

> **a** spinach and broccoli **b** seaweed **c** chocolate
> **d** insects **e** meat grown in a laboratory or factory

1 .... from stem cells will one day replace meat from farm animals in our diet.
2 In many parts of the world, people already eat .... This will soon be one of the vegetables everyone eats.
3 In many parts of the world, people eat .... , which are a great source of protein. They will soon become part of everyone's diet.
4 There may be a connection between eating .... and increased intelligence: people will eat more of it.
5 Eating genetically modified .... will help prevent disease.

2 Match each sentence with a photo.

3 Work in pairs. Discuss these questions, giving reasons for your answers.

1 Which of the foods in Exercise 1 would you …
  a be happy to eat or use?
  b be ready to try?
  c absolutely refuse to eat or use?
2 Which of these predictions do you think will come true?

Reading and Use of English | Part 6

1 Work in groups. You are going to read an article about a school in California where the students grow, cook and eat their own food. How do you think students benefit from this?

2 Read the article *Learning about food* carefully and note down the topic of each paragraph. An example has been done for you.

3 Six of the seven sentences below have been removed from the article. There is one extra sentence you do not need to use. <u>Underline</u> the words and phrases in the sentences which refer to something in another part of the article. (Sentences A and B have been done for you as examples.)

A Judging by the happiness in <u>this garden</u> among a mixed bunch of ordinary children, <u>the answer would have to be yes.</u>
B Keeping <u>notes in this way</u> is viewed as an essential part of experimental learning.
C One lesson, on European diets in the Middle Ages, ends with the children cooking roasted vegetables with herbs and garlic.
D The problem, according to some critics, is that these projects may be just too expensive to run.
E These two projects aim to provide all 10,000 students in Berkeley's public schools with good food while also placing food at the heart of the curriculum.
F We couldn't possibly produce enough food in this small space to feed all 300 children.
G Lessons like this one take place in the garden and kitchen and they form part of the curriculum.

Learning about food

A school in California finds a new way to teach students about healthy eating

School where students grow vegetables

Alice Waters – chef and restaurant owner – is sitting in the kitchen garden of the Martin Luther King School in Berkeley, California. The kitchen garden is called the Edible Schoolyard, and students at this public school are preparing a vegetable bed as part of a lesson. Later, they will cook what they pick as part of their school lunch. **1** ___ Each student receives between 18 and 40 hours' tuition a year in the Schoolyard, and as a result, what they eat at school has changed. A good part of the food grown here is used in the school's daily meals.

Waters has been fighting to improve children's diets for a decade, and in 1996 she started a campaign to raise funds for the Edible Schoolyard and the School Lunch Initiative. **2** ___ And Waters hopes that they will set an example for other parts of the country as well. "We have such a huge problem of bad eating habits in the United States that teaching about food cannot be left to parents," she says. "So many children generally are eating fast, cheap, easy food that something has to be done."

Marsha Guerrero, director of the School Lunch Initiative, explains how it all works. "This is mainly a teaching garden," she says. " **3** ___ " Nearby farms therefore also supply food as part of the regular lunches at the school. These are prepared using fresh organic ingredients when possible.

Typical classes in the Edible Schoolyard involve plenty of gardening activity. However, they are not a break from normal school work, as academic projects are always attached. In one lesson, the students are asked to choose one part of the garden as their personal spot for the entire year. They then observe and record in a journal what happens in this spot as time progresses. They record their observations of insect life, the soil and changes to the plants. **4** ___

Classes in the kitchen involve cooking lunch, but also link into classroom academic subjects. The food cooked here includes a range of dishes from pasta to stuffed vine leaves and delicious Italian omelettes filled with herbs and vegetables. The recipes are dictated by what vegetables are available. Science is taught through nutrition and cooking technique; geography through the effects of the seasons and eating habits around the world. **5** ___

Today's midday meal consists of homemade pesto and tomato sandwiches, with a big vegetable salad. Everyone is eating. Teo Hernandez, 13, says he has changed the way he eats. "I can now cook and grow things," he says. "I don't know yet if I will continue doing so in the future, but I know I can. I have changed my attitude to food; I like some herbs and lettuce and I use less salt. It's been fun, the teachers are nice – and there's no homework." Teo has been in the US for only three years, but his teachers say he has learned to speak perfect English in such a short time because he is so happy at school.

But has Alice Waters succeeded? Is the Edible Schoolyard model the way forward? **6** ___ "When kids become unhealthy due to bad diet, they become isolated," says Waters. "But eating such good food and picking, smelling and cooking the vegetables and fruit in this garden makes them care about what they eat – and it shows them that we care about them. Just seeing a child saying to another, 'Would you like some?' – that is the essential thing."

Adapted from the *Daily Telegraph*

4 Choose from the sentences A–G the one which fits each gap (1–6). When you place a sentence, check what the words and phrases which you underlined refer to.

5 Work in groups.

- Do you think all schools should teach students cookery and healthy eating habits? Why? / Why not?
- Did you study cookery at school? If so, how useful did you find the lessons?

Exam advice

- Read the text carefully before you look at the gaps, so you know what each paragraph is about. It helps to make a brief note in the margin.
- Read the sentences carefully one by one; can you recognise from the idea expressed in the sentence where it should go?
- Use words and phrases in the sentences which refer to something in the article to help you.

Vocabulary

food, dish and meal

1 Candidates often confuse *food, dish* and *meal*. Read the definitions on page 183. Then complete these sentences by writing one of the words in the correct form in the gaps.

1 A good part of the .... grown here is used in the school's daily ....
2 The .... cooked here includes a range of .... , from pasta to stuffed vine leaves and delicious Italian omelettes filled with herbs and vegetables.
3 Today's midday .... consists of homemade pesto and tomato sandwiches.

2 Each of these sentences contains a word which is often used wrongly by candidates. Cross out the wrong word and write the correct word.

1 I'm quite surprised, but I'm really enjoying English ~~meal~~. food
2 Moussaka is one of the most delicious meals you can eat in my country.
3 This beef food is really tasty, isn't it?
4 The meal in my country is delicious.
5 Too many people eat meals direct from the fridge, which is not always very healthy.
6 When I visit you, I could cook a food that is from my country.
7 The cost of your holiday includes two dishes a day: breakfast and dinner.

3 EP Complete these collocations by writing *food, dish* or *meal* in the correct gap. You will need to use one of the words twice. In one case, more than one answer is correct.

Some noun and adjective collocations with *food, dish* and *meal*:

1 a .... source/supply/shortage
2 organic/convenience ....
3 a(n) elaborate/simple .... or ....
4 a balanced/filling/light/heavy ....

Answers to Starting off, Exercise 1: 1 e, 2 b, 3 d, 4 c, 5 a

4 EP Complete these sentences by writing the correct form of a collocation from Exercise 3. In some cases, more than one answer may be possible.

1 At weekends, Santos likes to spend hours in the kitchen carefully cooking ......elaborate dishes...... containing many ingredients.
2 Growing populations may lead to .... in some countries.
3 I wouldn't call yoghurt and a banana a .... – it's more like a snack.
4 If we continue to overfish, we won't be able to rely on the oceans as a .... in the future.
5 Many people lead such busy lives that they tend to buy .... from supermarkets to save time.
6 My mum always tries to provide .... with fresh vegetables, pasta or potatoes and some meat or fish.
7 The hotel's .... is delivered directly from local markets every morning.
8 There's little evidence that .... is healthier than other types of food.

5 Work in pairs or groups. Imagine that students at your school or college have to do a project on the food people eat. Below are some places where they can spend time doing this.

- Talk to each other about what they might learn at each place.
- Decide which two places they should spend time at.

Places to learn about food
- a farm
- a restaurant kitchen
- a supermarket
- cookery classes
- a factory producing food

Grammar

so and *such*

1 Complete these sentences from Reading and Use of English Part 6 by writing *so*, *such* or *such a* in the gaps.

1 "We have .... huge problem of bad eating habits in the United States that teaching about food cannot be left to parents," she says. ".................... many children generally are eating fast, cheap, easy food that something has to be done."
2 Teo has been in the US for only three years, but his teachers say he has learned to speak perfect English in .... short time because he is .... happy at school.
3 "But eating .... good food ... makes them care about what they eat ..."

page 175 Language reference: *so* and *such*

2 Write *so*, *such* or *such a(n)* in the gaps in these sentences.

1 I always enjoy visiting his house because he makes .... lovely food.
2 There was .... much food on the table that we didn't know where to start.
3 I don't think eating a pizza at your place is .... good idea if your parents are at home.
4 It's difficult not to cook good food when the ingredients are .... fresh.
5 She's got .... little to say that most people find her rather dull.
6 It was .... scary film that I couldn't get to sleep when I went to bed.

3 Candidates often make mistakes with *so* and *such*. Some of these sentences are correct. Find and correct the mistakes.

1 I'll remember the meal for a long time because it was such delicious.
2 I can't study in a so much a noisy place.
3 It was such fun for all of us to be together.
4 They're so nice, talkative, funny people.
5 I'm glad to see you after so long time.
6 It's difficult to get by on such little money.
7 It's a pity that there were so few spectators at the football match.
8 There aren't many places in this town where you can listen to so good music.

4 For questions 1–6, complete the second sentence so that it has a similar meaning to the first sentence, using the word given. Do not change the word given. You must use between two and five words, including the word given.

1 This is the best meal I've ever eaten.
GOOD
I have .... meal before.
2 She spoke too quickly for us to understand.
THAT
She spoke .... could not understand her.
3 He was given a good grade because he gave an excellent answer to the question.
ANSWERED
He .... that he was given a good grade.
4 We all felt hungry because the organisers didn't give us enough food.
LITTLE
The organisers provided us .... that everyone felt hungry.
5 It was the most enjoyable party she had ever been to.
FUN
She had never .... a party.
6 It's hard to sleep with such noisy neighbours.
NOISE
The neighbours .... that it is hard to sleep.

Listening | Part 4

Exam information

In Listening Part 4, you:

- listen to an interview or a conversation and answer seven questions by choosing A, B or C.
- hear the recording twice.

This part tests your ability to understand main ideas, details, opinions, attitudes and specific information.

1 Work in pairs. You will hear an interview on local radio with a woman called Cherry, who runs a café. Before you listen, discuss these questions.

- Do you have a favourite café? What's it like? Describe the food and drink, the atmosphere and the service.
- How do you think it could be made even better?

2 Quickly read only the questions in 1–7 (do not read options A–C yet) and underline the main idea in each one.

1 Cherry started her café because she
A had recently lost her job.
B saw a business opportunity.
C wanted to achieve a dream.

2 What did Cherry consider most important when she chose the site for her café?
A It had no other cafés nearby.
B It had schools nearby.
C It had more space.

3 What does Cherry say about the décor of her café?
A It is changed regularly.
B It is easy to clean.
C It is welcoming.

4 How does Cherry behave with her customers?
A She tries to get to know them personally.
B She is always smiling and friendly.
C She treats them with respect.

5 One purpose of the back room is as a place for
A meeting new people.
B studying.
C people with no home.

6 Cherry believes food she serves should be
A healthy.
B reasonably priced.
C quick to prepare.

7 What do parents like about the café?
A the atmosphere
B the prices
C the food

3 ▶13 Now listen, and for questions 1–7, choose the best answer (A, B or C).

4 Work in pairs.

- Does Cherry's café sound the sort of place you would like to visit? Why? / Why not?
- Are there cafés in your town which are mainly for young people? How are they different from cafés for other types of customer?
- What things make a café attractive to young people?

Grammar

too and *enough*

1 Read these sentences from Listening Part 4. Write *too, too many, too much* or *enough* in the gaps.

1 Poor things, they've got .... free time and they're not eating well ....
2 We don't want to be going replacing furniture every five minutes. It'd just be .... expensive and I'd go broke!
3 I don't just serve, like, hamburgers and chips. That's not healthy ....
4 I don't do the cooking – Mikey does that 'cos I don't have .... time …
5 Actually, I don't see .... parents but the odd comment comes back.

➡ page 175 Language reference: *too* and *enough*

2 Complete these sentences by writing *too, too many, too much* or *enough* in the gaps.

1 I really enjoyed the meal, although I thought there were .... chips and not .... fresh vegetables.
2 Few schools spend .... time teaching students about nutrition.
3 A lot of people eat .... quickly to enjoy their food properly.
4 The school canteen is .... small for everyone to eat lunch at the same time.
5 Students don't take .... interest in their diets.

3 Candidates often make mistakes with *too, too many, too much, enough* and *very*. Rewrite these sentences correctly. More than one answer may be possible.

1 I liked the restaurant but the food wasn't enough.
2 Experts say that fast food is not too much good for you.
3 I don't have money enough to pay for your dinner.
4 We didn't like the hotel because it wasn't enough comfortable.
5 The food takes too much long to prepare, so customers become impatient.
6 Some people suffer from doing too hard work.
7 The food was not too much tasty.
8 I'm afraid the meal was too much expensive.

4 For questions 1–4, complete the second sentence so that it has a similar meaning to the first sentence, using the word given. Do not change the word given. You must use between two and five words, including the word given.

1 Few people can afford to eat in that restaurant.
TOO
That restaurant .... most people.
2 We ran out of petrol before we reached our destination.
ENOUGH
We did not have .... to our destination.
3 The news surprised her so much that she couldn't speak.
ASTONISHED
She .... the news to speak.
4 We did not go swimming because of the cold weather.
WARM
The weather .... us to go swimming.

5 Work in pairs. Imagine you have both been to a birthday party at a friend's house, but you didn't really enjoy yourselves. Discuss what was wrong with the party, e.g. *The house was too cold, so we were shivering to start with. There wasn't enough food, so we had to go out and get some more.*

You can talk about:

- the food
- the place
- the other guests
- the music
- how you felt.

Speaking | Part 4

Exam information

In Speaking Part 4, the examiner:

- asks you questions to find out your opinions on general topics related to Part 3.
- may also ask you to discuss questions with the other candidate and react to ideas and opinions which they express.

This part tests your ability to express and justify opinions, agree and disagree.

1 Martyna and Miguel are answering an examiner's question in Speaking Part 4. Read their answers, ignoring the gaps, and match the words and phrases in bold with the definitions a–g below.

Examiner: Do you think fast food is bad for you?

Martyna: I think it depends. I think the most important thing is to have **a balanced diet**, **(1)** .... you eat a variety of vegetables, meat, cereals and so on. I'm not sure it matters so much how long it takes to prepare, **(2)** .... I think fast food is just food which is prepared quickly. **(3)** .... , if you just **live on**, what's it called, **junk food**, for instance hamburgers and pizzas and things like that, **(4)** .... you probably need to **cut down** and have a more balanced diet.

Examiner: And Miguel, what do you think?

Miguel: I agree with Martyna. I think it's fine to eat fast food occasionally, **(5)** .... you have to balance it with other things like fresh fruit and vegetables **(6)** .... are in season and cut down on **dairy products** and **fat**. Also, I think that **(7)** .... you eat is only one part of a healthy **lifestyle**.

a solid or liquid substance obtained from animals or plants and used especially in cooking fat
b combination of the correct types and amounts of food
c do less of something
d food that is unhealthy but is quick and easy to eat
e foods made from milk, such as cream, butter and cheese
f only eat a particular type of food
g someone's way of living; the things that a person or particular group of people usually do

2 ▶ **14** Complete Martyna's and Miguel's answers by writing a word or phrase from this box in the gaps. Then listen to check your answers.

because	but	in other words	on the other hand
then	what	which	

3 Find words or phrases in Martyna's and Miguel's answers where they:

1 explain what they mean using different words
2 give a reason
3 give examples
4 balance one idea or opinion with another.

4 Pronunciation: grouping words and pausing (1)

When we speak, we say words in groups which form a meaning together, almost like one word, and we pause slightly between these groups of words.

1 ▶ **15** Listen to Miguel and Martyna answering the examiner's next question and use a (/) to mark where they pause.

Examiner: How can families benefit from eating together?

Miguel: Well, / the important thing is not eating, / it's spending time together / so that they can talk about what they have been doing during the day. They get the chance to exchange opinions and make plans as well, because everyone can contribute and that's what makes a rich, meaningful family life. Children learn ideas and attitudes from their parents, while parents keep up to date with their children and what they are thinking and doing.

Examiner: And Martyna, do you agree?

Martyna: Yes, I do. And also I think people cook better when they are cooking for several people than when they are just cooking for themselves, so that as a result, people who eat together eat more healthily.

2 Work in pairs. Read Miguel's and Martyna's answers aloud. While your partner is speaking, check where they pause and if the pause sounds natural.

3 Look at Martyna's and Miguel's answers in Exercise 1 and use a (/) to mark where you think they pause. Then listen again to check your answers.

4 Work in pairs. Read Martyna's and Miguel's answers aloud.

5 Write your answer to the question in the box in three or four sentences. Where necessary, use phrases to explain what you mean, give examples and reasons, and balance one opinion or idea against another.

> How can children and young people be encouraged to eat healthily?

When you have finished, mark where you think you need to pause when you speak.

6 Work in pairs and take turns to ask and answer the question in Exercise 5.

7 Think about how you can answer each of these questions. Then work in pairs and take turns to ask and answer the questions.

1 How important is it for people to be interested in the food they eat?
2 What, for you, is a healthy diet?
3 How are the things we eat nowadays different from the things our grandparents used to eat when they were young?
4 Do you think young people should learn to cook at school? Why? / Why not?

➔ page 198 Speaking reference: Speaking Part 4

Reading and Use of English | Part 1

Exam information

In Reading and Use of English Part 1, you read a text of 150–160 words with eight gaps and one example (0). You must choose the best option A, B, C or D for each gap.

This part tests your knowledge of the meanings of words, how they are used, collocations and the grammar connected with particular words.

1 You are going to read a short review of a restaurant in Manchester. Read the review quickly to find out what the writer liked about the restaurant, e.g. *the price*.

MosoMoso

I **(0)** ...tried... Moso Moso for the first time this month, and **(1)** .... that it was easily the best Chinese restaurant I've eaten in.

The surroundings were modern, yet it still felt airy and cosy. The waiters were very welcoming and informative, and not too rushed, as is often the **(2)** .... in some of the city's more popular restaurants.

As I was eating with a party of eight, we **(3)** .... to sample a good range of items on the menu, and between us couldn't find a single item that wasn't satisfying and delicious. Every **(4)** .... featured wonderful combinations of flavours. All the ingredients were clearly fresh and of the highest **(5)** .... and in my opinion, the seafood was particularly tasty. We felt that we were given very good **(6)** .... for money, because the meal **(7)** .... to about £15 per person which we thought was very reasonable.

All of us would highly **(8)** .... this restaurant and, as it is located just a short walk from our workplace, we will no doubt be back for many more lunches!

Adapted from the *Manchester Evening News*

2 For questions 1–8, read the review again and decide which answer (A, B, C or D) best fits each gap. There is an example at the beginning (0).

	A	B	C	D
0	A checked	B tried (circled)	C tested	D proved
1	A revealed	B noticed	C found	D knew
2	A reality	B case	C situation	D fact
3	A achieved	B succeeded	C managed	D reached
4	A plate	B dish	C food	D meal
5	A quality	B level	C condition	D choice
6	A price	B worth	C cost	D value
7	A arrived	B reached	C came	D rose
8	A recommend	B propose	C suggest	D advise

3 Work in groups. Where is the best place in your town for:

- a night out with your friends?
- a big family celebration?

Writing | Part 2 A review

1 Work in pairs. Read the Exam information and advice box on page 49, then read the writing task below and underline the points you must deal with.

You see this announcement in your local English-language newspaper.

> Can you recommend a local restaurant, café or snack bar? If so, why not write a review for our Food section? Tell our readers what the place and the food are like, and say why you think everyone in the family would enjoy eating there.
>
> All reviews published will receive vouchers for a free meal.

Write your **review**.

2 Answer these questions with a partner.

1 Which features below (a–j) do you think a review of a restaurant or snack bar should cover?
2 Which features does the review in Reading and Use of English Part 1 cover?

a The type of restaurant, café or snack bar
b The writer's general opinion of the restaurant, café or snack bar
c A description of its design and surroundings
d A description of the food
e A description of the other customers
f A description of the service
g An explanation of how to get there
h A recommendation
i An indication of the price
j The location

3 A review is a good opportunity to show your range of vocabulary. Complete the table below by writing each of the adjectives in the box from the review in Reading and Use of English Part 1 in the appropriate row. You can write some adjectives in more than one row.

airy cosy delicious fresh informative modern reasonable rushed satisfying tasty wonderful welcoming

the waiters / the service	
the interior	
the food and menu	
the price	
the restaurant in general	

4 EP Now add these adjectives to the table. You can add some of them to more than one row.

attractive cheerful colourful competitive delightful elegant exceptional exclusive original raw satisfactory superb well-balanced

5 Read this writing task and underline the points you must deal with.

> You see this announcement in your college magazine.
>
> Do you have a favourite restaurant, café or snack bar in town? If so, why not write a review for our 'Free Time' section, telling us what your favourite place is like and why you would recommend it to our students.
>
> The three best reviews will receive a prize of €50.
>
> Write your **review**.

6 Write a plan for your review and make notes on what you will put in each paragraph. Here are some things you can cover:

- Introduction: the name and type of place and where it is situated
- Your overall opinion of the place
- Particular dishes the place serves (and your opinion of them)
- The décor, the service, etc.
- Things you particularly like, such as the price
- A general recommendation

7 Work in pairs. Compare your plans.

8 Write your review. Write 140–190 words.

page 192 Writing reference: Writing Part 2 Reviews

Exam information and advice

- Writing a review tests your ability to describe and give your opinion about something you have experienced (e.g. a restaurant or a concert) and to make a recommendation to the reader.

When writing a review, you should think about what people want to know when they read the review, e.g. what sort of restaurant is it? What is the food like? Is it expensive?

Vocabulary and grammar review Unit 3

Vocabulary

1 Circle the correct word in *italics* in these sentences.

1 Welcome to the Intercity Hotel. I hope you had a pleasant *travel / journey*.
2 Sarah came back from her shopping *trip / journey* with lots of new clothes.
3 Among Brian's many interests, he lists foreign *journeys / travel* and climbing.
4 Do you know the *way / journey* to the cathedral?
5 It was a long, dangerous *trip / journey* to the South Pole.
6 I always stop for coffee at a café on my *journey / way* to work.
7 Are you all prepared for your forthcoming *trip / travel* to Egypt?
8 Many of our students have quite a long *travel / journey* to college each morning.

Grammar

2 For questions 1–6, complete the second sentence so that it has a similar meaning to the first sentence, using the word given. Do not change the word given. You must use between two and five words, including the word given.

1 During my visit to London, I took hundreds of photos.
WHILE
I took hundreds of photos .... London.

2 I didn't notice that my passport was missing until I reached the immigration desk.
LOST
When I reached the immigration desk, I noticed that .... my passport.

3 I've given up using the bus to go to school.
USED
I .... by bus, but I've given it up.

4 She was still at school when she passed her driving test.
GOING
She passed her driving test when .... school.

5 Paola and Antonio met for the first time at yesterday's party.
NEVER
Paola and Antonio .... before yesterday's party.

6 Pablo is no longer as frightened of spiders as in the past.
USED
Pablo .... frightened of spiders than he is now.

Word formation

3 EP Read this text. Use the word given in capitals at the end of some of the lines to form a word that fits in the gap in the same line.

Paradise Hotel

We had been promised an **(0)** ......exceptional...... holiday in a three-star hotel, so we made our reservation despite the **(1)** .... expense this involved. The website said it was an **(2)** .... three-star hotel which promised outstanding views of **(3)** .... mountain scenery. Imagine how disappointed we felt when we found that we had been given a room with a view over the kitchens, which was completely **(4)** .... When we went down for dinner the first evening, we found that the restaurant was so **(5)** .... that we had to wait for our table even though we had booked it in advance.

When we finally sat down for dinner, the waitress was tired, irritable and generally **(6)** .... So we decided to spend the **(7)** .... days of our holiday in a quieter hotel nearby. It wasn't as luxurious as our first hotel, but the view of the mountains and river was certainly **(8)** .... to a view of the kitchens!

(0)	**EXCEPT**
(1)	**CONSIDER**
(2)	**EXCLUDE**
(3)	**DRAMA**
(4)	**ACCEPT**
(5)	**ORGANISE**
(6)	**HELP**
(7)	**REMAIN**
(8)	**PREFER**

Vocabulary and grammar review Unit 4

Vocabulary

1 Complete this text by writing *food, dish* or *meal* in the correct form in the gaps. In some gaps, more than one answer is possible.

Last week, my boyfriend, Nigel, invited me out for a **(1)** .... in a restaurant. The **(2)** .... was not very good though. For my first course, I chose a **(3)** .... called 'Chef's special', which turned out to be a kind of pizza. Generally, I'm not very keen on fast **(4)** .... , and this **(5)** .... was quite disappointing because it wasn't very special. Nigel didn't enjoy his **(6)** .... very much either. Personally, I think we would have enjoyed ourselves more if I'd cooked a **(7)** .... at home – after all, I had plenty of **(8)** .... in the fridge.

Grammar

2 For questions 1–6, complete the second sentence so that it has a similar meaning to the first sentence, using the word given. Do not change the word given. You must use between two and five words, including the word given.

1 The food was so hot that we didn't really enjoy it.
TOO
The food was .... really enjoy.

2 The waitress spoke so quickly that we had difficulty understanding her.
ENOUGH
The waitress didn't speak .... understand her easily.

3 We didn't get a table at the restaurant because it was too full.
SO
The restaurant .... we couldn't get a table.

4 I asked for a second helping because the food was so delicious.
SUCH
It was .... I asked for a second helping.

5 Julio is not a very good cook, so he won't get a job in that restaurant.
ENOUGH
Julio doesn't .... to get a job in that restaurant.

6 We ate very late because Phil spent too much time preparing the meal.
TIME
Phil spent .... preparing the meal that we ate very late.

Word formation

3 EP Read this text. Use the word given in capitals at the end of some of the lines to form a word that fits in the gap in the same line.

Changing diets

Even in quite **(0)** ......traditional...... **TRADITION**
societies, eating habits are changing.
In the past, people used to prepare
good **(1)** .... meals **FILL**
from fresh ingredients and what was
readily available in markets, but
now **(2)** .... food is **CONVENIENT**
becoming **(3)** .... popular. **INCREASE**
Research shows that eating some
types of food too often may cause
health problems, so governments and
other **(4)** .... now offer **ORGANISE**
information about diet and nutrition in
the hope that it will **(5)** .... **COURAGE**
people from eating too much of the
same thing and have a generally more
(6) .... diet. **BALANCE**

On the other hand, some people argue
that despite the **(7)** .... of **APPEAR**
many traditional dishes from our menus,
in general our diets are not as repetitive
as they used to be. There is a much
wider **(8)** .... of products **CHOOSE**
available in supermarkets and other
shops than there was 20 years ago.

5 Study time

Starting off

Work in groups.

What aspects of school life do these photos show?
How can students benefit from these activities?
Which of these activities have you done?
Which did you enjoy most?

Listening | Part 1

1 EP You are going to hear people talking in eight different situations connected with studying. Before you listen, match these words or phrases (1–9) with their definitions (a–i).

1 tutor
2 research (verb)
3 learner
4 mark (verb)
5 admission
6 pass (noun)
7 sit (an exam)
8 course requirement
9 job prospects

a check a piece of work or an exam, showing mistakes and giving a number or a letter to say how good it is
b someone who is getting knowledge or a new skill
c something that is needed or demanded for a course
d study a subject in detail in order to discover new information about it
e successful result in a test or course
f take a test or exam
g the possibility of being successful at finding work
h university teacher who teaches a small group of students
i when someone is given permission to become a member of a club, university, etc.

2 Now read these questions and <u>underline</u> the main idea in each question (but not the options A, B or C).

1 You overhear a student talking about a course he has been doing. How does he feel about the course now?
A discouraged
B nervous
C satisfied

2 You hear a student complaining about a problem she has had. What was the problem with her essay?
A It had to be rewritten.
B It was similar to another essay.
C It was given a low mark.

3 You hear a student at a language school in Japan. What does she like most about the experience?
A attending language classes
B doing other activities after class
C meeting other language students

4 You hear an interview with a student who is thinking of studying abroad. What does she think will be the main benefit?
A living in a different culture
B becoming more independent
C getting a better qualification

5 You overhear the director of a school talking to students. Why is he talking to them?
A to explain something
B to remind them of something
C to cancel something

6 You hear a girl leaving a message about her first day at a new school. What surprised her about the school?
A the other students
B the teachers
C the classrooms

7 You hear two students talking about a lesson. What does the boy think about the lesson?
A It was too advanced.
B It was too long.
C It was too disorganised.

8 You hear a teacher talking to a student. What is he giving her advice about?
A sitting university exams
B choosing a university course
C paying for university fees

3 ▶16 Listen and, for questions 1–8, choose the best answer (A, B or C).

Exam advice

- Read the questions carefully, <u>underlining</u> the main ideas in the question as you read. This helps you to focus on what is being asked. In some cases, you may have to <u>underline</u> the whole question.
- The words you hear will usually be different from the words in the question; listen for the meaning rather than actual words.

Vocabulary

Phrasal verbs

1 EP Match these phrasal verbs from Listening Part 1 (1–8) with their definitions (a–h).

1 get over
2 live up to
3 hand back
4 get away with
5 point out
6 put off
7 turn out
8 look back

a be as good as something
b decide or arrange to delay an event or activity until a later time or date
c feel better after something or someone has made you unhappy, or get better after an illness
d be known or discovered finally and surprisingly
e return something to the person who gave it to you
f to think about something that happened in the past
g succeed in avoiding punishment for something
h tell someone about some information, often because you believe they are not aware of it or have forgotten it

2 Complete these sentences by writing a phrasal verb from Exercise 1 in the correct form in the gaps.

1 Franz hates writing essays and tries to .... writing them till the last moment.
2 I don't know how Charo .... copying her essays from the Internet, but the teacher never seems to notice.
3 Julia worked really hard for the test, but when the teacher .... it .... she found she'd got a very low mark. I hope she .... the disappointment soon because she's looking really depressed.
4 My mum is very ambitious for me and it's difficult to .... her expectations. I think when she .... at her youth, she feels she didn't study hard enough herself.
5 The exam .... to be easier than I expected and, just as you .... , it was all things we'd studied before.

find out, get to know, know, learn, teach and *study; attend, join, take part* and *assist*

3 Candidates often confuse the following words: *find out, get to know, know, learn, teach* and *study; attend, join, take part* and *assist*. Circle the correct word in *italics* in these sentences, then check your answers by reading the definitions on page 183.

1 I've been thinking of going to an Italian university and *learning / studying* international business for a year.
2 I only *found out / knew* in my tutorial just now when the tutor handed my essay back to me.
3 … the opportunity to live abroad would be extremely educational because I'd *learn / study* about the Italian way of life and way of thinking.
4 I *learn / know* Japanese from Japanese teachers.
5 I'm doing a karate course *learned / taught* in Japanese.
6 … I'm *knowing / getting to know* lots of local people.
7 They also organise lots of other things for us learners to *assist / take part* in after school.
8 There are clubs we can *assist / join* if we're interested …
9 You're expected to *join / attend* all your lessons …

4 Complete these sentences by writing the words from Exercise 3 in the correct form in the gaps.

1 Dimitri has been .... Spanish because he hopes to study in Seville next year.
2 I've .... a lot of interesting people from different countries while doing this course.
3 Maria hopes to .... chemistry when she goes to university.
4 While Karen was at summer camp, she .... how to windsurf.
5 The best way to .... the answer to this question is to look on the Internet.
6 I'd like to ring Kevin, but I don't .... his phone number.
7 I had a wonderful course tutor who .... me to speak Spanish really well.
8 The university has an accommodation officer who will .... students with finding somewhere to live.
9 Kostas .... a youth club because he wanted to meet people.
10 It was the first time he had .... in a marathon, so people were surprised when he won.

Grammar

Zero, first and second conditionals

1 Read the sentences (1–6) below. Which …

a refer to something which the speaker thinks is possible?
b refer to something which the speaker is imagining, thinks is improbable, or thinks is impossible?
c refer to something which is generally true?

1 If you speak a bit of the language, it's much easier to make friends.
2 If I went, it might make it more difficult for me to get a good degree.
3 If for any reason you can't make it to a tutorial, try to let your tutor know.
4 If I lived in Italy, I'd learn about how Italians live and think.
5 If your tutor has to cancel a tutorial or put it off, he or she'll try to tell you the week beforehand.
6 Your tutors will organise you into groups and suggest research unless you prefer working alone.

→ page 164 Language reference: Conditionals

2 Match the beginning of each sentence (1–10) with its ending (a–j).

1 I won't mention your name
2 I'd travel round the world
3 We don't allow people to do the course
4 I'll have to buy the book
5 If I decide to study abroad,
6 If I see her,
7 If I wasn't so busy,
8 If I went to study in Australia,
9 I'd take a taxi
10 If students come to class regularly,

a I won't see my girlfriend for several months.
b they usually get good results.
c I'd go to the cinema with you.
d I wouldn't come back.
e I'll tell her you called.
f if I had the money.
g unless I can find it in the library.
h unless you want me to.
i if I could afford one.
j unless they have the right qualifications.

3 Candidates often make mistakes with first and second conditionals. Find and correct one mistake in each of these sentences. There may be more than one way to correct some sentences.

1 If I say that technology has not changed the way we study, I would be lying.
2 If I live near my school, I would go there by bicycle or even on foot.
3 If we study together, I think we would be able to test each other at the same time.
4 If we'll have any free time during the term, we can organise a school excursion.
5 If you'll have any problems on your course, please contact your tutor, who will sort them out.
6 If there will be something that interests you, do write back, and I'll do my best to tell you.
7 If I buy a computer, I would have to spend all day in front of it.
8 If we take a good rest, we would be full of energy and we could do everything better.
9 If you'll decide to stay until Christmas, you'll find Athens very exciting.
10 I'd like to say that if more people travelled by bicycle, the atmosphere will be better.

4 Complete the second sentence so that it has a similar meaning to the first sentence, using the word given. Do not change the word given. You must use between two and five words, including the word given.

1 We will not be able to finish the project without your help.
ASSIST
Unless .... project, we will not be able to finish it.
2 You cannot use the swimming pool unless you become a member of the sports club.
JOIN
You can only use the swimming pool .... the sports club.
3 Stella will not participate in the concert because she is feeling ill.
PART
If Stella was not feeling ill, she .... the concert.
4 It will be necessary for us to postpone the match if the weather does not improve.
PUT
Unless the weather gets better, we .... the match.
5 Your English improves because your teacher shows you your mistakes.
UNLESS
Your English would not get .... out your mistakes.
6 I will only play in the basketball match if I recover from my cold.
GET
Unless .... , I will not play in the basketball match.

5 Work in pairs. Take turns to ask each other these questions.

- If you could study anywhere in the world, where would you go?
- If you studied in a different country, what do you think would be your biggest problem?
- If you could change one thing in your life, what would it be?
- If, one day, you became famous, what do you think you'd be famous for?
- How will you celebrate if you pass all your exams this year?

Reading and Use of English | Part 7

1 Work in pairs. You are going to read extracts from four reports written by secondary-school students from different countries. Each student has written about an educational exchange he/she went on to another country. Before you read, discuss these questions.

1 How do you think students benefit from going to school in another country for a term (or even a year)?
2 What problems do each of the pictures show?
3 If you were doing an educational exchange, how would you deal with each problem?

1

2

3

4

2 Now underline the main idea in each question 1–10.

Which person

was surprised by the different approach to education? 1 ☐
enjoyed cooperating with their host family? 2 ☐
believes they are more adult as a result of the exchange? 3 ☐
feels the exchange has helped to equip them for the future? 4 ☐
felt a responsibility to take as much advantage as possible of exchange? 5 ☐
had a different attitude to attending school while abroad? 6 ☐
wanted a change from their normal school life? 7 ☐
had not expected to be able to do an exchange? 8 ☐
had mixed feelings about the type of school? 9 ☐
changed their opinion of people as a result of the exchange? 10 ☐

Exam advice

- Before you read the sections, read the questions carefully, underlining the main ideas.
- Read the first section and find which questions it answers.
- Deal with each section in turn in this way.
- If you have any time left at the end, go back and check what you have written and fill in any questions you missed.

3 For questions 1–10 above, choose the students A–D on page 57 and underline the words which give you the answer. The students may be chosen more than once.

4 Work in groups. Look at this post on an international student forum. Think about the experiences of the students you have just read about and decide what Anna should do.

Anna
I'm 16 years old and I'm interested in coming to your country for a few months to learn the language. I know a little of the language, but I'd like to speak it much better because I might decide to study it at university in future. What do you think I should do? Should I do an educational exchange and find a family with people my own age to stay with, or would it be better to stay at home and do an online course or go to a language school in my town?

At school abroad

Have you ever thought of studying abroad? Four students who studied abroad relate their experiences …

A Divya Singh from Cardiff went to Chile

I went to a talk given by a couple of older students who had been on an exchange programme the previous year, and it occurred to me that if I could persuade my mum, this would be just the sort of break from normal school routine that I needed. I filled in my application while holding out little hope of being selected. However I was, and was soon immersed in a totally different educational culture, which helped me to appreciate many aspects of my school back home. Another great advantage of my year abroad was that I picked up Spanish much more quickly than in classes back home and, because my teachers were pretty demanding, I even feel confident writing it now. As a result, I'm considering doing Spanish and Latin American studies at university and perhaps after that going into the diplomatic service.

B Bruce Brown from Sydney went to England

Although my parents had insisted that I went, I knew what a sacrifice they were making to pay for my year abroad, so I was determined to make the most of the opportunity. My host family was really welcoming, but what I found hard to get used to were the seemingly endless days of grey drizzle and the fact that it got dark so early in winter. Even so, I took every chance to get out and meet people, make friends and get a real, in-depth experience of English life. At the same time, I was keen to make an impact at school and get good grades, although I found the schoolwork quite challenging and not really the highlight of my stay. Even so, I learned far more than I expected, made a lot of friends and came away with the impression that the British are a lot more interesting than I had been given to expect by people back home.

C Nelson Grace from Boston went to New Zealand

I lived on a farm on South Island, where my host family had a vast flock of about 3,000 sheep. Being a city boy, the experience of farming life was totally novel, but I loved it and took every opportunity to go out and help with the work of the farm. I also got involved in lots of sporting activities with my school, including sailing, rugby and skiing – all firsts for me. I found New Zealanders so enthusiastic about everything that I used to get up with a buzz of excitement and, unlike back home, I actually looked forward to going into school every day. I also think I matured a lot during my year abroad. I'm not so dependent now on my family or my teachers to make me study, and I've learned to get on with all sorts of different people, even if they're not my type. I've also learned a bit about the value of money!

D Carmen Echevarria from Bilbao went to Scotland

After four years in a state secondary school in Bilbao, it was a huge shock to find myself in a private all-girls school in the Highlands of Scotland, where everyone wore uniforms. Studying there was a complete revelation to me: gone were the hours spent in the evenings memorising huge numbers of useless facts for tests the next day which I would forget as soon as the test was over. Instead, we spent a lot of time discussing issues, solving problems and writing creatively. I missed my friends back home, but really appreciated learning to think in new ways and seeing that education could be so creative. I missed not sharing my classes with boys, but on the other hand, we probably concentrated harder and may have felt more relaxed about the opinions we expressed.

Reading and Use of English | Part 3

1 EP Form nouns from these verbs.

Verb	Noun
qualify	1 qualification
intend	2
respond	3
adjust	4
compare	5
exist	6
demand	7
develop	8
behave	9
advise	10
appear	11
know	12

2 EP Each of these nouns has been formed from a verb. Write the verb next to each noun.

Verb	Noun
1 agree	agreement
2	assessment
3	feeling
4	involvement
5	investigation
6	confusion
7	preference
8	approval

➔ page 181 Language reference: Word formation

Exam advice

Read the text quickly to see what it is about.

- Read before and after the gap to decide:
  - what meaning the word has
  - what type of word you need (noun, verb, adjective or adverb).
- Think about how you need to change the word in capitals to form the word you need.
- When you have finished, read the completed text to check it makes sense.

3 EP Read the text below.

- Decide what type of word (verb, noun, adjective or adverb) you need for each gap.
- Then, use the word given in capitals at the end of some of the lines to form a word that fits in the gap in the same line.

Culture shock for international students

Students going to study in another country usually have to make a number of cultural	
(0) adjustments . They may find it difficult to form	ADJUST
(1) .... with local people and they will	FRIEND
certainly have to get used to a **(2)**	VARY
of new things including food, the climate and the language. An extra difficulty may be the	
different **(3)** .... which their teachers	EXPECT
and tutors have of them in **(4)** .... with	COMPARE
their home country. They may be	
(5) .... for the amount of work they	PREPARE
have to do on their own or the fact that their tutors are looking for originality and a capacity	
for **(6)** .... thought rather than an ability	DEPEND
to memorise large quantities of information. Equally, they may sometimes be surprised by	
the **(7)** .... of their fellow students who,	BEHAVE
although usually friendly and **(8)** .... ,	WELCOME
may sometimes seem a little immature. As time passes, international students will find that things become easier and what was unfamiliar to start with will eventually seem normal.	

4 Work in groups. How do schools benefit from having visits from exchange students?

Speaking | Part 1

1 17 Work in pairs. Complete this extract of two candidates doing Speaking Part 1. Then listen to check your answers.

Teacher: Nikolai, what is your favourite subject at school?
Nikolai: I find biology very interesting. That's **(1)** .... I enjoy all science subjects a lot and **(2)** .... I can get good enough marks in my final exams, I'll study medicine **(3)** .... I go to university. Also, I've got a really excellent biology teacher, **(4)** .... makes the subject much more fun.
Teacher: And you, Martyna, how do you think you'll use English in the future?
Martyna: Well, I think English is an absolute necessity now and you just can't get by without it. It'll help me to find a job, and **(5)** .... my work involves travelling, it'll really be essential. I'd like to work in business, **(6)** .... I think English is really necessary for that too.
Teacher: Thank you. Nikolai, can you …

2 Work in pairs.

1 How many reasons does Nikolai give for his answer?
2 How many situations does Martyna mention for using English?
3 Why is it good to combine ideas and reasons in your answers?
4 Why is it good to sound interested and enthusiastic?

3 Think how you can answer these two questions, combining your ideas and reasons for them. Then work in pairs and take turns to ask and answer the questions.

- What is/was your favourite subject at school? Why?
- How do you think you'll use English in the future?

4 **Pronunciation:** word stress (2)

With some related words, the stress is different depending on whether it is a noun, a verb or an adjective.

1 18 Listen to these words. Which syllable is stressed?

necessary necessity

2 Decide which syllable is stressed in each of these words.

satisfying / satisfactory educate / education
exam / examination explain / explanation
graduate / graduation possible / possibility
prefer / preference refer / reference
relative / relation institute / institution

3 19 Now listen to check your answers. What do you notice about where we stress words ending in

- *-tion?*
- *-ity?*

4 Work in pairs. Take turns to read the words aloud.

5 Think about how you can answer these two questions using three or four words from Pronunciation Exercise 2 in your answers.

- What do you particularly like about the school where you study?
- What plans and ambitions do you have for your education in the future?

6 Work in pairs. Take turns to ask and answer the questions above. While you listen to your partner, pay attention to whether they use the correct stress on the words from Pronunciation Exercise 2 that they use. Correct them where necessary.

7 Work in pairs. Decide whether you will be Student A or Student B and take some time to think about how you will answer your questions. Then take turns to ask your partner the questions in their box.

Questions for Student A

- Can you describe the school you go (went) to?
- What would you like to study in the future if you had the chance? Why?
- How much homework do students in your country generally do?
- Can you tell me what you most enjoy about learning English?
- Tell me about the best teacher you have ever had.

Questions for Student B

- Do you prefer studying alone or with other people? Why?
- Can you remember your first day at school? Tell me about it.
- Would you like to study in a different country? Why? / Why not?
- How important are exams in your country?
- How important is learning English to you?

Exam advice

- Listen carefully to the question and make sure your answers are relevant.
- Where possible, give reasons for your answer and/or add some extra information.

Writing | Part 1 An essay

1 Read this writing task and discuss the essay question with a partner. Make a note of all your ideas and opinions from the discussion.

In your English class, you have been talking about what subjects should be compulsory at secondary school.

Now your English teacher has asked you to write an essay.

Write an essay using **all** the notes and give reasons for your point of view.

Essay question
All young people should study a foreign language as part of their education.
Do you agree?

Notes
Write about:

1. working life
2. travel and holidays
3. .... (your own idea)

2 Work alone and write a plan for your essay. Then compare your plan with your partner's.

3 Read Marina's essay plan and then answer the questions below.

Para. 1: Brief intro – present situation: more contact with other countries, more travel – my view: essential

Para. 2: necessary to get a job; useful for international work

Para. 3: going abroad – speaking with local people: more enjoyable + you learn more

Para. 4: using the Internet– mainly in English: essential information for all aspects of life – give examples

Para. 5: conclusion – my opinion: people who can't speak f. lang. have fewer opportunities.

1 Has she repeated words or phrases from the task in her plan? Why? / Why not?
2 How long do you think it took her to write the plan?
3 Has she covered all the points in the task? Why is this important?

4 Work in groups. Read the three opening paragraphs below (1–3).

- Which paragraph do you think is best? Why?
- What is wrong with the other two paragraphs?

1
Although most young people spend many hours at school learning a foreign language, usually English, for most of them the result is that they do not learn to speak it well and all this time is wasted. Instead, they could be learning mathematics or computer science, which are both really useful subjects. Is learning a foreign language a useful school subject? I will give you my opinion at the end.

2
In the past, only educated people in high society learned to speak foreign languages. This was mainly because only they could afford an education. However, as time has passed, education has become available to all children, and foreign-language learning has become increasingly common. Why do young people have to study foreign languages, and how do they benefit from doing so? That's the question.

3
In the modern world, we have to work and communicate with people from other countries. For this reason, I believe that learning a foreign language is an essential part of modern education.

5 Match these teachers' comments (a–c) with each of the opening paragraphs in Exercise 4.

a
- A good opening paragraph. You've stated your point of view clearly and directly and related it to the present situation.
- It's just two sentences, so plenty of space for the rest of the task!

b
- The history of language learning is not relevant to the task.
- Your question is <u>not</u> the question in the task, so also irrelevant. Stick carefully to the writing task.
- Your intro is 63 words – you now have a maximum of 120 words for dealing with the task. If you don't deal with the task exactly, you won't pass the exam!

c

- You've started the essay with an opinion, not an introduction to the topic. Will your final opinion be different?
- The paragraph is too long.
- You don't appear to have planned the essay – you've just started with the first idea that occurred to you. Remember: you'll lose marks if your essay is not well planned and organised.

6 Now write your own opening paragraph for the task in Exercise 1.

7 Complete Marina's answer below by writing the words and phrases from the box (which she uses for linking her ideas together) in the gaps.

a further point is that | also | do so | for all these reasons | for example when | if | it | these opportunities | with the result that

In the modern world, we work and communicate with people from other countries. For this reason, I believe that learning a foreign language is an essential part of modern education.
Nowadays, many jobs are international, **(1)** .... people have to be able to communicate in English. **(2)** .... people are likely to work in different countries during their careers, **(3)** .... their companies send them abroad to work. **(4)** .... will not arise for people who cannot speak a foreign language.
In their free time, many people like to travel and, **(5)** .... they can speak to local people, they enjoy their holidays more and learn about the places they visit. If they cannot speak a language, they probably stay in their own country and miss seeing other places.
(6) .... we all use the Internet in English for study and work. **(7)** .... gives us information about things which are interesting and useful to us.
(8) .... , it is essential for young people to learn a foreign language. If they do not **(9)** .... , they will have fewer opportunities.

page 167: Language reference: Linking words and phrases

8 Work in pairs. Read this writing task and:

- discuss your ideas and opinions
- make a note of any useful points
- write a plan for your essay.

In your English class, you have been talking about studying abroad.

Now your English teacher has asked you to write an essay.

Write an essay using all the notes and give reasons for your point of view.

Essay question
All young people who have the opportunity should study in a foreign school or college for a year. Do you agree?

Notes
Write about:

1. what they learn
2. growing up
3. .... (your own idea)

Write your **essay**.

9 Write your essay following your plan. You should write between 140 and 190 words. You can use Marina's essay in Exercise 7 as a model.

Exam advice

Make sure that you:

- read the question carefully and underline the key words to make sure that you know exactly what to do
- answer the question exactly
- deal with all the points below the question
- include your own idea.

Write a brief first paragraph which:

- states why the question is important
- briefly indicates your point of view.

6 My first job

Starting off

Work in groups.

1 Which of the jobs in the photos would be best for a student in their free time? Which job would be best during their holidays?

2 Which job would suit you best? Which would suit you least? Why?

Listening | Part 3

1 Work in pairs. You are going to hear five young people talking about their first job. For each speaker (1–5), you will have to choose from the list of options (A–H) which feelings or opinions they describe. Before you listen, paraphrase each option in your own words.

A I feel people enjoy chatting to me.
I get the impression people like talking to me.
B I find it surprisingly hard work.
C I'm learning a lot from the people I meet.
D I might have the opportunity to achieve an ambition.
E I feel I'm gaining useful skills.
F I enjoy some parts of the job more than others.
G I enjoy the financial independence.
H I feel frustrated with things I can't deal with.

Speaker 1 [ ] 1
Speaker 2 [ ] 2
Speaker 3 [ ] 3
Speaker 4 [ ] 4
Speaker 5 [ ] 5

2 ▶20 Now listen. For speakers 1–5 above, choose from the list (A–H) what each speaker says. Use the letters only once. There are three extra letters which you do not need to use.

Exam advice

- Before you listen, read each option carefully and think about what it means.
- Listen for the general idea of what each speaker is saying.
- Wait until each speaker finishes before you choose an answer.
- Remember that the speakers may talk about something connected with other sentences, but there is only one correct sentence for each speaker.

3 Work in groups.

- Would you be interested in doing any of the jobs the speakers talked about? Why? / Why not?
- What job would be 'a dream come true' for you?

Vocabulary

work or *job*; *possibility*, *occasion* or *opportunity*; *fun* or *funny*

1 Candidates often confuse the following words: *work* or *job; possibility, occasion* or *opportunity; fun* or *funny.* Read these sentences from Listening Part 3 and circle the correct word in *italics*. Then read the definitions on page 183 to check your answers.

1 This is my first student *job / work*, and I'm a part-time hospital porter.
2 It's hard physical *job / work*, but I think I expected that when I started.
3 They have the *possibility / occasion / opportunity* to talk about things outside the hospital.
4 On some *possibilities / occasions / opportunities*, I've also been left on my own in charge of the whole hotel.
5 It isn't a very well-paid *job / work* and it's not exactly fun, but then first *jobs / works* usually aren't.
6 The people are really *fun / funny*, so there are lots of laughs on set.
7 There's even the *possibility / occasion / opportunity* that I'll be given a small part.

2 Circle the correct word in *italics* in these sentences.

1 I know he was trying to be *fun / funny*, but none of his jokes made us laugh.
2 The trip was *fun / funny* – we should do it again sometime.
3 I don't think there's much *possibility / opportunity* of him being chosen for the job.
4 I only wear these smart clothes on special *occasions / opportunities*.
5 Did you get a(n) *possibility / opportunity* to chat to Matt yesterday?
6 She's just filled out a form applying for a summer *job / work*.
7 I'm hoping to study engineering and to find *job / work* in the construction industry when I finish.
8 One of my *jobs / works* was to count the money at the end of the day.

3 Work in pairs. Complete the diagram below by grouping these words which form adjective collocations with *job* and *work* according to meaning. In some cases, more than one answer may be possible.

badly paid challenging demanding ~~fascinating~~ ~~full-time~~ ~~hard~~ holiday manual office ~~outdoor~~ part-time permanent pleasant responsible ~~skilled~~ temporary tiring tough weekend ~~well-paid~~ worthwhile

a .... job / .... work

1 ....well-paid....
2 ....

3 ....hard....
4 ....
5 ....
6 ....
7 ....

12 ....full-time....
13 ....
14 ....
15 ....
16 ....
17 ....

8 ....outdoor....
9 ....

18 ....fascinating....
19 ....
20 ....
21 ....

10 ....skilled....
11 ....

4 Work in pairs. Describe each of these jobs using two or three adjectives from Exercise 3. (Put the adjectives which express your opinion first and the adjectives which express a fact afterwards, e.g. *Being a lifeguard at a swimming pool is a pleasant, outdoor, temporary job.*)

- waiter
- doctor
- social worker
- babysitter
- accountant
- the job you would like to do in the future

Reading and Use of English | Part 5

1 You are going to read an extract from the autobiography of Lucy Irvine, whose first job was in her father's hotel. Before you read, work in groups. What do you think are the advantages and disadvantages of working with your parents?

2 Read the extract quickly to answer these questions.

1 What was Lucy's job?
2 What part of her job involved making things?

Lucy's first job

When I was just 16, my father bought an old guesthouse in the village where we lived and decided to turn it into a luxury hotel. At the early stages of the hotel, he experimented with everything. None of us had ever worked in a hotel before, but my dad had a vision of what guests would like to see. His standards were uncompromisingly high and he believed that in order to achieve those standards the most important thing was work.

For a month that summer, my name was down on the duty roster as waitress at breakfast and dinner, which included laying the tables in the dining room beforehand and hoovering and glass polishing afterwards. This gave me the middle of the day free for studying because, predictably, my school report had not lived up to my father's high expectations.

Like all the other waitresses, I was equipped with a neat little uniform and instructions to treat the guests as though they were special visitors in my own home. Although I did not feel comfortable with this, I did not express my feelings. Instead I concentrated all my attention on doing the job as well as, if not better than, the older girls.

I soon learned how to tackle the two most daunting installations in the kitchen: the dishwasher and the chef, Gordon. He had an impressive chef's hat and a terrifying ability to lose his temper and get violent for no clear reason. His breath was strong and fishy, and I avoided close contact with him and always grabbed the dishes he set down with a forbidding expression on my face which was transformed into a charming smile in the brief space between kitchen and dining room.

Breakfast waitressing was, I found, more enjoyable than the dinner shift. The guests came wandering into the dining room from seven thirty onwards, staring with appreciation at the view of sea and islands through the dining-room window. If the day looked promising, I would note down requests for boats and packed lunches along with their breakfast orders. It was a matter of pride to me that everyone got their order promptly, and I took pleasure in my ability to get on with the people at each table.

It was funny how differently people behaved in the evenings, dressed up and talking with louder, colder voices, not always returning my smile. However, that all changed when Dad, who was keen to make full use of my potential, created a special role for me which made me feel considerably more important.

It began with a few modest trays of cakes for the guests' packed lunches and progressed swiftly to fancy cakes for afternoon teas. I found that recipes were easy to follow and it was amusing to improvise. This led to the climax: a nightly extravaganza known as Lucy's Sweet Trolley. Every evening, I made a grand entrance, wheeling before me a trolley carrying the most extraordinary collection of puddings, cakes and other desserts ever to grace a Scottish hotel. Most were things I had invented myself and I had cooked all of them. Some – Jacobite Grenades, Mocha Genghis Khan and Goat's Milk Bavarios to name a few – were undeniably strange. It was Dad's idea that I should dress smartly and stop at each table and recite the name of each dish.

Adapted from *Runaway* by Lucy Irvine

3 **Read these questions and copy out (or underline) the parts of the text which provide the answers.**

1 In paragraph 1, what does Lucy say the people working at the hotel had in common?
2 What does the writer mean by *daunting* in line 24?
3 What did Lucy do while she carried food to the dining room?
4 Why did Lucy enjoy serving breakfasts more than dinners?
5 What was special about the food on Lucy's Sweet Trolley?

4 **For questions 1–6, choose the answer (A, B, C or D) which you think fits best according to the text. Use the words you underlined in Exercise 3 to help you.**

1 What did the people working at the hotel have in common?
A They all understood the guests' expectations.
B They all shared the same goals.
C They all lacked experience.
D They were all hard-working.

2 What does the writer mean by *daunting* in line 24?
A disgusting
B frightening
C interesting
D strange

3 What did Lucy do while she carried food to the dining room?
A She smiled at Gordon in a friendly way.
B She avoided touching Gordon.
C She checked the food Gordon gave her.
D She started to look more friendly.

4 Lucy enjoyed serving breakfasts more than dinners because the guests were
A more demanding.
B more friendly.
C more punctual.
D more relaxed.

5 What was special about the food on Lucy's Sweet Trolley?
A It was inspired by traditional recipes.
B It was prepared along with food for picnics.
C It was made following her father's instructions.
D It contained a number of new creations.

6 What impression does Lucy give of her job throughout the passage?
A She found many opportunities to laugh.
B She looked for ways of doing it better.
C She found all aspects of it enjoyable.
D She could do it with little effort.

Exam advice

- First read the text quickly to get a general idea of what it is about.
- Read the first question, find where it is answered in the text and read that section carefully more than once before you read the options A, B, C and D.
- Read each of the options A, B, C and D carefully and choose the one which matches what the text says.

5 **Work in pairs.**

- Would you enjoy doing a job like Lucy's? Why? / Why not?
- Which parts of her job would you enjoy more and which would you enjoy less?
- Do you think being a waiter is a good holiday job for a teenager? Why? / Why not?

Speaking | Part 2

1 Work in pairs. When you compare photos, you can say what the photos have in common as well as what is different about them. Discuss how you could answer the examiner's instructions below to say:

- which things are similar
- which things are different.

> I'd like you to compare the photographs and say what you think the people are learning from doing these two types of work.

What are the people learning from doing these two types of work?

2 How could you use these words or phrases to talk about the photos?

a involve b deal with c not well-paid d coaching
e full-time f part-time g keep somebody in order
h work under pressure i keep cool

3 ▶21 Listen to Nikolai and Antonia doing this part of the test. Which photo do they use each word or phrase with? Write 1, 2 or B (both) by each word or phrase (a–i).

4 Which of these strategies (a or b) does Nikolai use when doing the task?

a He describes the first photo and answers the question before moving on to the second photo and doing the same.
b He points out similarities as well as differences between the two photos and switches between them as he answers.

5 Listen again. Which of these phrases does Nikolai use? Tick (✓) the ones you hear.

- Both photos show … ✓
- Both the jobs in the photos involve … / … neither of them …
- Anyway, the first photo shows …
- While the girl in the first photo …
- … whereas in the second photo … / … whereas the boy's …
- Another thing in the second photo is …
- I think both can …
- On the other hand …
- not just … but also …

6 Pronunciation: sentence stress (2)

We can use stress to contrast ideas or information.

1 Which ideas or information does Nikolai contrast in this sentence?

Anyway, the first photo shows a girl serving young people in a restaurant, whereas in the second photo a boy is working with children.

2 ▶22 Listen to the sentence and underline the stressed words.

3 ▶23 Decide which words are stressed in these sentences. Then listen to check your answers.

- The girl's job may be full time, // whereas the boy's is probably part time.
- The girl can learn how to keep customers happy, // while the boy has to keep children in order.
- He'll probably learn not just to deal with children, // but also their parents.
- I'd prefer to coach children than work in a restaurant // because really I enjoy being in the fresh air more than being indoors.

4 Work in pairs. Student A: read the first half of each sentence up to each // using the same stress as above. Student B: read the second half of the sentence using the same stress as above.
Student A: The girl's job may be full-time ...
Student B: ... whereas the boy's is probably part-time.

7 Work alone.

- Write three sentences to compare the photos and say which job you think is more difficult. Use phrases from Exercise 5 in your sentences.
- When you are ready, work in pairs and take turns to read your sentences aloud using stress to contrast your ideas.

8 Work in pairs.

Student A: Do the speaking task in Exercise 1 on page 66.
Student B: Time your partner and make sure they speak for one minute.

9 Work in pairs.

Student B: Follow the examiner's instructions in the next column.
Student A: Time your partner and make sure they speak for one minute.

Then change roles.

"Here are your photographs. They show people doing different part-time jobs. I'd like you to compare the photographs and say what you think the people might enjoy about doing these jobs."

What do the people enjoy about doing these jobs?

Exam advice

- Compare the general differences between the two photos and also spend time answering the printed question.
- You can talk about one photo first and then the other (as you saw in Unit 2), or both at the same time (as in this unit).
- Keep speaking till the examiner says 'Thank you'.

Grammar

Countable and uncountable nouns

1 Most of these sentences contain mistakes which are often made by candidates. Two of them are correct. Find and correct the mistakes.

1 Could you please send me some informations about the job?
2 I hope you don't mind if I give you an advice about how to apply for the job.
3 She's just found a work as an ambulance driver.
4 Public transport is still the best way to get around the city.
5 The hotel also provides accommodations for its employees.
6 Congratulations! The news about your job is very good.
7 He works in a shop selling furnitures.
8 Sorry to hear about the accident. Did it do many damages?
9 Unfortunately, when we arrived at the airport terminal, we couldn't find our luggages.
10 Everyone loves the band, because they play such fantastic musics.

➡ **page 165 Language reference:** Countable and uncountable nouns

2 Candidates often make mistakes with countable and uncountable nouns. Circle all the *uncountable* nouns in each list.

1 accommodation hotel luggage suitcase scenery
2 advice information knowledge news suggestion
3 accident bus damage transport
4 bed furniture
5 dish food meal
6 homework job service task work
7 equipment tool
8 instrument music

3 Complete these sentences by writing a word from the box in the gaps. In some cases, more than one answer may be possible.

piece bit deal number amount

1 Can I give you a .... of advice about shopping in this town?
2 During the storm, quite a large .... of trees were blown down.
3 Have you brought that .... of equipment I asked for? The amplifier, I mean.
4 I've just been given a great .... of news – I've passed my exams!
5 Seb put a great .... of effort into organising the party.
6 There were a large .... of guests at the party, judging by the .... of food that was eaten!

Articles

4 Look at the underlined examples from the reading text in extracts 1–6. Then match them with the rules for articles (*a, an, the*) below (a–f).

1 When I was just 16, my father bought an old guesthouse … (lines 1–2) b
2 … my father bought an old guesthouse in the village where we lived … (line 2)
3 At the early stages of the hotel, he experimented with everything. (line 4)
4 … but my dad had a vision of what guests would like to see … (line 6)
5 … the most important thing was work. (lines 8–9)
6 … the most important thing was work. (lines 8–9)

a No article is used when using uncountable nouns in the singular.
b *a* and *an* are used with singular countable nouns mentioned for the first time.
c *the* is used when it's clear who or what we are referring to from the context.
d No article is used when talking in general and in the plural.
e *the* is used with superlative adjectives and adverbs.
f *the* is used with things mentioned before.

➡ **page 163 Language reference:** Articles

5 Complete this text by writing *a, an, the* or '–' if no article is needed in the gaps.

I was just 18, and it was (1) .... first time I had worked in (2) .... office. It was (3) .... summer holidays and I had just finished (4) .... school. I thought it would be (5) .... good way of earning (6) .... bit of money before I went to (7) .... university in (8) .... autumn. I spent most of (9) .... day keying (10) .... information into the company's database. Although I found (11) .... job rather boring, I earned (12) .... good salary.

6 Candidates often make mistakes with articles. Correct the mistakes in these sentences. Some sentences contain more than one mistake.

1 Have you heard a latest news about Bayern Munich in the Champions' League?
2 I bought my first motorcycle at my age of 16.
3 I'm hoping to visit your town the next year.
4 She found a lot of useful information on Internet.
5 My mum had difficulty parking in city centre on Saturday.
6 I think that bicycles are most effective means of transport.
7 The money can cause a lot of problems.
8 I really enjoy listening to the music of all sorts on my iPod.
9 When I visit the foreign cities, I really like the shopping for clothes.
10 I'm having wonderful time with my friends.
11 I've got a plenty of spare time at this moment, so we can have a dinner together if you like.
12 We can provide an accommodation for you in a comfortable hotel.

Reading and Use of English | Part 2

1 Read this article quickly, ignoring the gaps. What activities does the programme include?

A new summer programme

This summer, a group of 16-year-old students are taking (0) ...*part*... in a three-week programme designed to teach them new skills and (1) .... them used to working with people they have never met before. (2) .... things go according to plan, in two years' time, nearly one in six teenagers will be involved in the programme with (3) .... eventual aim of offering it to (4) .... young person in the country. (5) .... far, our group has spent two weeks living (6) .... from home (many for the first time), initially on an outdoor course, with activities (7) .... as rock climbing, rafting and trekking, and then spending a week in self-catering accommodation where they are planning and setting up a volunteering project. At the moment, the students are putting their plans into action not (8) .... by cooking for themselves, but also by organising a night outside sleeping rough in order to raise money for a local homeless shelter.

Adapted from *The Independent*

2 Read the text again and think of the word which best fits each gap (1–8). Use only one word in each gap. There is an example at the beginning (0).

3 Check or complete your answers using these clues.

1 a verb
2 a conditional
3 an article
4 a synonym of *all*
5 a synonym of *up to now*
6 the opposite of *at home*
7 a synonym of *for example*
8 *not .... but also*

4 Work in groups.

1 Do you think all 15–17-year-olds should get experience of:
- living away from home?
- doing outdoor activities?
- cooking for themselves?
- helping other people?

Why? / Why not?

2 Which of the experiences above are the most useful for them to have?

Exam advice

- Read the text quite quickly to get a general idea what it is about.
- Look at the words before and after the gap and decide what type of word you need (an article, pronoun, preposition, etc.).
- When you've chosen a word, read the completed sentence to make sure it makes sense.
- Words may sometimes be part of fixed phrases, e.g. *in order to*, *as far as I know*, etc.

Writing | Part 2 A letter or email

1 Read this writing task and underline the three points you must deal with in your reply.

> You have received an email from an English friend, Rosie. Read this part of the email.
>
> I'm doing a college project on jobs students do. Can you help me by describing the sort of jobs students do in your country, any problems they have and the best way to find a good student job?
>
> Thanks,
>
> Rosie
>
> Write your **email**.

2 Work in pairs. Discuss what you can say to answer the three points. Note down your ideas as you speak.

3 Write a brief plan for your reply (in note form).
- How many paragraphs do you need?
- What ideas or information will you include in each paragraph?

4 Read Pablo's email to Rosie, ignoring the spelling mistakes, and answer these questions.

1 How does Pablo begin and end his email?
2 How do we know the subject of each of the three main paragraphs straight away?

Hi Rosie

It's good to hear from you.

In Spain, many students find part-time or casual work as waiters or kitchen workers in cafés or restaurans quite easely. Students usually do these sorts of jobs in the evenings, at weekends or in the summer.

Students who work have two main problems. First, it can be quite difficult for students to combine employment with the large amount of homework and studing for exams wich they have to do. Second, although they have to work extremely hard, the jobs are often not well payed. On the other hand, the money is usefull becaus it helps them to continue with their corses and have some pocket money.

Finding a job is usually straightforward, especialy if you live in a big city, or in an area which is visited by tourists. Many places put an advertisment in the window saying that they are looking for staff, so you just walk in and ask to speak to the manager. For many people, this is the most effective way of finding a job because they'll take you on immediately!

I hope this helps and good luck with your project.

Cheers,

Pablo

5 Pablo's email contains ten spelling mistakes often made by candidates. Find and correct the mistakes, e.g. ~~restaurans~~ restaurants

6 Decide whether these words are spelled correctly or not. Where they are spelled wrongly, write the correct spelling.

accomodation *accommodation*	experience
embarassing	begining
oportunity	comunicate
confortable	excelent
convenient	foward
greatful	preffer
believe	recieved
enviroment	recomend
necesary	wich

page 176 Language reference: Spelling

7 Read the writing task below and:

- underline the points you must deal with in your answer
- write a short plan.

You have received an email from an American friend, Bob. Read this part of his email.

> I'm doing a project in college on people's first jobs. Can you help me by describing your first job (or the first job of someone you know well), when you did it, what you learned from it and any problems you had with it?
>
> Thanks
>
> Bob

Write your **email**.

8 Write your email. You should write between 140 and 190 words.

page 189 Writing reference: Emails and letters

Exam advice and information

Writing Part 2 tests your ability to respond to a letter or email you have received, often from an English-speaking friend.

When writing a letter or email for this task:

- read the letter/email in the task carefully and underline the points you must deal with
- use the underlined points to write a plan, dealing with one point in each paragraph
- write following your plan.

Vocabulary and grammar review Unit 5

Vocabulary

1 Complete these sentences by writing a phrasal verb from page 53 in the correct form in the gaps.

1 It's getting harder for students to .... copying essays from the Internet, because teachers check up.
2 Our science teacher is ill, so she has .... our test until she has .... her infection and is back at work.
3 Piotr works hard because he wants to .... his parents' ambitions for him.
4 When I .... to when I first started secondary school, I realise that I didn't expect to enjoy studying chemistry, but it has .... to be quite interesting.
5 When my teacher .... my essay, she .... that I hadn't answered the question exactly and that there was a lot which was irrelevant.

2 Circle the correct word in *italics* in these sentences.

1 Mario is thinking of taking driving lessons to *know / learn* how to drive.
2 Ludmila wants to *know / study* biology at university.
3 Sven is *teaching / learning* me how to ski.
4 If you *join / assist* this club, you will *know / get to know* people from all over the world.
5 You should *attend / assist* lessons every day if you want to get high marks.
6 Sayed decided to *assist / take part* in the debate on human rights.

Grammar

3 Complete the second sentence so that it has a similar meaning to the first sentence, using the word given. Do not change the word given. You must use between two and five words, including the word given.

1 He won't pass the test because he doesn't work hard enough.
HARDER
If he worked .... pass the test.
2 Studying abroad will make you more independent.
BECOME
If you .... more independent.
3 Sandra only goes to lessons because she wants to meet other students.
ATTEND
If Sandra didn't want to meet other students, ... lessons.
4 I'll lend you my book if you take care of it.
AFTER
If you .... , you can borrow it.
5 I can't tell you the answer because I don't know.
WOULD
If I .... tell you.
6 He's not very enthusiastic because he's tired.
SO
If .... , he'd be more enthusiastic.

Word formation

4 EP For questions 1–8, read this text. Use the word given in capitals at the end of some of the lines to form a word that fits in the gap in the same line. There is an example at the beginning (0).

It is sometimes said that 'Your schooldays are the happiest days of your life', and people often feel that this should be a period of
(0) enjoyment . However, exams often affect — ENJOY
students' happiness, and many students
express a **(1)** .... for alternative methods — PREFER
of assessment, where the work they do throughout the year counts towards their final mark. They say that exams test short-
term memory and **(2)** .... which is — KNOW
forgotten immediately after the exam. Also, assessing coursework as part of the final mark
changes students' **(3)** .... , making them — BEHAVE
more responsible about studying. There are some students, however, who prefer final
examinations, saying that in **(4)** .... they — COMPARE
only have to work hard for two months a year and so they have more time for their leisure
(5) .... They say that some students — ACT
receive **(6)** .... with their coursework — ASSIST
from their parents, so it is not an accurate
(7) .... of how hard they have worked or — MEASURE
of their real **(8)** .... in the subject they are studying. — ABLE

Vocabulary and grammar review Unit 6

Vocabulary

1 Complete the sentences below by writing a word from the box in the gaps.

fun funny job occasion occasion opportunity possibility work

1 Andrea's birthday was a great .... – I won't forget it for a long time.
2 Excuse me! I have to get to .... and I'm already late.
3 Helena, you did an excellent .... arranging the meeting so efficiently!
4 My boss has lost his temper on only one .... as far as I can remember.
5 I didn't find working in the office much .... because my colleagues weren't very friendly.
6 Olga sees her part in this film as a great .... to show she can act in English as well as in Russian.
7 Polly took us to see a very .... film which made us laugh a lot.
8 You have no .... of getting a more responsible job with your qualifications.

Grammar

2 Complete the second sentence so that it has a similar meaning to the first sentence, using the word given. Do not change the word given. You must use between two and five words, including the word given.

1 I found my first day at work so enjoyable.
FUN
I .... my first day of work.
2 Were you able to speak to your teacher after class?
OPPORTUNITY
Did you .... to your teacher after class?
3 Sandra may be able to study in Canada next year.
POSSIBILITY
Sandra may .... in Canada next year.
4 We didn't expect the news to be nearly so good.
MUCH
The news .... we expected.
5 Patricia helped us a lot with her advice.
DEAL
Patricia provided us .... helpful advice.
6 William has only spoken to his boss once during the year.
OCCASION
William has only spoken to his boss .... all year.

3 Complete these sentences by writing one word in each gap. In some cases, more than one word may be possible.

1 Drive carefully! I paid a great .... of money for that car.
2 I heard an interesting .... of news on the radio this morning – they're giving us a day's holiday next month.
3 I'd like to offer you a little .... of advice: don't go up to the castle at midday as it gets very hot.
4 That's a really useless .... of equipment – you should throw it away!
5 There are a large .... of shops in the town centre where you can buy souvenirs.

4 Complete this story by writing *a*, *an*, *the* or '–' if you think no article is needed in the gaps.

I was travelling around Europe by **(1)** .... train one summer when I was about 18 years old and I arrived in **(2)** .... city (I can't remember **(3)** .... name) just as it was getting dark. I went looking for somewhere to stay such as **(4)** .... youth hostel, but the only one I found was full, and they couldn't recommend anywhere else for **(5)** .... cheap accommodation. As usual, I had **(6)** .... problem with **(7)** .... money: I didn't have enough for **(8)** .... hotel. I wandered round **(9)** .... city looking for **(10)** .... park to sleep in. It was very dark when I came to **(11)** .... pair of **(12)** .... imposing gates leading into what looked like **(13)** .... park. I went inside, and fortunately I had **(14)** .... excellent sleeping bag, which I unrolled and climbed inside. Then I ate some bread, which was **(15)** .... only food I had. When I woke up and looked around me, I had **(16)** .... enormous surprise when I saw I had been sleeping in **(17)** .... someone's back garden!

7 High adventure

Starting off

1 ....

2 ....

3 ....

4 ....

5 ....

6 ....

1 Match these adventure sports with the photos.

canoeing / kayaking   mountain biking   parasailing   rock climbing   snowboarding   windsurfing

2 Work in groups.

1 Which of these sports do you think is the most dangerous? Which is the least dangerous?
2 Which have you tried? Which would you like to try? Why? / Why not?

Listening | Part 2

1 Work in pairs. You are going to hear Gary giving a talk about adventure racing as part of a school project. Read this text and discuss what type of information you need for each gap.

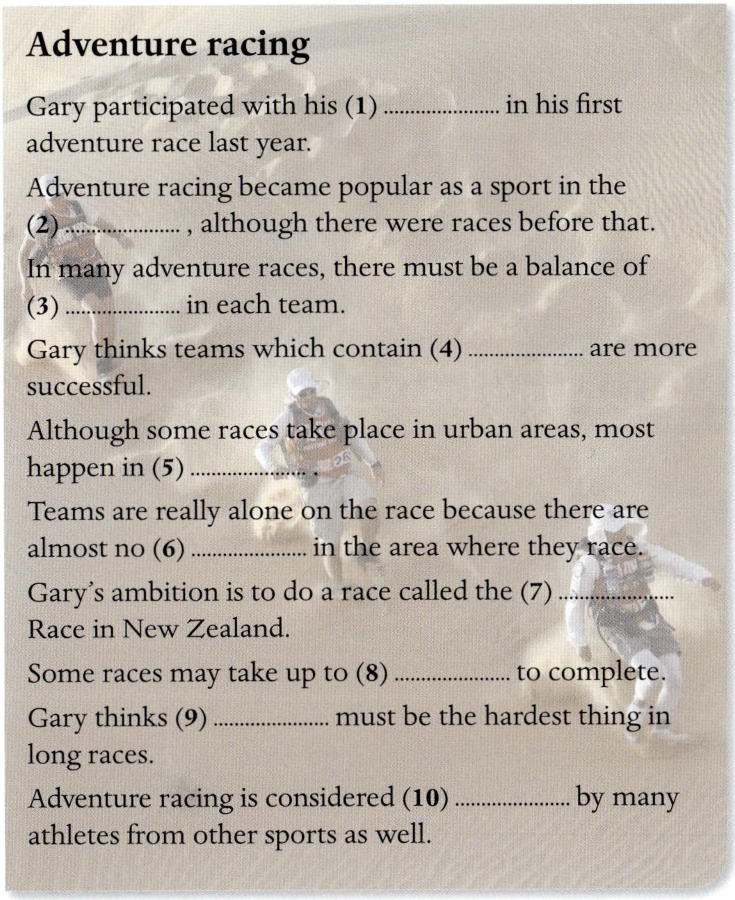

Adventure racing

Gary participated with his **(1)** .... in his first adventure race last year.

Adventure racing became popular as a sport in the **(2)** .... , although there were races before that.

In many adventure races, there must be a balance of **(3)** .... in each team.

Gary thinks teams which contain **(4)** .... are more successful.

Although some races take place in urban areas, most happen in **(5)** ....

Teams are really alone on the race because there are almost no **(6)** .... in the area where they race.

Gary's ambition is to do a race called the **(7)** .... Race in New Zealand.

Some races may take up to **(8)** .... to complete.

Gary thinks **(9)** .... must be the hardest thing in long races.

Adventure racing is considered **(10)** .... by many athletes from other sports as well.

2 ▶ **24** Listen and, for questions 1–10, complete the sentences with a word or short phrase.

Exam advice

Before you listen:

- look at the incomplete sentences, including any words which come after the gap.
- think about what type of information you need for each gap (a date, a job, etc.).
- think about what type of word(s) you need for each gap (a noun (phrase), verb (phrase), etc.).

3 Work in groups.

- What do you think are the advantages of racing in teams?
- What are the main difficulties of adventure racing?

Vocabulary

Verb collocations with sporting activities

1 Complete these extracts from Listening Part 2 by writing an appropriate verb in the correct form in the gaps.

1 Adventure racing is a sport you .... in teams.
2 Anyway, it's not like just .... jogging or running or something like that.
3 The races are .... in all sorts of different places.
4 The majority are .... in mountains or deserts.
5 Many people who are at the top of their sport in other fields are now .... because they find that, rather than .... as individuals … they need to work as a team.

2 Use the table of collocations below to complete these sentences. In some cases, more than one answer may be possible.

1 I think local governments should .... competitions for schools in their area where any student over 15 can ....
2 I would encourage people to .... swimming two or three times a week because I think it's an excellent way of .... exercise.
3 People who enjoy team sports often .... basketball or football, whereas people who enjoy individual sports .... golf or .... windsurfing.

verb	sport
hold / organise / compete in / enter / take part in	a race / a competition / a tournament / a championship
do / take	exercise
go*	jogging / cycling / skiing / swimming / windsurfing
play**	football / golf / basketball
do***	sports / athletics / gymnastics / judo / weightlifting

* for sports that end in *-ing* and are usually or often done outdoors
** for sports which are considered games
*** for other sports which do not use *go* or *play*

3 Work in pairs.

- How do you take exercise?
- What sports have you tried, and how much did you enjoy them?

Reading and Use of English | Part 6

1 Work in pairs. You are going to read an article by an adventure racer. Before you read the whole article, read the title and the subheading in *italics*. What do you expect to find out by reading the article?

2 Read the article quite carefully and make a short note in the margin about the subject of each paragraph. An example has been done for you.

Are you ready for an adventure race?

Rebecca Rusch has competed in several Eco-Challenge races, where teams of four men and women race non-stop over a 500 km course which includes trekking, canoeing, horse riding, scuba diving, mountaineering and mountain biking.

need for experience

Obviously, I did not feel so ready for the early races in my career as the races we have done recently. There is a lot to be said for just gaining experience. Just getting out there and getting your feet wet teaches you the right skills and attitude.

It's often not the most physically prepared or the fittest teams that win. The ones who come first are the teams who race intelligently and adapt to unexpected situations. **1** ____ The only way to develop those qualities is to get out and race or do long training trips with your team-mates and friends.

Adventure races are such a huge challenge that when you enter a race you always think, "Am I ready? Did I train enough? Did I forget something?" I remember one race in particular, my very first Eco-Challenge and only my second race ever. **2** ____ A 24-hour race seemed like an eternity to me. My background was cross-country running in high school and college where a two- or three-mile race seemed long. Most of my fear was due to lack of experience and knowledge. I really had no idea what I was getting into because I had never done a 24-hour race before. **3** ____

In preparation for Australia, I tried to approach my training in a methodical way. Looking back, I wasn't methodical at all. In fact, what I did involved simply running, biking and paddling a kayak as much and as hard as I could. I was also working at the same time. In reality, I was training a couple of hours a day during the week to get fit and at weekends training with the team for perhaps four hours. **4** ____ I spent the rest of the time worrying about how slow I was.

So, we went to Australia and entered the race. We didn't plan a strategy at all, but just ran as fast as possible from the start. I just tried to keep up with my team-mates, who were more experienced than I was. **5** ____ It was a furious 36 hours. We arrived at a few of the check points in first place and were among the top five. I knew we didn't belong there.

To cut a long story short, two of my team-mates decided not to continue the race after just a day and a half. One was suffering hallucinations and feeling ill. He was just too tired to carry on. **6** ____ We had been going so fast that he felt uncomfortable asking us to stop so he could take care of his blisters. The other two of us, feeling fresh still, had to drop out with the rest of our team. Four days later, we watched in disappointment as the winners crossed the finishing line. I knew that our team had not been prepared or realistic about the pace we could keep, but not finishing that race was the most valuable lesson I could have learned.

I promised then to come back one day and finish the race. That was seven years (and thousands of race miles) ago.

Adapted from *Adventure Sports Journal*

3 Six sentences have been removed from the article. Read the sentences below one by one. As you read each sentence:

- underline words and phrases which you think refer to something in the article
- decide which gap (1–6) it fits.

There is one extra sentence which you do not need to use.

A Another had severe problems with his feet.
B I kept my mouth shut and followed them.
C We won it even so, and were invited to compete in the Eco-Challenge in Australia.
D His encouragement helped me to complete it.
E That was how much I had prepared.
F When I did it, I felt totally afraid and unprepared.
G To achieve this, you have to be flexible and patient.

4 Work in pairs.

- Do you prefer team sports or individual sports? Why?

Exam advice

- Pay attention to pronouns (*we*, *that*, *it*, etc.), adverbs (*however*, *even so*, etc.) and other reference words/phrases in the sentences which have been removed. Decide what they refer to before you place the sentence in a gap.
- Work methodically through the sentences, reading them and placing them one by one when you're sure they are right.

Grammar

Infinitive and verb + *-ing*

1 These sentences (some of which are from the article you have just read) are examples of when to use the infinitive and when to use the verb + *-ing* form. Decide which sentence (a–i) is an example (1–10) for each of the rules on this page. You can use some of the sentences as examples for more than one rule.

a **Not finishing** that race was the most valuable lesson I could have learned.
b I promised then **to come back** one day and finish the race.
c In fact, what I did involved simply **running, biking** and **paddling** a kayak as much and as hard as I could.
d There is a lot to be said for just **gaining** experience.
e I was training a couple of hours a day during the week **to get fit**.
f There are medical teams **to take care of** injured runners.
g He was just too tired **to carry on**.
h It's no use **entering** a race if you haven't prepared properly.
i Two of my team-mates decided **not to continue** the race after just a day and a half.

Using the infinitive and verb + *-ing*

The **infinitive** is used:

1 to say why you do something (sentence .....e.....)
2 to say why something exists (sentence ....)
3 after *too* and *enough* (sentence ....)
4 after these verbs (there is a more complete list on page 166): *agree, appear, ask, arrange, decide, expect, fail, help, promise* (sentences .... and ....)
5 The negative is formed by placing *not* before the infinitive (sentence ....)

The **verb + *-ing*** is used:

6 after prepositions (sentence ....)
7 as subjects or objects of a verb (sentence ....)
8 after these verbs (there is a more complete list on page 166): *admit, enjoy, finish, involve, mind, postpone, risk, suggest* (sentence ....)
9 after these expressions: *it's no good, it's not worth, it's no use, it's a waste of time, spend time, can't help* (sentence ....)
10 The negative is formed by placing *not* before the verb + *-ing* (sentence ....)

➡ **page 166 Language reference:** Infinitive and verb + *-ing* forms

2 Complete these sentences by writing the verb in brackets in the correct form in the gaps.

1 Carlos has suggested .... (*start*) a five-a-side football team. What do you think?
2 I don't think the weather is good enough .... (*go*) sailing this afternoon.
3 We've decided .... (*hold*) the race early in the morning before it gets too hot.
4 .... (*train*) is essential if you want to perform well.
5 I've joined a gym .... (*get*) myself fitter.
6 If you train too hard, you risk .... (*injure*) yourself before the race.
7 It's no good .... (*run*) in a marathon if you're not wearing the right shoes.
8 She was disqualified from the race for .... (*push*) an opponent.

3 Circle the correct form in *italics* in each of these questions.

1 What sport would you advise someone *to do / doing* in order to make friends?
2 What sport would you choose *to learn / learning* if you had plenty of time and money?
3 If someone needed to get fit, what sport would you suggest *to do / doing*?
4 What sports do you avoid *to take part in / taking part in* and why?

4 Work in pairs. Ask and answer the questions in Exercise 3, giving your opinions.

5 Candidates often make mistakes with the infinitive and verb + *-ing*. Some of these sentences are correct. Find and correct the mistakes.

1 Students are not allowed running along school corridors.
2 Few people choose spending their time taking exercise.
3 The Internet means that we spend more time sitting at home, but we cannot imagine to live without it.
4 Being fit and healthy does not mean to run 20 km a day.
5 Many students would prefer to cycle to school than go by school bus.
6 Many people only think about take exercise when they are overweight.
7 Unless they try to compete as a team, they will not succeed to win the competition.
8 Doing a sport is a good alternative if you are bored to sit and read a book.
9 It may be good to use a bicycle instead of going by public transport.
10 There are several good reasons for ride a bike.

Reading and Use of English | Part 4

1 Work in pairs. For questions 1 and 2, choose the correct answer A–D. Why are the other answers incorrect?

1 Why don't we start jogging if we want some exercise?
TAKING
He suggested .... in order to get some exercise.
A that they should take up jogging
B taking up jogging
C to take up jogging
D going jogging

2 She won the match without difficulty.
EASY
She found .... the match.
A it easy to win
B that it was easy to win
C she could easily win
D it simple to win

2 Now do these Part 4 questions. Use the clues below each question to help you.

1 Marianne prepared for the race by training every evening.
READY
Marianne trained every evening .... for the race.
- Can you think of an expression with *ready* which means *prepare*?
- Why did Marianne train every evening?
- Do you use the verb + *-ing* or an infinitive to say why she trained every evening?

2 I found it impossible not to laugh at his efforts.
HELP
I .... at his efforts.
- You need an expression with *help* which means 'find it impossible'.
- Your answer needs to be in the same tense.

3 Cycling on the pavement is prohibited.
USE
Cyclists .... the pavement.
- How do you use *allowed* to mean it's prohibited?
- Do you use the verb + *-ing* or an infinitive after *allowed*?

3 Now do these Part 4 questions.

1 We'd like all our students to participate in the sports programme.
PART
We are keen on all our students .... the sports programme.

2 Buying the equipment for this sport is cheaper than hiring it.
MORE
It's .... the equipment for this sport than to buy it.

3 You should have phoned her to tell her the game was cancelled.
GIVE
You were supposed .... to tell her the game was cancelled.

4 Mateo managed to win the race.
SUCCEEDED
Mateo .... the race.

5 'I'll never get angry with the referee again,' said Martin.
TEMPER
Martin promised never .... the referee again.

6 Tanya found windsurfing easy to learn.
DIFFICULTY
Tanya .... to windsurf.

Exam advice

- Use the word in CAPITALS without changing it.
- Count the words. Contractions (*isn't, don't,* etc.) count as two words.
- Read both sentences again at the end to check that they mean the same and contain all the same information/ideas.

4 Check your answers by looking at these clues for each of the questions in Exercise 3.

1 Did you use a fixed phrase which means *participate*?
2 Have you used an opposite of *cheap*? Did you use an infinitive or a verb + *-ing*?
3 Did you use an expression which means *phone* (*give her a ...*)?
4 *Managed* is followed by an infinitive. Is *succeeded* also followed by an infinitive? Do you also need a preposition?
5 Can you remember an expression with *temper* which means *become angry*?
6 You cannot write *did not have any difficulty in learning* because it's seven words.

Listening | Part 4

1 Work in pairs. You will hear an interview with someone who went on a paragliding course. Before you listen, look at the photo.

- Do you think paragliding is a risky sport?
- Would you like to try it? Why? / Why not?

2 Read these questions and underline the main idea in each one.

1 Why did Hannah want to try paragliding?
A She had seen other people doing it.
B She wanted to write an article about it.
C She was bored with the sport she was doing.

2 Why did Hannah choose to do a paragliding course in France?
A The location was safer.
B The course was cheaper.
C The weather was better.

3 Hannah says that the advantage of learning to paraglide from the sand dune is that
A you are unlikely to fall in the sea.
B you can land comfortably on the sand.
C you cannot fall too far.

4 How did Hannah spend the first morning of her course?
A She learned to lift her paraglider.
B She flew to the bottom of the dune.
C She watched other people paragliding.

5 When she started flying, her instructor
A shouted at her from the ground.
B talked to her over the radio.
C flew next to her.

6 When you land after paragliding, it feels like
A jumping from a seat.
B falling from a horse.
C falling from a bicycle.

7 What, for Hannah, is the best reason to go paragliding?
A It's exciting.
B It's unusual.
C It's quiet.

3 25 For questions 1–7, listen and choose the best answer (A, B or C).

Exam advice

- When you listen, wait until the speaker has finished talking about an idea before you choose your answer.
- Listen for the same idea to be expressed, not the same words.

Vocabulary
look, see, watch, listen and hear

1 Candidates often confuse the following words: *look, see* and *watch,* and *listen* and *hear.* Complete these sentences from Listening Part 4 by writing *look, see, watch, listen* or *hear* in the correct form in the gaps.

1 I spend my life .... people doing different sports.
2 I was .... down the course, planning my next shot or something, when I .... these paragliders floating down.
3 In fact, I .... to my instructor, Chantalle, through an earphone.
4 It was generally very quiet, calm and civilised, except when she raised her voice to shout at other flyers to keep away from me. And then you really .... her!

2 Read the definitions on page 184. Then circle the correct word in *italics* in these sentences.

1 I *looked at / watched* my watch and saw that it was time to leave.
2 I really enjoy *looking at / watching* horror films.
3 We live near a motorway and can *listen to / hear* the traffic non-stop.
4 I've been *looking at / watching* our holiday photos.
5 Did you *watch / see* Buckingham Palace when you were in London?
6 She knew the policeman was *looking / watching* what she did.
7 Ivan was in the kitchen, so he didn't *listen to / hear* the telephone when it rang.
8 Marisa looks so relaxed when she's *listening to / hearing* music on her MP3 player.

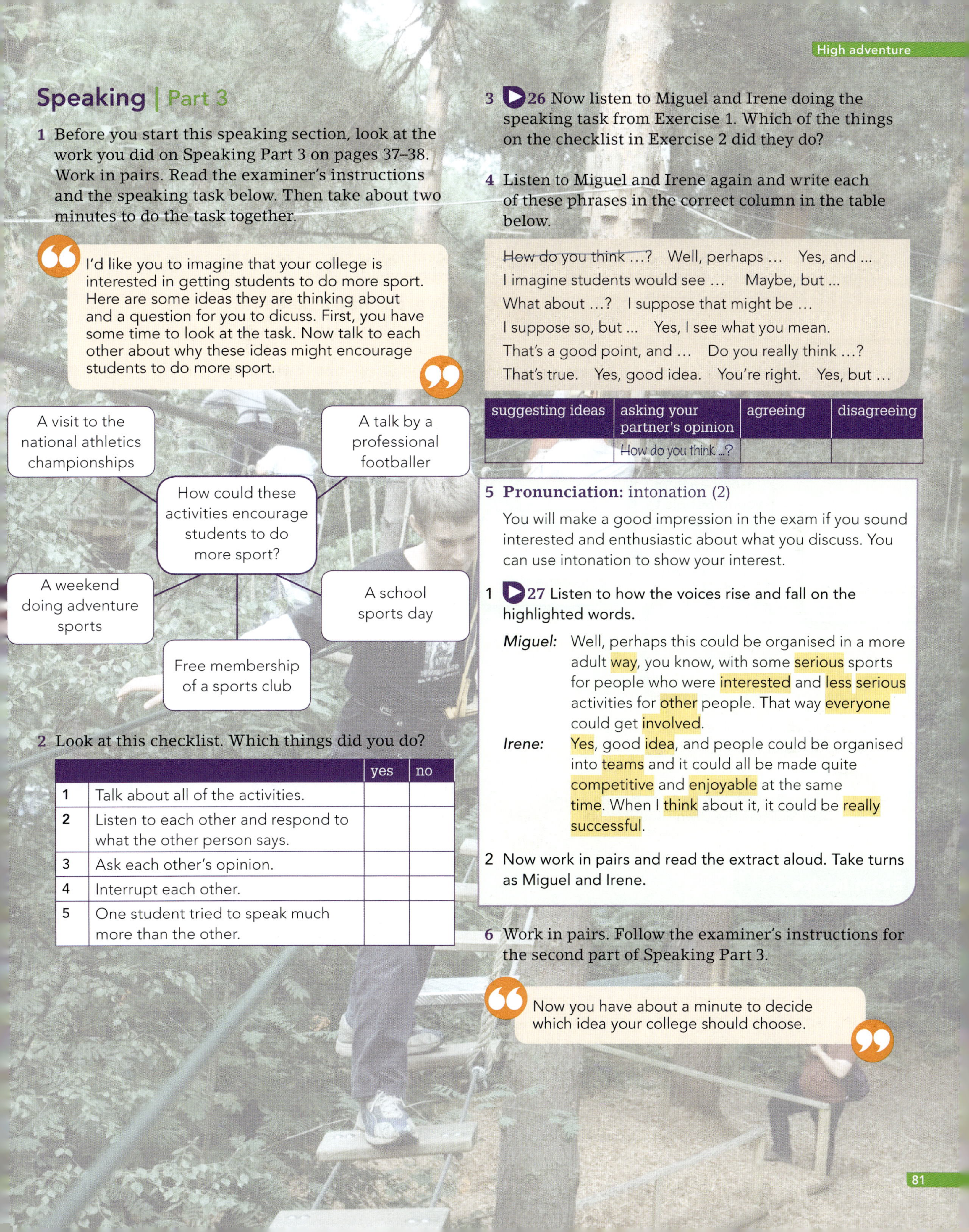

Speaking | Part 3

1 Before you start this speaking section, look at the work you did on Speaking Part 3 on pages 37–38. Work in pairs. Read the examiner's instructions and the speaking task below. Then take about two minutes to do the task together.

> I'd like you to imagine that your college is interested in getting students to do more sport. Here are some ideas they are thinking about and a question for you to dicuss. First, you have some time to look at the task. Now talk to each other about why these ideas might encourage students to do more sport.

How could these activities encourage students to do more sport?

- A visit to the national athletics championships
- A talk by a professional footballer
- A weekend doing adventure sports
- A school sports day
- Free membership of a sports club

2 Look at this checklist. Which things did you do?

		yes	no
1	Talk about all of the activities.		
2	Listen to each other and respond to what the other person says.		
3	Ask each other's opinion.		
4	Interrupt each other.		
5	One student tried to speak much more than the other.		

3 ▶26 Now listen to Miguel and Irene doing the speaking task from Exercise 1. Which of the things on the checklist in Exercise 2 did they do?

4 Listen to Miguel and Irene again and write each of these phrases in the correct column in the table below.

~~How do you think …?~~ Well, perhaps … Yes, and …
I imagine students would see … Maybe, but …
What about …? I suppose that might be …
I suppose so, but … Yes, I see what you mean.
That's a good point, and … Do you really think …?
That's true. Yes, good idea. You're right. Yes, but …

suggesting ideas	asking your partner's opinion	agreeing	disagreeing
	How do you think …?		

5 Pronunciation: intonation (2)

You will make a good impression in the exam if you sound interested and enthusiastic about what you discuss. You can use intonation to show your interest.

1 ▶27 Listen to how the voices rise and fall on the highlighted words.

Miguel: Well, perhaps this could be organised in a more adult way, you know, with some serious sports for people who were interested and less serious activities for other people. That way everyone could get involved.

Irene: Yes, good idea, and people could be organised into teams and it could all be made quite competitive and enjoyable at the same time. When I think about it, it could be really successful.

2 Now work in pairs and read the extract aloud. Take turns as Miguel and Irene.

6 Work in pairs. Follow the examiner's instructions for the second part of Speaking Part 3.

> Now you have about a minute to decide which idea your college should choose.

7 Work in pairs.

1 Take about two minutes to do the first part of this speaking task.

I'd like you to imagine that a town wants young people to spend their free time in ways which are useful for them. Here are some ideas that they are thinking about and a question for you to discuss. Talk to each other about how these ideas would provide useful ways for young people to spend their free time.

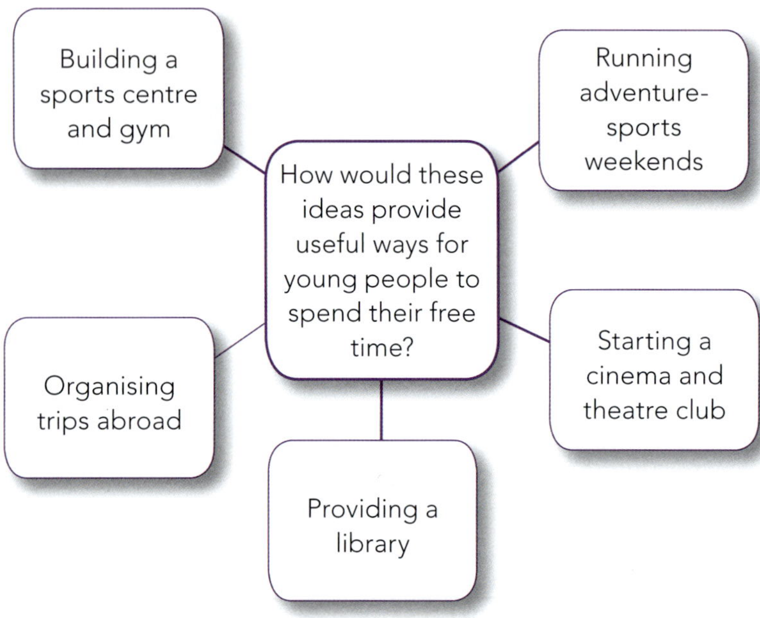

2 Now follow the examiner's instructions for the second part of Speaking Part 3.

Now you have a minute to decide which two facilities the town should build.

Exam advice

When you discuss the first part of the task, you needn't talk about all of the options, but you should make suggestions, ask your partner's opinion and respond to your partner's ideas.

When you discuss the second part of the task, it's not necessary to reach agreement, but you should:

- discuss which option(s) to choose and give reasons for choice(s)
- listen and respond to what your partner says. Don't be afraid to disagree politely – this can lead to a good discussion.

Writing | Part 2 An article

1 Read this writing task and underline the points you must deal with in your answer.

> You see this notice on your college noticeboard.
>
> The editors of the college magazine would like contributions to the magazine on the following subject:
>
> **A great way to keep fit.**
>
> Describe a sporting activity or form of exercise you enjoy, how you started and why you would recommend it to other people.
>
> The writer of the best article will receive ten tickets to the local cinema.
>
> Write your **article**.

2 Work in pairs.

- Discuss the ideas each of you could express to deal with the points you have underlined in the task.
- Which ideas would you use in your article?

3 Read the article on page 83, which was written by Nacho Pallas.

- What does he enjoy about his way of taking exercise? Why?

Rugby: rough but fun

I love playing rugby. I started playing the game at school when I was just nine years old. It was compulsory to do a sport three afternoons a week, and in winter the boys had to play rugby. I immediately found I enjoyed it, *despite* not being as big as other boys my age. *However*, I was quite athletic, so I could often run past my opponents and score points by being more agile than them.

Although it's quite a rough game with complicated rules, it keeps you fit because you have to run for 80 minutes, so you also have to train several times a week. For people who are competitive and enjoy playing in a team, it's great fun. You can play it at any level, but if you want to win a trophy, you'll need someone to coach you so that you learn the best tactics and learn to work effectively together.

Although you can sometimes get hurt, I would recommend the game to anyone who enjoys ball games, running and keeping fit. *However*, if you decide you don't want to actually play, it's a great sport for spectators as well.

4 Look at the structure of the article. In which paragraph does Nacho deal with these points?

1 He describes a sporting activity.
2 How he started.
3 Why he would recommend it.

5 Study how the words and phrases in *italics* in Nacho's article are used. Then complete these sentences by writing *although, however* or *despite* in the gaps.

1 .... the swimming pool is quite far from where I live, I try to go there three times a week.
2 .... being given tickets to the football match, we decided to watch it on TV.
3 .... I'd love to be a professional footballer, I don't think I'm talented enough.
4 He was very easy to talk to .... being a famous tennis star.
5 Ten per cent of British teenagers dream of becoming sports stars. .... , very few will achieve their ambition.
6 I won the game .... I'd never played badminton before.
7 .... feeling very tired, she managed to finish the race.
8 I didn't enjoy the match. .... , our opponents played very well.

➔ page 168 Language reference: Linking words for contrast

6 EP Study how Nacho used the words in the box in his article. Then use them in the correct form to complete the sentences below.

athletic   opponents   competitive   rough   trophy
coach   spectators

1 Although Valery enjoys .... sports, he prefers taking exercise on his own.
2 Ice hockey is a .... game where players often get hurt.
3 If I was more .... , I might be able to win a few more races.
4 Our .... for the next match are last year's champions.
5 We need someone to .... our team so that they learn to play better.
6 Few .... watch adventure sports because they take place in remote areas.
7 We're rated as one of the top teams despite never having won a single ....

7 Now write your own answer to the writing task in Exercise 1.

- Before you start writing, make a brief plan.
- Try to use structures and vocabulary you have studied in this Writing section and this unit.
- Write between 140 and 190 words.
- Read through your article when you have finished to improve it and to check it for mistakes.

Exam advice

- Write a plan before you start writing the article.
- Organise your ideas into paragraphs, and use linking words such as: *however, despite, in addition, for example* and *on the other hand.*

Before you write:

- think about what the people reading the article will find interesting, enjoyable or useful
- write a plan by:
  – underlining all the points you must deal with
  – organising your ideas into paragraphs so that you cover everything you've been asked to do. Often each underlined point will form the topic of a paragraph.

8 Dream of the stars

Reading and Use of English | Part 7

1 You will read a newspaper article about five actors at the beginning of their careers. Before you read, discuss this question in pairs.

- What are the advantages and disadvantages of working as an actor?

2 Read questions 1–10 and underline the main idea in each question.

Which actor

believes actors must be ready to accept negative comments?	1
feels that they have learned a lot from people already working in the theatre and TV?	2
says that listening to other people's suggestions improves their acting?	3
has always been excited by having people watching their acting?	4
had planned to enter a different profession before training to become an actor?	5
prefers working in theatre rather than in cinema or television?	6
did not want to work outside the theatre initially?	7
feels worried about performing in front of some important people?	8
originally tried to train as an actor somewhere else?	9
wasn't so interested in acting in the theatre initially?	10

3 Now read the newspaper article. For questions 1–10, choose from the people A–E.

Exam advice

- Many of the sections may say quite similar things. You will have to read carefully to decide which section answers the question exactly.
- Guess difficult words from the context when you think it will help you to answer a question.
- Underline phrases in the texts which give you the answers and check them against the questions.

4 Work in groups.

- Have you ever performed in public (e.g. acting, speaking in public, dancing, doing a sport)?
- How did you feel about the experience? What did you enjoy about it? What did you dislike?

Starting off

1 Work in groups. Look at the photos and compare these different types of star. Talk about:

- income/money
- preparation and training
- length of career
- the advantages and disadvantages of being famous.

2 If you could be a star, what sort of star would you like to be? Why?

Five young actors

The curtains open in the theatre as a group of young actors make their way on to the stage. These are some young Edinburgh-based actors doing the final performance of their drama course.

A Scott Hoatson

22-year-old Scott is already a step ahead of his classmates, as he has been offered a year-long contract with the National Theatre of Scotland's under-26 theatre group. He was discovered by someone from the theatre while performing in plays in Edinburgh and St Andrews, but he admits the students' final performance in front of directors and agents is still nerve-wracking. "It's so important for all of us. The fact that there are artistic directors from the big theatres who come to watch makes it such a big opportunity. There's so much happening in Scotland at the moment. There are a lot of opportunities up here, so it makes sense to stay closer to home. When I started the course, I thought that stage acting was the only thing I wanted to do, but now I want to do everything I can – whether it's on stage, TV, film or radio."

B Kim Gerard

21-year-old Kim got her first taste of performing as a ballet dancer when she was just two and has been hooked on performing ever since. Although her ballet days are now behind her, she admits that it gave her a great introduction to the profession. "It was just so exhilarating to get up on stage and perform in front of an audience. Acting is the only thing that I have ever really wanted to do, and this course has let me do my training close to home. Even though I'd done some theatre before, I always wanted to get into TV. I really liked the idea of being a famous, well-paid TV star in a drama series. But now, I've realised acting on stage is just as good."

C Allan Scott-Douglas

Although 23-year-old Allan has been interested in performing since his early teens, it was only in his second year of a primary teaching degree at Edinburgh University that he decided to pursue a career as an actor. "I kind of got into it by accident," he admits. "I was more of a singer, but I ended up doing musical theatre and absolutely loved it. I'm pretty much open to anything. I suppose my heart will always belong to theatre, as there's a live audience there in front of you, but the film and TV work we've done has been great fun too, so I'd love to do some more. If you want to achieve your ambitions as a young actor, you've got to go where the work is. If I'm offered a job down in London, there's no way I'd ever be able to turn it down."

D Romana Abercromby

26-year-old Romana says she got involved with a lot of drama productions when she was still at school. "When I left school, I realised that it was the only thing I wanted to do. I tried applying to drama schools down in London, but after being rejected by them, I took a year out to go travelling. This course has given us so many useful skills and brought us into contact with so many actors and directors who have told us all about the industry. And we've been able to gain some experience with TV as well as stage acting, which has been great. When it comes down to finding work, if it's in Scotland, that's great, but I'd love to travel around, too."

E Neil Thomas

20-year-old Neil was just seven years old when he joined an after-school youth theatre company, which gave him his first taste of acting on stage. "I went once or twice a week and adored it," he says. "I was always keen to show off at school, so it was the perfect outlet for me to perform properly. I've had the chance to do a lot of different types of acting, and the training has been invaluable. It's intense, but everyone knows that's the nature of the career and you have to be prepared. People will give you all sorts of advice about your acting, which helps you to strip away your bad habits. In our profession, you have to be prepared for brutal criticism, because that's what you'll expect when you start working."

Adapted from *The Scotsman*

Vocabulary

Verb collocations with *ambition, career, experience* and *job*

1 Complete these extracts from Reading and Use of English Part 7 by writing a word or phrase from the box in the correct form in the gaps.

achieve gain offer pursue turn it down

... it was only in his second year of a primary teaching degree at Edinburgh University that he decided to **(1)** .... a career as an actor.

If you want to **(2)** .... your ambitions as a young actor, you've got to go where the work is. If I'm **(3)** .... a job down in London, there's no way I'd ever be able to **(4)** ....

And we've been able to **(5)** .... some experience with TV as well as stage acting, which has been great.

2 EP Complete these groups of collocations by writing *an ambition, a career, experience* or *a job* in the gaps.

1 *gain / get / have / lack* ....
2 *apply for / find / leave / look for / offer / turn down* ....
3 *abandon / build / launch / make / pursue / start out on* ....
4 *abandon / achieve / fulfill / have / realise* ....

3 Complete Dean's story by writing a verb from Exercise 2 in the correct form in the gaps. For some gaps, more than one answer may be possible.

I've always enjoyed performing in front of people and I'd like to **(1)** .... a career as an actor. If I could **(2)** .... my first ambition of going to drama school, I'd **(3)** .... the knowledge and experience which is needed if I'm going to **(4)** .... a job in the theatre. Acting is a very competitive profession, and you have to **(5)** .... your career step by step until, hopefully, a well-known director recognises your talent and **(6)** .... you a job which really **(7)** .... your career on the stage.

4 Work in pairs. Tell each other about your ambitions and the careers each of you would like to follow.

play, performance and *acting*; *audience, (the) public* and *spectators*; *scene* and *stage*

5 Candidates often confuse these words: *play, performance* and *acting; audience, public* and *spectators; scene* and *stage*. Circle the correct word in *italics* in each of these sentences. Then check by looking at the text in Reading and Use of English Part 7 again.

He was discovered by someone from the theatre while performing in **(1)** *plays / performances* in Edinburgh and St Andrews, but he admits the students' final **(2)** *acting / performance* in front of directors and agents is still nerve-wracking.

When I started the course, I thought that stage **(3)** *acting / playing* was the only thing I wanted to do.

It was just so exhilarating to get up on **(4)** *stage / scene* and perform in front of **(5)** *a public / an audience*.

6 Read the definitions on page 184 and look at the photos. Then complete each of these sentences by writing one of the words or phrases in the gaps in the correct form. Use each word only once.

1 The garden in all its glory is now open to ...*the public*...
2 He wrote his latest .... in under six weeks.
3 The thing I enjoy most about .... is the chance to work in films on location.
4 She gave a superb .... as Lady Macbeth.
5 The .... were clearly delighted with the performance.
6 The actor forgot what he was supposed to say in the final .... of the play.
7 The show ended with all the performers singing on .... together.
8 He broke the world 400-metres record in front of over 40,000 cheering ....

audience

spectators

the public

Grammar

at, in and *on* in phrases expressing location

1 Candidates often confuse *at, in* and *on* when saying where something is located. Complete these sentences from Reading and Use of English Part 7 by writing the correct preposition in the gaps.

1 The curtains open .... the theatre ...
2 He was discovered by someone from the theatre while performing in plays .... Edinburgh ...
3 '... now I want to do everything I can – whether it's .... stage, TV, film or radio.'
4 Romana says she got involved with a lot of drama productions when she was still .... school.
5 ... it was only in his second year of a primary teaching degree .... Edinburgh University that he decided to pursue a career as an actor.

page 172 Language reference: Prepositions – *at, in* and *on* to express location

2 Write the correct preposition in the gaps in these sentences written by candidates in the exam.

1 Every morning, we got up early and went to walk .... the mountains.
2 Every year, many people are injured .... the roads because of bad driving.
3 I am studying English .... school, and a spell in your country would be a great chance for me to improve.
4 I think that your cinema is the best .... the city.
5 I was alone .... home, my parents were .... a party and my sister was .... a friend's house.
6 Despite spending two hours a day commuting, I prefer living .... the outskirts of London.
7 The seaside is the ideal place for a family holiday because children can swim .... the sea as well as play .... the beach.
8 Our next destination was Italy, where we spent one week .... the seaside.
9 The journey was a good one, and I met an old friend .... the train.
10 You can waste a lot of time .... a car .... traffic jams.

Listening | Part 2

1 Work in pairs. You are going to hear a student called Julie giving a talk to students in her year about the time her father was on a television quiz show. Before you listen, read the sentences and decide:

- what sort of information you need in each gap (a person, a number, type of transport, etc.)
- what sort of word(s) could go in each gap (noun, adjective, verb, etc.).

Ten minutes of fame

A TV producer invited Julie's aunt to the quiz show while she was working in the **(1)** .... belonging to the family.

She didn't go because she was worried that she would be too **(2)** .... to answer any questions.

Julie's father used a **(3)** .... to travel to the show.

When he went to the show, he forgot to wear a **(4)** ....

He prepared for the show by learning large numbers of **(5)** .... from the newspapers.

The contestants were asked to wait in the **(6)** .... for the show to begin.

He competed against a **(7)** .... , a bus driver and a bank employee.

The contestants were asked questions on **(8)** .... during the show.

The show was broadcast almost **(9)** .... after it was recorded.

Julie's father won a **(10)** .... and a toy elephant.

2 ▶28 Listen and, for questions 1–10, complete the sentences with a short word of phrase.

Exam advice

- Be careful to choose the right information from what you hear, e.g. if you need to write a type of animal in the gap, the speaker will probably mention other animals which are not the correct answer.
- Write exactly the word(s) you hear without changing them in any way.
- Read the completed sentences to make sure the words fit grammatically and match what the speaker said.
- Make sure you haven't repeated ideas expressed elsewhere in the text.
- Answer every question, even if you're not sure.

3 Work in groups.

- How would you feel if you were invited to take part in a quiz programme?
- What would you like to win?
- Have you ever won anything in a competition?

Grammar

Reported speech

1 Look at these two sentences from Listening Part 2. What do you think Julie's aunt's and sister's exact words were?

1 She said she was afraid she'd get too nervous and be unable to speak when they asked her questions!
   a 'I'm afraid I'll get too nervous and be unable to speak when they ask me questions!'
   b 'I'm afraid I got too nervous and was unable to speak when they asked me questions!'

2 My elder sister, who was only 11 at the time, told her she should go because it was the chance of a lifetime.
   a 'You'll go because it's the chance of a lifetime.'
   b 'You should go because it's the chance of a lifetime.'

➔ page 173 Language reference: Reported speech

2 For questions 1–6, complete the second sentence so that it has a similar meaning to the first sentence, using the word given. Do not change the word given. You must use between two and five words, including the word given.

1 'Last night I saw a fantastic film,' said Phil.
PREVIOUS
Phil told me that the .... a fantastic film.

2 'I'll return quite late from the theatre tonight,' said Elena.
BACK
Elena warned me that .... quite late from the theatre that night.

3 'I won't be late for the show,' said Lucy.
ARRIVE
Lucy promised she .... time for the show.

4 'You can't borrow my camera, Mike,' said his father.
ALLOWED
Mike's father told him he .... his camera.

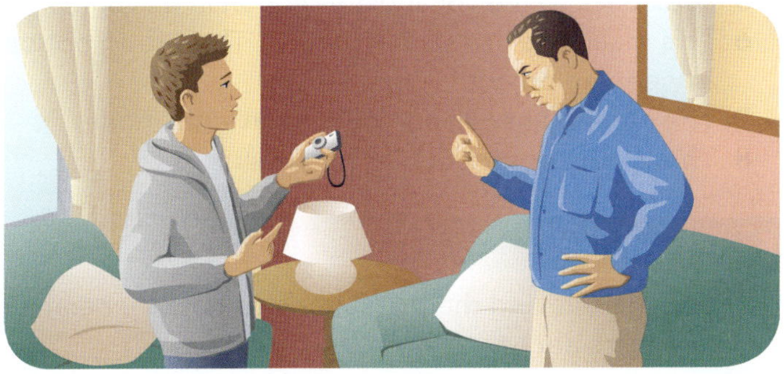

5 'I know I got several answers wrong in this exercise,' Hannah said.
MISTAKES
Hannah admitted that she .... in the exercise.

6 'I really enjoyed the play,' Katie told George.
FOUND
Katie told George that she .... very enjoyable.

3 Circle the correct form of the verb in *italics* in each of these sentences from Listening Part 2.

1 Anyway, when she was asked, she just refused *to even consider / even considering* it.

2 Well, he saw his opportunity and offered *to go / going* on the show himself.

3 He had to ask the producer *do you have / if they'd got* a spare one at the studio he could borrow.

4 In fact, I don't think we've ever had an encyclopedia in the house, though I suggested *to buy / buying* one for the occasion.

➡ **page 174 Language reference:** Reported speech – reporting verbs

4 Complete these sentences by writing the verb in brackets in the correct form in the gaps.

1 She admitted .... (*steal*) the watch.
2 Susan accused Brian of .... (*lie*).
3 Mark's mother agreed .... (*buy*) him a new car.
4 The children apologised for .... (*break*) the window.
5 Peter has invited me .... (*visit*) him in Switzerland this summer.
6 Ewan persuaded his mother .... (*buy*) him a new bike.
7 Karen has promised .... (*visit*) me after the summer.
8 I would recommend .... (*install*) new computers in the office.
9 Can I remind everyone .... (*send*) me an email if you're not coming to class next week?
10 Martin warned me .... (*not use*) the machine.

5 For questions 1–6, complete the second sentence so that it has a similar meaning to the first sentence, using the word given. Do not change the word given. You must use between two and five words, including the word given.

1 'You really should see that film, Pablo,' his friend said.
ADVISED
Pablo's friend .... the film.

2 'Why don't we go swimming this afternoon?' said Marie.
SUGGESTED
Marie .... afternoon.

3 'Don't leave the light on when you go to bed,' my father said to me.
SWITCH
My father .... the light when I went to bed.

4 'Don't forget to post the letter,' Silvia told Natasha.
REMINDED
Silvia .... the letter.

5 'You haven't been paying attention to me,' our teacher told us.
ANY
Our teacher accused us .... notice of him.

6 'I'll try as hard as I can to pass the exam,' said Paola.
BEST
Paola promised .... to pass the exam.

Reading and Use of English | Part 1

1 Work in pairs. You are going to read an article about how people make money from YouTube. Before you read, discuss these questions.

- What things do you most enjoy on YouTube?
- Why do many people prefer YouTube to watching television?

2 Read the article quickly. How do people make money on YouTube?

Back 111

YouTube millionaire celebrities

Geeks, musicians, teenage boys in their bedrooms – (0) ..anyone.. can now become a global internet sensation and a millionaire in the (1) .... In between the amusing videos of animals doing strange things and skateboarding accidents, people are building (2) .... by uploading videos.

In (3) .... years, there have been many success stories of people who started at home with just a webcam and have now huge followings. With over 100 million visitors to YouTube every month, advertisers have started (4) .... on the most popular video makers to take advantage of their loyal (5) .... Last year, 'YouTuber' Michael Buckley (6) .... that he was making over $100,000 a year from YouTube advertisements alone.

The YouTube payment system works on a pay-per-click basis. Effectively, the amount of money you (7) .... is determined by the number of views you get. A video of around a million views, which is (8) .... for popular YouTubers, may bring in about a thousand dollars.

adapted from the *Daily Mail*

3 For questions 1–8, read the article again and decide which answer (A, B, C or D) best fits each gap.

	A	B	C	D
0	A someone	B anyone (circled)	C everyone	D all
1	A way	B process	C method	D manner
2	A work	B jobs	C careers	D occupations
3	A recent	B last	C past	D latest
4	A aiming	B directing	C focusing	D pointing
5	A public	B people	C watchers	D spectators
6	A informed	B told	C reminded	D announced
7	A gain	B pay	C win	D earn
8	A conventional	B typical	C traditional	D everyday

4 Now check your answers to Exercise 3 by using these clues.

1 This phrase means 'one thing happens as a result of the other'.
2 This will be a part of their whole working life.
3 Notice the sentence uses the present perfect.
4 Only one option is followed by this preposition.
5 Look back to the vocabulary section in this unit.
6 This means he has said it publicly. The wrong options all need an object.
7 The correct answer is a collocation with 'money'.
8 This is normal for popular YouTubers.

Exam advice

- Read the title and the text quickly to get a general idea of what it's about.
- Deal with the gaps one by one. Read carefully before and after the gap. The words in each option will be similar in meaning, but only one will fit correctly into the gap.
- Check that the word fits into the sentence grammatically by looking at prepositions and other grammatical structures.
- If you are not sure which option is correct, reject the options you think are wrong and choose from the others.
- When you have finished, read the whole text quickly again to check your answers.

5 Discuss one of these questions in groups.

1 Have you ever uploaded something onto a video-sharing website such as YouTube? If so, what?
2 What would you like to upload onto YouTube? Why? / Why not?

Vocabulary and grammar review Unit 8

Vocabulary

1 Choose the best word, A, B, C or D, for each gap.

1 The flying display attracted about 50,000 ..... despite the rain.
A public B assistants C spectators D audience
2 As a police officer, I get a lot of questions from members of the ..... asking how to get to one place or another.
A people B public C audience D spectators
3 During the musical, the ..... clapped at the end of every single song.
A audience B spectators C public D attendants
4 British actress Amanda Haslett gave a superb ..... as Lady Macbeth at the Globe Theatre last night.
A play B act C performance D acting
5 If you're interested in a career in ..... , you must be prepared to work hard for little money.
A acting B playing C performance D stage
6 That play is much better on the ..... than in the film version.
A theatre B play C scene D stage
7 Vera is thinking of pursuing a ..... in the music industry.
A work B job C career D position
8 It's more important to do a job you enjoy than one where you ..... a lot of money.
A win B earn C gain D pay

Grammar

2 Complete each of the sentences below by writing a word or phrase from the box. In some cases, more than one answer may be possible. You can use the words and phrases more than once.

although	despite	even though	however
in spite of	whereas	while	

1 .... Eva wanted to pursue a career in acting, she couldn't find a job.
2 Max gave a wonderful performance in the school concert .... his headache.
3 .... Jason dreams of being a footballer, Eva wants to work in the theatre.
4 .... not being very talented, she became a highly successful Hollywood star.
5 They spent millions on the film. .... , not many people were interested in going to see it.
6 I enjoy watching documentaries .... my brother prefers soap operas.
7 He insisted on playing loud music .... it was nearly two o'clock in the morning.
8 People of all ages go to rock concerts, ... classical music concerts are mainly attended by people over 50.

3 For questions 1–6, complete the second sentence so that it has a similar meaning to the first sentence, using the word given. Do not change the word given. You must use between two and five words, including the word given.

1 Although it was dangerous, she went swimming.
THE
In spite .... she went swimming.
2 The theatre was full, despite the high price of the tickets.
EXPENSIVE
Although .... , the theatre was full.
3 Although he felt ill, he went to work.
DESPITE
He went to work .... well.
4 She enjoys her job in spite of her low salary.
EVEN
She finds her job enjoyable .... low.
5 'I've been asleep all afternoon.'
HAD
Helen admitted that .... whole afternoon.
6 'I'll phone when the concert finishes.'
CALL
Martin said he .... end of the concert.

9 Secrets of the mind

Starting off

1 Work in pairs. Find nine things which might make people happy by matching these words and phrases.

1 being admired	a a loving family
2 being part of	b in your studies or work
3 doing really well	c by the people around you
4 falling	d live well
5 having enough money to	e friends
6 having lots of	f in a nice neighbourhood
7 having lots of time to spend	g in love
8 living	h on the things you enjoy doing
9 not having to	i work too hard

2 Which of the things in Exercise 1 do you think are essential for happiness? Which do you think are not so important?
Are there any other important things which make people happy?

3 Work in pairs. Take turns to do the task below.

- Student A should look at photos 1 and 2.
- Student B should look at photos 3 and 4.

> The photos show people who are happy. Compare the photos and say why you think the people might be happy.

Why might the people be happy?

Reading and Use of English | Part 5

1 You are going to read an article by a psychologist about happiness. Read the article quickly to find out what he thinks makes people happy.

Article | Video | Picture gallery

The secrets of happiness

Mihaly Csikszentmihalyi has devoted his life to studying happiness. He believes he has found the key.

I've been fascinated by happiness most of my life. When I was a small boy, I noticed that though many of the adults around me were wealthy and educated, they were not always happy and this sometimes led them to behave in ways which I, as a child, thought strange. As a result of this, I decided to understand what happiness was and how best to achieve it. It was not surprising, then, that I decided to study psychology.

On arrival at the University of Chicago 50 years ago, I was disappointed to find that academic psychologists were trying to understand human behaviour by studying rats in a laboratory. I felt that there must be other more useful ways of learning how we think and feel. Although my original aim had been to achieve happiness for myself, I became more ambitious. I decided to build my career on trying to discover what made others happy also. I started out by studying creative people such as musicians, artists and athletes because they were people who devoted their lives to doing what they wanted to do, rather than things that just brought them financial rewards.

Later, I expanded the study by inventing a system called 'the experience sampling method'. Ordinary people were asked to keep an electronic pager for a week which gave out a beeping sound eight times a day. Every time it did so, they wrote down where they were, what they were doing, how they felt and how much they were concentrating. This system has now been used on more than 10,000 people, and the answers are consistent: as with creative people, ordinary people are happiest when concentrating hard.

2 Read this article in one minute ignoring the gaps. What does the writer say are the advantages of using local shops and shopping online?

Shopping online versus shopping locally

Most people want a busy shopping street (0) ....in.......... their town with butchers, bookshops, boutiques, cafés and restaurants, (1) .... makes it depressing to see so many shops becoming vacant. Experts predict that (2) .... to 40% of shops will be forced to close in the next five years.

No one wants to see their high-street shops disappear, (3) .... why would people want to shop locally? Internet shopping sites offer discount prices along with 24/7 shopping and deliveries. (4) .... to a recent report, some products, such as toys, are as (5) .... as 60% cheaper online.

Local shops should be more (6) .... clubs which provide personal service and social relationships, and each shop should be seen (7) .... something unique. To meet this need, in some parts of the world shops shut for hours during the day, then do excellent business in the evening, when they aim to give customers (8) .... more satisfying experience than they would ever have from shopping online.

3 Work alone. Decide which word best fits each gap. Where you are not sure, think of the type of word (preposition, article, etc.) you need. When you have finished, compare your ideas with the rest of the group.

4 Work in pairs.

- Do you or members of your family ever buy things online? If so, what are your favourite websites for online shopping?

Exam advice

- Answer the questions you find easy first. Go back to the more difficult questions later.
- Pay careful attention to the meaning of the text to help you think of the right word.
- Read to the end of each sentence before deciding what the missing word might be.
- Answer all the questions. If you can't decide what word to write, think what type of word you need (preposition, pronoun, etc.) and guess.
- When you have finished, check your answers by reading the completed text again.

Grammar

as and *like*

1 Look at these sentences (a–c) and answer the question below.

a Tom has two jobs: he's a teacher and a football referee. As a teacher he's very easy-going, but as a referee he's really strict.
b Mark is a social worker, but he spends so much time with young people that sometimes he feels like a teacher.
c Shops should be more like clubs which provide personal service and social interaction, and each should be seen as something unique.

Which, *as* or *like*, means ...
1 he is / they are (a teacher / something unique, etc.)?
2 he is similar to / they are similar to (a teacher / club, etc.)?

➔ page 163 Language reference: *as* and *like*

2 Complete these sentences by writing *as* or *like* in the gaps.

1 He has a weekend job .... a shop assistant.
2 He was regarded by his teachers .... one of the most brilliant students they had ever taught.
3 Tanya's father gave her a car for her 18th birthday .... she'd done so well in her exams.
4 I find subjects .... physics and chemistry very difficult.
5 I shall be on holiday next week, ... you know.
6 I'm afraid I don't study .... much .... I should.
7 I'm speaking to you .... a friend.
8 My English teacher is lovely. She's .... a mother to me!
9 Several cities in Switzerland, such .... Zurich and Berne, have reputations .... excellent places to live.
10 How embarrassing! Donna came to the party wearing exactly the same clothes .... me!

Reading and Use of English | Part 5

1 Work in groups. You will read a story called 'My greatest influence' written by a teenager from Texas. Before you read, discuss these questions.

- Who or what has had the greatest influence on you?
- How have they / has it influenced you?

2 Read the story quite quickly to find out what happens.

My greatest influence

By Rachel S., Colleyville, Texas

Sundays, I walk to the supermarket. Mother hands me the grocery list and puts money in my pocket, hoping it will be enough. She's had a hard day, and I've had a hard week. Nothing out of the ordinary happens when I get to the store. I grab the bread, some milk, and other things on the list. As I turn to head out, I see it, all pinks and yellows. It looks gorgeous in the window, and I'm sure if I were to try it on, it would be a perfect fit. I smile for a moment and turn away, bitter that I could never own such a dress as that. Instead, I grab the last item and check out.

Outside, traffic zooms by, an artificial breeze across my face. The sun beats down, making me sweat. These paper sacks in my arms are not the easiest things to carry. Yet, even with all these distractions, I cannot stop thinking about that pretty sundress in the window of the market. It is not fair that I can never have what I want. I work so hard to help my family and yet I get nothing in return, just another grocery list or errand to do.

In my anger, I fail to realize the tear that had been growing along the bottom of one of the sacks. Its contents spill out everywhere so that I must drop everything else just to chase after the soup cans and apples rolling across the sidewalk. Suddenly, I see a pair of hands that do not belong to me. They hold out to me a can of green beans. I follow them up the forearms, from the shoulders, and to the face of this stranger. His skin is tanned and wrinkled from so many years in the sun. His clothes are mismatched, borrowed or stolen. But his eyes are soft and kind.

I pause in silence, only able to stare at him. "Huh ... thanks," I say, coming to my senses, and I take the can from him. No other words are spoken as he continues to help me recover my purchases and get back on my feet. There is an awkward silence between us. Not knowing what else to say in this sort of situation, I tell him "thank you" one more time and am on my way because I have many other chores to finish. Suddenly, he speaks for the first time, and all he says is "Have a good day, ma'am." And then he gives me the biggest, most gap-toothed smile I have ever seen. Right then, he looks years younger—and I feel a fool.

Look at me, feeling sorry for myself because I do not get what I want! Do I not think others are in the same boat, or worse? I am but one person out of the billions that exist on this earth, so who am I to think that I deserve more than I already have?

To say that I try to follow the example of just one person would be to oversimplify things. The human character is much more complex than that. Just as our world is shaped by many different outside sources, so, too, have I been influenced by many familiar and unfamiliar faces.

It is not a matter of who, but what, has been the greatest influence in my life. I do not wish to be that homeless man on the street, for he has taught me with one genuine smile that my life is enough, and that there are worse things out there than not having a pink and yellow sundress. But it is his selfless character that continues to mold me.

My mother will hand me the grocery list today. I will make the same journey to the supermarket, and most likely, I will get the same items as last time. And I will probably see something I want but cannot have. But before I start to feel sorry for myself, I will remember the kind stranger with the gap-toothed grin, I'll grab the last item, and check out.

Source: *www.teenink.com 'My Greatest Influence'*

3 For questions 1–6, choose the answer (A, B, C or D) which you think fits best according to the text.

1 What impression do we have of Rachel in the first paragraph?
A She enjoys doing the family shopping.
B She comes from a family with not much money.
C She never buys herself new clothes.
D She is in a hurry to get home.

2 She feels angry as she walks home because
A she is expected to do too much.
B she dislikes the area where she lives.
C her family pay little attention to her.
D she is not rewarded for her effort.

3 Rachel only speaks briefly to the man who helps her because
A she thinks he has a criminal past.
B she has never met him before.
C she doesn't like the way he's dressed.
D she's in a hurry to do other work.

4 What does Rachel mean by 'others are in the same boat' in line 43?
A She has similar ambitions to other people.
B She deserves to be treated the same as other people.
C She lives in similar circumstances to other people.
D She can share her problems with other people.

5 Who, according to Rachel, has had the greatest influence on her?
A the homeless man
B her mother
C many different people
D her family as a whole

6 Which of these phrases best summarises the lesson Rachel has learned?
A She shouldn't complain about her situation.
B She shouldn't envy other people.
C She can be poor but happy.
D She should value her family more.

4 To understand a text, you often need to understand exactly what the writer is referring to at different points in the text. Which noun phrase (a or b) does each of these words/phrases refer to?

1 it (line 2)
a the grocery list
b the money

2 it (line 6)
a the list **b** the dress

3 these distractions (line 14)
a the traffic, the sun, the sacks
b the dress, the window, the supermarket

4 everything else (line 21)
a the other sacks **b** the spilled contents

5 them (line 25)
a the soup cans and apples **b** the hands

6 him (line 30)
a the stranger **b** a friend

7 others (line 43)
a other people **b** other strangers

8 that (line 49)
a following the example of just one person
b oversimplifying things

9 what (line 52)
a a familiar face **b** one genuine smile

Exam advice

- The answers to the questions come in the same order in the text, so, for example, you will locate the answer to question 2 after question 1.
- The final question may refer to the whole passage: in this case, consider the general message, but also skim the text for words which support your choice.

5 Work in groups.

- Do you think Rachel was right to feel angry that she couldn't have the dress? Why? / Why not?
- If they can afford it, how much pocket money should parents give their children at these ages: 13, 15 and 18? Why?
- What is the best age for young people to have their own bank account? When should they have their own credit card?
- Should young people be encouraged to save? Why? What for?
- Do you think teenagers should earn some of the money they need by doing housework or taking a part-time job? Why? / Why not?

Vocabulary
arrive, get and reach

1 Candidates often confuse *arrive, get* and *reach*. Circle the correct word in *italics* in each of these sentences. Then check your answers by reading the definitions on page 185.

1 Nothing out of the ordinary happens when I *arrive / get / reach* to the store. I grab the bread, some milk, and other things on the list.
2 The plane was late taking off and has only just *arrived / got / reached*.
3 When they *arrived / got / reached* the top of the mountain, they were unable to see anything due to the thick cloud.

2 Complete these sentences with *arrive, get* or *reach* in the correct form. In some cases, more than one answer may be possible.

1 Stop writing when you have .... 190 words.
2 The traffic was so bad that they didn't .... to the concert till after it had started.
3 She's driving home and she'll phone me when she .... there.
4 What time do you normally .... to school in the morning?
5 When they .... at the hotel, they went straight to their rooms.
6 When you .... the end of the road, turn left.

3 Complete the sentences below with an adverb / adverbial phrase from the box to form collocations with *arrive*.

finally	in time	on time	safe and sound	shortly	unannounced

1 Mum was worried that we might have an accident because of the snow, but we arrived home .... , much to her relief.
2 Sandy was late for the refreshments, but he arrived .... to hear the speeches.
3 The airline has a great reputation for punctuality, with 90% of flights arriving ....
4 The train that will be arriving .... at Platform 13, just two minutes after its scheduled time, is the Orient Express from Paris.
5 Uncle Kamal arrived .... in the middle of lunch, so we had to set an extra place for him at the table.
6 We were very late because of the traffic and when we .... arrived, the shop was closed.

Listening | Part 4

1 Work in pairs. You are going to hear a student interviewing two teenagers about a new shopping centre they've been researching for a school project. Before you listen, why do many people prefer shopping centres? Make a list of your ideas.

2 07 Listen to the interview once. How many of your ideas from Exercise 1 do they mention?

3 Read questions 1–7. How many can you answer already?

1 Where is the shopping centre situated?
A in the city centre
B on the edge of the city
C in the countryside

2 The location was chosen because
A it would not harm the environment.
B it was easy to get permission to build there.
C it was easy for people to reach.

3 What is the main attraction of the shopping centre?
A It's a convenient place to do the shopping.
B It's attractive to the whole family.
C It offers high-quality goods at low prices.

4 Kerry particularly enjoys the shopping centre's
A feeling of luxury.
B good security.
C friendly atmosphere.

5 Salim says families argue when they go shopping because
A they don't enjoy the same things.
B they can't agree on what to buy.
C they find each other's company stressful.

6 How are the shops organised?
A Each shop in the centre chooses its own location.
B Each section of the centre has a variety of shops.
C Similar shops in the centre are located near each other.

7 What innovation does Salim describe for making shopping easier?
A electric vehicles
B moving walkways
C automatic delivery systems

4 Listen again. For questions 1–7, choose the best answer (A, B or C).

Vocabulary and grammar review Unit 10

Vocabulary

1 Read the text and decide which answer (A, B, C or D) best fits each gap.

According to recent research, teenagers are very **(0)** ...B... to price. They hunt for **(1)** .... and consider high prices a personal insult. They plan their shopping and do not just **(2)** .... into shops and buy on impulse. Interestingly, parents have a lot of **(3)** .... both over how much teenagers spend on clothes and what they buy, even if the teenagers have **(4)** .... the money themselves from a part-time job; in short, teenagers worry about their parents' reaction to the clothes they **(5)** .... Shops operate in a highly **(6)** .... environment, so they make sure to **(7)** .... for young people's tastes by having a wide range of fashion clothes in **(8)** .... at any one time.

0	A sensible	B sensitive	C affected	D considerate
1	A values	B cheapness	C bargains	D decreases
2	A jump	B pop	C enter	D pass
3	A impact	B importance	C pressure	D influence
4	A earned	B won	C gained	D acquired
5	A invest	B achieve	C purchase	D obtain
6	A competent	B competitive	C contested	D combative
7	A offer	B cater	C sell	D supply
8	A stock	B shelf	C place	D existence

Grammar

2 Complete the second sentence so that it has a similar meaning to the first sentence, using the word given. Do not change the word given. You must use between two and five words, including the word given.

1 Manu didn't succeed in completing the crossword.
ABLE
Manu .... off the crossword.

2 We need to use less paper.
AMOUNT
We need to cut .... paper we use.

3 Katya found the climb so tiring that she fell asleep at the top.
WORN
Katya .... the climb that she fell asleep at the top.

4 Pierre was unable to suggest an answer to the problem.
COME
Pierre .... an answer to the problem.

5 Did you manage to collect Paz from the station?
PICK
Were you .... from the station?

6 When Alexis reached the cinema, the film had finished.
GET
Alexis did not .... the film was over.

3 Write *as* or *like* in each of the gaps.

When my grandfather left school at the age of 14, he got his first job **(1)** .... an office assistant. In those days, he was extremely thin, **(2)** .... he wasn't paid very much and couldn't afford to eat a lot. But he was in the same situation **(3)** .... a lot of boys at that time, **(4)** .... most children left school at that age and had to look for a job. I have one or two photos of him from that time, and he looks just **(5)** .... me, but thinner! When he grew older, he worked at all sorts of things, such **(6)** .... reporting for a local newspaper and working **(7)** .... a part-time mechanic. **(8)** .... many people of his generation, he worked hard all his life, but he always found time for the things he enjoyed, **(9)** .... walking in the country or spending time with his grandchildren. I hope I'll be **(10)** .... him when I'm an old man!

11 Medical matters

1 Here I am, in my 80s and still quite .... – I mean I go shopping, visit my friends and go to the cinema when I want to. What more can you ask for?

2 I do an hour's .... in the morning before going to college, and in the evening I usually have time for a couple of hours' sport, so I really think I'm very fit.

3 I do .... the occasional cold or other .... I'm a doctor, so I can't really avoid them, but I .... them pretty quickly and they don't usually stop me going to work.

4 I visit the doctor regularly once a year for a .... Once or twice I've needed .... for something she's found, but it's never been anything very serious.

5 I never go to the doctor and in fact I don't even know my doctor's name. I'm lucky, I've never had a day's .... in my life.

6 I'm very careful to eat a .... – only a little meat and plenty of fresh fruit and vegetables – and I'm careful about not .... weight, so I do a reasonable amount of exercise as well.'

Starting off

1 Work in pairs. Complete what each of the people says about their health by writing the words or phrases from the box in the gaps.

active	balanced diet	catch	check-up	get over
illness	infection	putting on	treatment	workout

2 13 Work in pairs. Listen to the first part of what each speaker (A–F) says about their health and, when you hear the 'beep', predict which extract (1–6) from Exercise 1 comes next.

Example: A 2

3 14 Now listen to the complete extracts to check your answers to Exercises 1 and 2.

4 Work in pairs.

- Which speaker do you think has the healthiest lifestyle?
- Which speakers say something you agree with? Why?

Listening | Part 3

1 You are going to hear five people talking about a visit to their family doctor. Before you listen, answer the questions in the Exam round-up box.

Exam round-up

How much do you remember about Listening Part 3? Circle the correct option in *italics* in these sentences.

1 You listen to *four / five* speakers and you must choose the statement which best summarises what they say from *seven / eight* options.
2 Before you listen, you should *read and think about the meaning of each option / read through the options, then wait patiently for the listening to begin.*
3 The speaker will *express the same idea / use exactly the same words* as in the question.

2 Match the words and phrases (1–9) with their definitions (a–i).

1 cure
2 diagnose
3 examination
4 heal
5 prescribe
6 sick note
7 surgery
8 treat
9 vaccination

a an injection to prevent someone getting a disease
b piece of paper on which a doctor writes that a patient is ill and has permission not to go to school or work
c say what medical treatment someone should have
d recognise and name the exact character of a disease or a problem, by making an examination
e use drugs, exercises, etc. to cure a person of a disease or heal an injury
f when a doctor looks at a patient carefully in order to discover the problem
g make someone with an illness healthy again
h make or become well again, especially after a cut or other injury
i a place where you can go to ask advice from or receive treatment from a doctor or dentist

3 15 Now listen and tick ✓ the words and phrases from Exercise 2 as you hear them.

4 Listen again. For speakers 1–5, choose from the list (A–H) what each speaker says about their visit. Use the letters only once. There are three extra letters which you do not need to use.

A I wasn't given enough attention by the doctor at first.
B I was told by the doctor that I needed to relax.
C I was irritated by what the doctor said.
D I wish I hadn't gone to the doctor at all.
E I felt better after the visit.
F I asked for a specialist to deal with my problem.
G I agreed with the doctor's diagnosis.
H I arrived late for my doctor's appointment.

Speaker 1 [ ] 1
Speaker 2 [ ] 2
Speaker 3 [ ] 3
Speaker 4 [ ] 4
Speaker 5 [ ] 5

5 Work in pairs.

- What can people do when they are unhappy with their doctor?
- Which do you think is more important: dealing with the medical problem or treating the patient well?

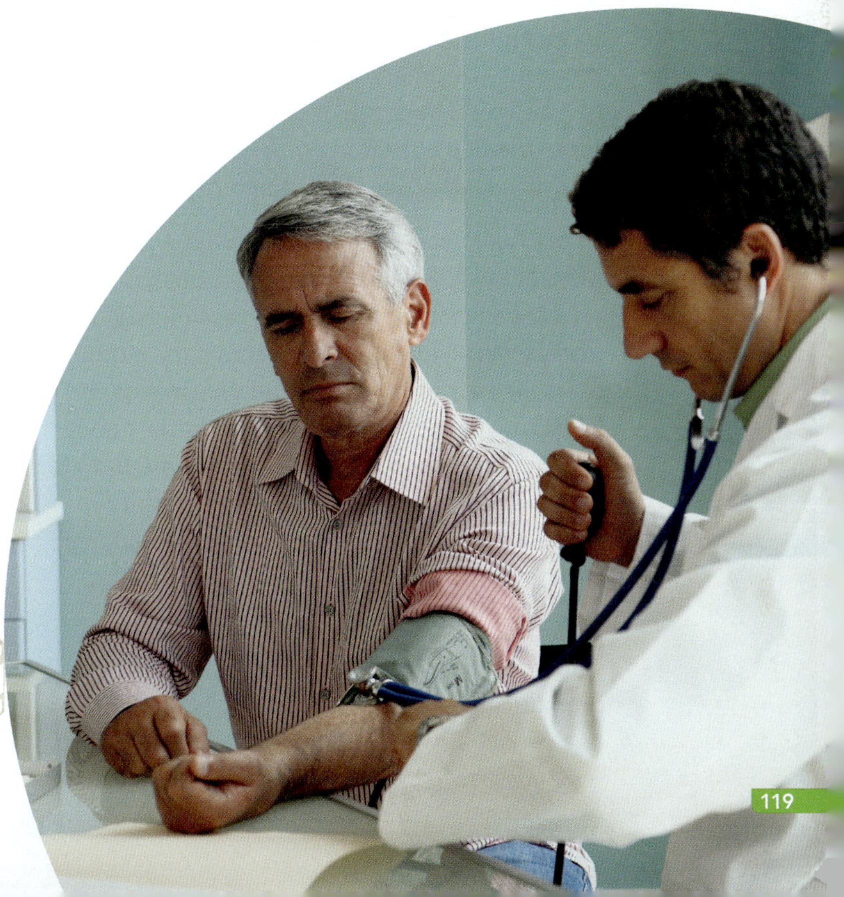

Reading and Use of English | Part 6

1 Work in groups. You will read an article about studying medicine. Before you read, discuss these questions.

- What attracts young people to become doctors?
- How do you think studying medicine might be different from studying other subjects at university?

2 Read the article carefully, ignoring the gaps. Note the subject of each paragraph in the margin as you read.

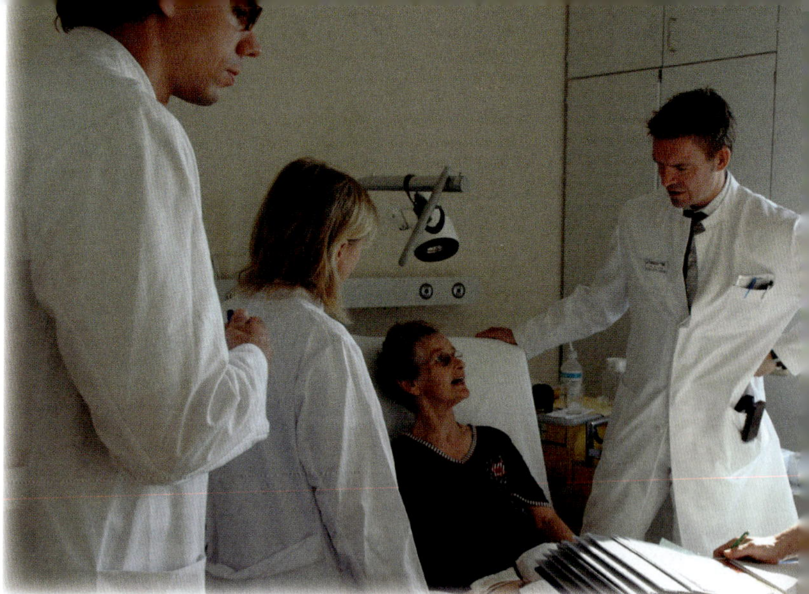

What's it like to study medicine?

Dr Fred Clough recounts his experience

How studying medicine is different

Medicine isn't quite like other degrees. I spent the first three years studying and attending lectures on anatomy, cell biology and pathology (what happens when the body goes wrong). I found when I got to medical school that I was required to memorise far more than I had had to at secondary school and put in far longer hours, especially around exam time.

As well as the lessons and lectures, I had individual weekly classes with my tutor, who also gave me work to do. **1** These classes soon became a high point in my week. We used to spend the hour discussing such things as the properties of different medicines or the topic of an essay whose title was *Doctors can learn more medicine from treating patients than from studying textbooks. Do you agree?* **2**

In my final year, I studied for an extra degree in Physiological Sciences. I was also able to pursue areas of interest, which in my case included neuroscience, and take supplementary modules in the history of medicine and pharmacology. Most universities now expect you to do some academic research as well. However, I felt incredibly lucky that I had the opportunity to work in laboratories where I rubbed shoulders with Nobel Prize winners. **3**

As a clinical student, in other words as a student in a hospital, my timetable changed dramatically. I was expected to dress smartly, as I spent every day with patients as a functioning part of a medical team. **4** These included surgery, medicine, dermatology, neurology and many more.

I moved to a London hospital for my clinical training, and had some very memorable experiences, such as delivering my first baby and visiting a prison psychiatric ward. **5** I was permitted to walk into any ward or any operating theatre and observe, learn, ask questions and speak to patients, whereas practising doctors are all rushed off their feet. Students can often take time to really investigate a patient's condition more deeply, and may even be able to inform the doctors and nurses of some very important detail that has been overlooked and which might lead to the patient being misdiagnosed. **6** Everyone teaches each other at whatever level, and now I also help secondary-school students who are preparing entrance exams for the top medical schools.

Medicine is a very time-intensive degree. However, being thrown in at the deep end of some of the most challenging situations I have ever been in, and having to deal with patients from all areas of life, continues to inspire me and satisfy me on a daily basis.

Adapted from *The Independent*

Exam advice

- If you can't think of a word, explain what the thing is used for or what it looks like.
- Try to use vocabulary relevant to the topic.
- If possible, avoid hesitating too often.

4 Pronunciation: intonation (3)

We tend to use more intonation on stressed words than on unstressed words.

1 ▶ 17 Work in pairs. Look at this extract from Antonia's answer. Underline the words you think she stresses. Then listen to check your answers.

OK, so both photographs show people doing things which might be good for their sanity, sorry, I mean their health. In the first photo I can see someone who looks as if he's, um, what's the word, he's commuting by bicycle in busy traffic.

2 ▶ 18 Listen to the extract with two different intonations.

- In which version, a or b, does the speaker sound more certain and confident?
- Does the voice rise or fall on the final stressed word in each sentence? What does this show?

3 Take turns to read the extract in Exercise 1 aloud. Your partner should say whether your intonation is more like version a or b.

4 ▶ 19 Decide which words will be stressed in these two extracts. Then listen to check your answers.

a I'd say there are some problems with the idea of health in the first photo because of the danger from the traffic, especially because he's cycling in the night, I mean the dark, and the, um, I can't think of the word, but it's a type of smoke which comes from the cars.

b On the other hand, if you live in the city, it's a good way of getting exercise. In the second photo, the kids should remember that they need to eat a mixed, sorry, a balanced diet, not just salad and fruit.

5 Does the speaker sound more certain and more confident in extract a or b? Why? Take turns to read these extracts aloud.

5 ▶ 20 Work in pairs.

- Student A: Listen to the examiner's instructions and do the Speaking Part 2 task in Exercise 2.
- Student B: Listen and complete the checklist in Exercise 2 for your partner. When your partner has finished, give feedback.

6 ▶ 21 Now, Student B should listen to the examiner's follow-up question and answer it.

7 ▶ 22 Work in pairs. Student B should listen to the examiner's instructions and do this task. Student A should complete the checklist in (Speaking) Exercise 2 and give feedback at the end.

Why is it important for these people to deal with their problems?

8 ▶ 23 Now Student A should listen to the examiner's follow-up question and answer it.

Writing | Part 1 An essay

1 Work in groups. Look at this discussion question. Discuss and note down at least three healthy or unhealthy aspects for each discussion point (a–e). When you have finished, change groups and report what your group decided.

> Do you think modern lifestyles are healthy or not?
> Talk about:
> a the environment and health
> b diet
> c work activities
> d information, e.g. about exercise, diet
> e free-time activities.

2 Work in pairs. Read the writing task in the next column.

- Underline the main ideas in the task.
- Decide which points from your discussion you would include in your answer and write a plan.

> In your English class, you have been talking about whether modern lifestyles are healthy or not.
>
> Now your English teacher has asked you to write an essay.
>
> Write an essay using **all** the notes and give reasons for your point of view.
>
> **Essay question**
> Modern lifestyles can seriously endanger our health. Do you agree?
>
> **Notes**
> Write about:
>
> 1. *food*
> 2. *physical activity*
> 3. .... *(your own idea)*
>
> Write your **essay**.

3 Work in pairs. Discuss what the strong points and weak points of this essay are. Then say what comments you would write at the end if you were this student's teacher.

It seems strange that although we know a lot about how to live healthily, many people continue to do things which may be harmful to their health.

There are many parts of our lifestyles which enable us to live healthily. For instance, we all know about the importance of eating a balanced diet and taking regular exercise. Moreover, in rich countries we have easy access to good-quality fresh food and suitable sports facilities, so it should be easy to adopt healthy living habits.

However, there are things which prevent people from having a healthy lifestyle. For example, industry and traffic have led to serious environmental pollution. What is more, we spend a lot of time sitting down, and this often means we have less time for activities which keep us fit. For example, there are many people who spend many hours sitting in front of computers working, studying, or playing computer games. In addition, many people do not eat the right sort of food.

4 Work in pairs. Read these concluding paragraphs and decide which one is most suitable for the essay in Exercise 3. Why?

1 All in all, I believe that we have to find ways of living which are as healthy as possible. Also, I think people should try to drive more carefully.

2 In conclusion, I would agree with the statement because although we have plenty of opportunities to follow a healthy lifestyle, in practice we often choose a less healthy alternative.

3 To summarise, modern lifestyles have good and bad aspects, but the lifestyle we choose depends on us. However, often our health depends on factors which we cannot control.

5 Match each of these teacher's comments (a–c) to one of the concluding paragraphs in Exercise 4.

a A good brief final paragraph where your opinion is clearly stated and you summarise the main arguments of your essay.

b This concluding paragraph doesn't seem to sum up the arguments you expressed in the main part of the essay, but it sums up other arguments. What a pity, because it's well written!

c You're giving an opinion which is not exactly connected with the essay question. Also, your final sentence introduces a new argument which hasn't been dealt with in the main part of the essay, so it's not really a conclusion.

6 If you're not sure how to begin a paragraph, you can begin with a sentence which:

- says what the paragraph will contain
- relates the paragraph to the previous paragraph.

Look at the opening sentences (a and b) from the sample answer in Exercise 3.

1 What will each paragraph contain?
2 Which word relates one of the paragraphs to the previous paragraph?

a There are many parts of our lifestyles which enable us to live healthily.
b However, there are things which prevent people from having a healthy lifestyle.

7 Write opening sentences for paragraphs which will contain:

1 three advantages of living in the country
2 some disadvantages of living in the country
3 reasons exercise is important
4 dangers of taking too much exercise.

8 Work in groups. Discuss whether you agree or disagree with the essay question in Exercise 9. You can talk about:

- diet
- sport and exercise
- free-time activities.

9 Do this writing task. Write between 140 and 190 words. Before you write, make a plan.
When you write, you can use the essay in Exercise 3 as a model.

In your English class, you have been talking about how interested young people are in health and fitness.

Now your English teacher has asked you to write an essay.

Write an essay using **all** the notes and give reasons for your point of view.

Essay question
Young people generally don't pay enough attention to their health and fitness. Do you agree?

Notes
Write about:

1. *physical exercise*
2. *other habits which affect health*
3. .... *(your own idea)*

Write your **essay**.

Exam advice

- Your concluding paragraph should summarise your opinion and the reasons for it.
- Don't include new arguments or ideas in your final sentence because you won't be able to support them with reasons or examples.
- Be careful not to spend too long on Part 1, or you won't have time to do Part 2 well.

12 Animal kingdom

Starting off

Work in pairs.

Imagine you are planning an article for your college magazine on the importance of animals in our lives. First, discuss what role each animal in the photos plays in our lives and how these roles benefit people.

Then decide which two photos would be best for the magazine article.

Listening | Part 1

1 Work in pairs. Before you listen, answer the questions in the Exam round-up box.

Exam round-up

How much do you remember about Listening Part 1? Circle the correct option in *italics* in each of these sentences.

In Listening Part 1:

1 you hear *six / eight* extracts; the extracts are on *the same subject / different* subjects.
2 you hear each extract *once / twice*.
3 you *read and hear / read but don't hear* the question before the extract.
4 you should underline the main idea *in the question only / in the question and each of the options.*
5 you should answer *while you listen / after you have heard the whole of each piece.*

2 24 You are going to hear people talking in eight different situations. For questions 1–8, choose the best answer (A, B or C). As you hear the question, underline the main idea.

1 You overhear a conversation between two women about animals. Which animal does she think her family will choose?
A a cat
B a dog
C a horse

2 You hear part of a television programme about zebras. What does the presenter say about their appearance?
A All members of a family of zebras have the same stripes.
B Zebras can recognise each other by their stripes.
C Male and female zebras have similar stripes.

3 You overhear a conversation between a boy and a girl about birds in the girl's garden. How does the girl's mother feel about birds?
A She enjoys watching them.
B She likes feeding them.
C She worries about them.

4 You overhear part of a conversation in which a girl and a boy are talking about dogs. What is the boy doing?
A recommending having a dog
B complaining about his dog
C suggesting where to keep a dog

5 You hear a woman giving part of a lecture about animal rights. She says zoos
A are no longer necessary in modern times.
B should only be for endangered species.
C should be closely supervised.

6 You hear a girl talking about some animals she worked with. When she was with them, she felt
A frightened.
B relaxed.
C strange.

7 You hear a boy talking about hippos. What does he say about them?
A They are more dangerous than he previously thought.
B They often attack people for no reason.
C They are easily frightened.

8 You hear a woman talking to her husband about a circus. She is talking to him in order to
A make a suggestion.
B make a complaint.
C remind him of something.

Vocabulary

avoid, prevent and protect; check, control, keep an eye on and supervise

1 Candidates often confuse the following words: *avoid, prevent* and *protect; check, control, keep an eye on* and *supervise*. Circle the correct word in *italics* in these extracts from Listening Part 1.

1 I mean, we'd have to *check / control / supervise* her quite closely to start with to make sure she was safe. At least until we know she can *check / control / keep an eye on / supervise* it.
2 … we really got him to *avoid / prevent / protect* us from burglars.
3 Well, all that barking might *avoid / prevent / protect* a burglary.
4 … the more modern zoos need to be strictly inspected to make sure that the animals are kept in the best conditions possible. That way diseases and other problems can be *avoided / prevented / protected*.
5 I had to *check / control / keep an eye on* them as well, because they could be quite rough when playing with each other …

2 Read the definitions on page 185. Then complete these sentences (1–10) by writing one of the words in the correct form in the gaps. In some cases, more than one answer may be possible.

1 This cream is perfect for .... you from insect bites.
2 Can you .... the children while they're in the swimming pool, please, to make sure they're safe?
3 You need to .... your dog, especially when you're walking with it in busy streets.
4 The new law .... people from building houses near the National Park.
5 There was a man who was .... the tickets as people walked into the stadium.
6 I think we should set out early to .... the worst of the traffic.
7 You ought to be wearing a hat to .... your head from the sun.
8 It's the chemistry teacher's responsibility to .... students when they're doing experiments to make sure nothing explodes!
9 Make sure you .... your answer for mistakes before you hand it in.
10 We should always respect the forces of nature because we will never be able to .... them.

3 Complete each of the sentences below with an adverb/verb collocation from the box in the correct form.

avoid … at all costs check … carefully
closely supervise heavily protect
narrowly avoid properly protect strictly control
successfully prevent

1 Ben .... the bear from attacking them by making a lot of noise.
2 Juan .... an accident when a dog ran in front of the car.
3 Rhinos are an endangered species and need to be .... by game wardens.

4 The number of visitors to the game reserve is .... to avoid upsetting the animals.
5 Tourists visiting the park need to be .... to make sure they don't go near the wild animals.
6 When it rains heavily, you should .... crossing the river .... , as the current can be very strong.
7 You need to .... your route .... on the map before you start, as you could easily get lost.
8 The camp is .... with a high fence and an alarm to prevent dangerous animals from getting in.

Grammar

Third conditional and mixed conditionals

1 Look at this sentence from Listening Part 1 (extract 7) and then decide whether the statements (1–3) are true (T) or false (F).

If he hadn't reacted quickly, the hippo would have killed him.

1 The man reacted quickly.
2 The hippo killed him.
3 The speaker is talking about the past.

2 Now look at these sentences and answer the questions below.

a *I think if they'd had more acrobats, we'd have enjoyed the circus more.*
b *I think if they had more acrobats, we'd enjoy the circus more.*

Which sentence (a or b) … ?
1 means: *They don't have enough acrobats, so we don't enjoy the circus very much.* ....
2 means: *They didn't have enough acrobats, so we didn't enjoy the circus very much.* ....
3 has this form: *if* + past simple, *would* + infinitive ....
4 has this form: *if* + past perfect, *would have* (*been/done/enjoyed*, etc.) ....
5 is second conditional (see pages 54–55) ....
6 is third conditional ....
7 has the same form as *If he hadn't reacted quickly, the hippo would have killed him* in Exercise 1 ....

page 165 Language reference: Conditionals – third conditional

3 Candidates often make mistakes with tenses in third conditional sentences. Complete each of these sentences by writing the verb in brackets in the correct form.

1 If Martin had concentrated on his work, he .... (*finish*) it earlier.
2 If I .... (*know*) that the train was going to be so late, I .... (*catch*) an earlier one.
3 If there had been a swimming pool in the garden I .... (*go*) swimming in it.
4 John could have spoken to Emma if the phone .... (*not be*) broken.
5 We wouldn't have become friends unless you .... (*sit*) next to me on the school bus.
6 If you had been there, you .... (*enjoy*) yourself, too!
7 Sorry! I .... (*not make*) so much noise if I'd known you were asleep.
8 We .... (*not hear*) the burglar downstairs unless the dog had barked.

4 Work in pairs. Answer these questions in any way you like.

- What would have happened if you'd got up an hour later this morning?
- Where was the last place you went on holiday? What would you have done if you hadn't gone on holiday there?
- What was the last exam you passed? What would have happened if you'd failed the exam?

5 If you want to talk about past and present time in the same conditional sentence, you can combine second conditional with third conditional. Look at these two extracts from Listening Part 1. Which part of each sentence (a or b):

- is second conditional, and which part is third conditional?
- refers to present time and which part refers to past time?

1 Probably, [if we lived in a safer area,]a [they wouldn't have bought a dog.]b

2 [I'd be happier,]a [if my parents had bought a house in the country.]b

page 165 Language reference: Conditionals – mixed conditionals

6 Complete these sentences by writing the verb in brackets in the correct form (second or third conditional) in the gaps.

1 My dad doesn't have a car, so he didn't drive me to my dancing lesson yesterday. If my dad .... (*have*) a car, he .... (*drive*) me to my dancing lesson yesterday.
2 Katie feels nervous about the test because she didn't study last weekend. If she .... (*study*), she .... (*not feel*) nervous about the test.
3 Our dog barks too much, so we didn't take him on holiday with us. If our dog .... (*not bark*) so much, we .... (*take*) him on holiday with us.
4 Karl was very rude to me, so we are no longer friends. If Karl .... (*not be*) so rude to me, we .... (still be) friends.

7 For questions 1–4, complete the second sentence so that it has a similar meaning to the first sentence, using the word given. Do not change the word given. You must use between two and five words, including the word given.

1 Marcelo often misses school, so his teacher did not let him go on the school trip.
ALLOWED
If Marcelo went to school more often, his teacher .... to go on the school trip.
2 We were late leaving home, so we missed the concert.
EARLIER
If we .... , we would not have missed the concert.
3 I did not ask my geography teacher any questions in class because she is quite frightening.
LESS
If my geography teacher was .... asked her some questions.
4 Franz did not understand because the guide spoke too quickly.
MORE
If the guide .... , Franz would have understood.

Reading and Use of English | Part 1

1 Work in pairs. You will read a short article by someone who worked in a circus. Before you read, discuss these questions.

- Are circuses popular in your country? Why? / Why not?
- What other traditional forms of entertainment are popular in your country? Why?

2 Before doing Reading and Use of English Part 1, answer the questions in the Exam round-up box.

3 Read the article quickly without paying attention to the gaps. What animals do Nell and Toti have in their circus?

My sister's circus

My sister and brother-in-law, Nell and Toti, **(0)** ...own... a circus. It is **(1)** .... Giffords Circus, and it tours some of the loveliest parts of south-west England. Circuses have always been a part of Nell's life, even when we were children. When she **(2)** .... Toti, she had already worked in **(3)** .... circuses in Britain and Europe. She had ridden elephants, but what she really **(4)** .... for was a circus of her own. If the word 'circus' **(5)** .... you of clowns and lions, think again. The show is **(6)** .... on traditional travelling circuses and aimed at a rural **(7)** ....
There are no wild animals, but horses play a leading role in performances, which are a mixture of theatre, dance, traditional circus acts and clowns. I had visited Nell at the circus a lot, but this time I was going to **(8)** .... the summer there.

Adapted from the *Daily Telegraph*

Exam round-up

How much do you remember about Reading and Use of English Part 1? Complete the information below with these words and phrases.

eight   after   all the questions   the text quickly   you have finished   the options

1 There are .... questions in this part. You must choose A, B, C or D.
2 Read .... before attempting the questions.
3 Read the words before and .... the gaps carefully.
4 Try all .... in the gaps before deciding.
5 Read the text again carefully when ....
6 Answer ....

4 For questions 1–8, read the text again and decide which answer (A, B, C or D) best fits each gap. There is an example at the beginning (0).

	A	B	C	D
0	A belong	B keep	C own	D possess
1	A called	B known	C named	D titled
2	A encountered	B knew	C met	D saw
3	A few	B number	C plenty	D several
4	A desired	B longed	C wanted	D needed
5	A recalls	B recollects	C remembers	D reminds
6	A based	B built	C put	D set
7	A spectator	B public	C viewer	D audience
8	A be	B pass	C spend	D stay

5 Work in pairs.

- Many people think it's cruel to use animals in circuses. Do you agree?
- Do you think it's cruel to keep animals in zoos? Why? / Why not?

Grammar

wish, if only and *hope*

1 Read these sentences (a–f) and answer the questions (1–8) below.

a My aunt has a white cat, and I wish I had one too.
b I wish the dog next door wouldn't bark, especially at night.
c I wish it had made some kind of scratch on my skin to show my friends.
d If only I was back in Italy!
e We get quite a variety of birds at this time of year. I always hope the cats don't get them.
f I hope you enjoy your holiday and have good weather!

1 In which sentences is the speaker talking about something in the present?
2 In which three sentences is the speaker saying he/she would like the present situation to be different?
3 In which sentence is the speaker complaining about an activity which is annoying?
4 What tenses are possible after *wish* and *if only* when referring to present time?
5 In which sentence is the speaker talking about something which happened in the past?
6 What tense is used after *wish* (and *if only*) when referring to past time?
7 In which sentence is the speaker talking about something in the future?
8 What tense can be used with the verb after *hope* when we talk about the future?

➜ page 180 Language reference: *wish, if only* and *hope*

2 Candidates often confuse *wish* and *hope*. Read these sentences and decide when *wish* is used correctly and when you should use *hope*. If you think a sentence is correct, write *correct*.

1 It was lovely seeing you and I wish to see you again very soon in my house.
2 Going to the theme park together was great and I wish you enjoyed the experience.
3 I wish I'd visited you last summer when I had the chance.
4 I'm looking forward to having news from you soon and I wish you have a good time in New York.
5 My neighbour's children are always shouting; I wish they wouldn't be so noisy.
6 The performance was really good but I wish more people will come next time.
7 I don't get many letters from you and I wish you'd write to me more often.
8 We wish you enjoy your stay at our hotel while you're here in Tokyo.

3 For questions 1–5, complete the second sentence so that it has a similar meaning to the first sentence, using the word given. Do not change the word given. You must use between two and five words, including the word given.

1 It's a pity I can't cook well.
BETTER
I wish I .... cook.

2 I regret not studying harder when I was at school.
STUDIED
If only .... when I was at school.

3 I want the neighbours to stop making so much noise.
MAKE
I wish the neighbours .... noise.

4 What a pity that they cancelled the match!
CALLED
If only they .... the match.

5 I'm sorry you didn't meet my brother.
WISH
I .... my brother.

Reading and Use of English | Part 7

1 Work in pairs. Before you read, answer the questions in the Exam round-up box.

Exam round-up

How much do you remember about Reading and Use of English Part 7? Say whether the following statements are true (T) or false (F). If a statement is false, correct it.

1. In this part, there are 12 questions.
2. You have to match the questions with different texts or different parts of a text.
3. You should read the text(s) carefully before you read the questions.
4. You should underline the main ideas in the questions.
5. If you can't find an answer, leave the gap blank.

2 Work in groups. You will read a newspaper article about people who have been attacked by animals. Before you read, discuss these questions.

- Are there any dangerous wild animals in your country?
- What do you think you should do if you see a dangerous animal?

3 Now read questions 1–10 carefully and underline the main idea in each.

Which person

didn't immediately realise he'd been injured?	1
was unwilling to injure the animal?	2
believes his behaviour caused the attack?	3
gave advice which was ignored?	4
was with people who lacked the knowledge to help him?	5
was considered to have missed an opportunity?	6
regrets the result of his encounter?	7
thinks he might not have been injured at another time of day?	8
was happy at first to see the animal which later attacked him?	9
was surprised to eventually escape?	10

4 Now read the article and, for questions 1–10, choose from the people (A–D). Each person may be chosen more than once.

5 Work in pairs. What should people do to protect themselves when they are in places where there are dangerous animals?

Surviving an animal attack

No matter how well prepared you are as a traveller, animals can still attack you. Our advice? Keep your distance!

A Colin Bristow

I was working as a safari guide in Botswana with four American clients. There was a sudden movement to my left, and a charging elephant crashed through some small trees less than 20 feet away. I always brief my clients that you should never take your eyes off a dangerous animal or show signs of fear or panic. I turned to face it and was immediately knocked over by one of the clients screaming 'run, run' at the top of his voice. I landed on my back between the exposed roots of a large acacia tree. My backpack tangled with one of the roots so that I couldn't move. The elephant was kneeling over me smashing his thick trunk into the roots on either side of my body. Elephants have poor eyesight and this may have been what saved me. I managed to free myself from my backpack and I ran for my life hardly daring to believe that the elephant wasn't chasing me.

B Chris Haslam

I was camping on a beach in Mexico. It was sunset and I was walking along the coast looking for firewood when I noticed a dead cactus which was perfect for the fire. I bent to lift it and perhaps because of the fading light, failed to notice the danger. I felt the slightest prick against my middle finger, which I thought I'd brushed against a cactus spine. It was a scorpion. The pain was intense and sudden. By the time I arrived back at camp, my lips were numb and I was shaking. In the absence of qualified medical opinion, my companions carried on with their game of cards.

The next morning, I showed the sting to a local.

'Did you play cards with the others last night?'

'Course not,' I replied. 'I was too ill.'

He raised his eyebrows. 'Too bad. Scorpion stings are very lucky, *muchacho*.'

C Baz Roberts

On our penultimate night on the Arctic ice as we were returning from the Pole, I was just falling asleep when Paul's voice woke me: 'Guys, there's a bear in the camp. I'm serious!' I leant forward on my knees to unzip the tent door. Directly in front was a polar bear about ten metres away. It heard the sound of my tent zip and turned to face me, all 600 kilos or so of him.

Due to melting ice, the polar bear's habitat is under threat and may one day disappear. As an intruder in their fragile world, I wanted to avoid causing it any harm. I started screaming and waving my arms. When he got about one metre away, I threw a large jar of coffee powder into the bear's face. If he hadn't turned and walked off at that moment, we wouldn't have survived.

D Zebedee Ellis (aged six)

I was at a zoo and dinosaur park with Mummy and Daddy two years ago. I had eaten about 400 tons of ice cream and now I wanted to see more animals. In a large open area next to a pond, daddy saw some big fat pelicans, all full of fish. 'There you are!' he said. 'Some animals for you to annoy.'

I was very pleased and danced up and down in front of them. Then one big pelican tried to eat my T-shirt. I think it went for me because I was moving around so much and that made it nervous, but I really wish it had made some kind of scratch on my skin to show my friends.

Adapted from the *Sunday Times*

Speaking | Parts 3 and 4

1 25 Work in pairs. Look at the speaking task below and listen to Miguel and Irene doing the task.

1 What is going wrong?
2 What can Irene do to put things right?

What would students find interesting and useful about each of these subjects?

- choosing a pet
- protecting animals in danger
- working with animals
- strange and amazing animals
- how animals communicate

2 26 Now listen to Miguel and Irene doing the task again. What phrases does Irene use to interrupt?

3 Work in pairs. Do the speaking task in Exercise 2, but take turns playing the role of a very talkative student and a student who wants to interrupt.

4 27 Now listen to the examiner and do the second part of Speaking Part 3.

5 28 Part 4 questions are on topics related to Part 3. Listen to Irene answering two Part 4 questions.

1 Which of these strategies does she use?
   a She just gives her opinion.
   b She expresses a range of ideas, but doesn't say which she agrees with.
   c She summarises other people's opinions, then gives her own.

2 Complete the table below by writing these phrases from Irene's answer in the correct column.

I'm not sure that I agree   People often suggest that
Some people say that   That's a difficult question
~~I think that's true~~   That's quite interesting

comment on the question	introduce other people's opinions	say whether you agree or disagree with the other people's opinions
		I think that's true

3 Work in pairs. Think of two more phrases you can add to each column of the table.

6 **Pronunciation:** word stress (3)

We sometimes pronounce individual words differently, depending on whether we stress them or not.

1 29 Listen to these phrases from Irene's answers again and underline the highlighted words which are stressed.

That's a difficult question. Some people say that it's cruel to keep animals in zoos where they don't have the freedom that they'd have in their natural habitat.

They say that animals get stressed and can't relax, but I'm not sure that I agree. I think they can. If animals have some space, they can have a nice relaxed life in a zoo.

That's quite interesting. People often suggest that children learn to be responsible because they have to look after the animal.

I think that's true and also, from my experience, I think that it's an extra relationship which develops children's ability to love and care about the animals and the people around them.

2 Listen again and notice how the pronunciation of the highlighted words changes depending on whether they are stressed or not.

3 Work in pairs. Take turns to read the sentences in Exercise 1 aloud.

4 30 Listen to each of these sentences being read twice, once with the highlighted words stressed and once with the highlighted words unstressed. Then work in pairs and take turns to read both versions of the sentences aloud.

a Looking after animals takes time and money.
b He was very tired, I admit.
c Where were you yesterday?
d Dogs can be very noisy.

7 Work in pairs and take turns to ask and answer these Part 4 questions.

1 What pet do you think is most suitable for young children? Why?
2 How can children benefit from having an animal to look after?
3 Which is better: to live in the country or to live in a large town? (Why?)
4 Why is it important to protect animals and other wildlife?
5 Do you think animals should be kept in zoos? (Why? / Why not?)

Exam advice

- Answer the questions in Speaking Part 4 with your opinion backed up with an example from your own experience if possible.
- Be prepared to discuss with your partner – you will gain marks if you have a conversation rather than just speaking one at a time.

Writing | Part 2 A letter or email

1 Work in pairs. Read this exam task and discuss the questions below.

> You have received a letter from your British friend, Les. Read this part of the letter.
>
> I'm thinking of visiting your country this summer. I'd be interested in seeing some beautiful scenery. Also, we'd like to see some wildlife. Can you advise me on where to go, what to see and the best way of getting around?
>
> Best wishes,
>
> Les
>
> Write your **letter**.

1 What three things must you deal with in your letter?
2 What advice would you give Les about your country?
3 What style would you use: formal or informal? Why?

2 Work in pairs. Write a plan for your letter.

3 Read Manolo's reply to Les's letter and answer these questions.

1 How does Manolo show that he has read Les's letter?
2 Has he answered all three things from the question? What advice did he give about each?
3 Does he give reasons for his advice?
4 What style does he use: formal or informal?

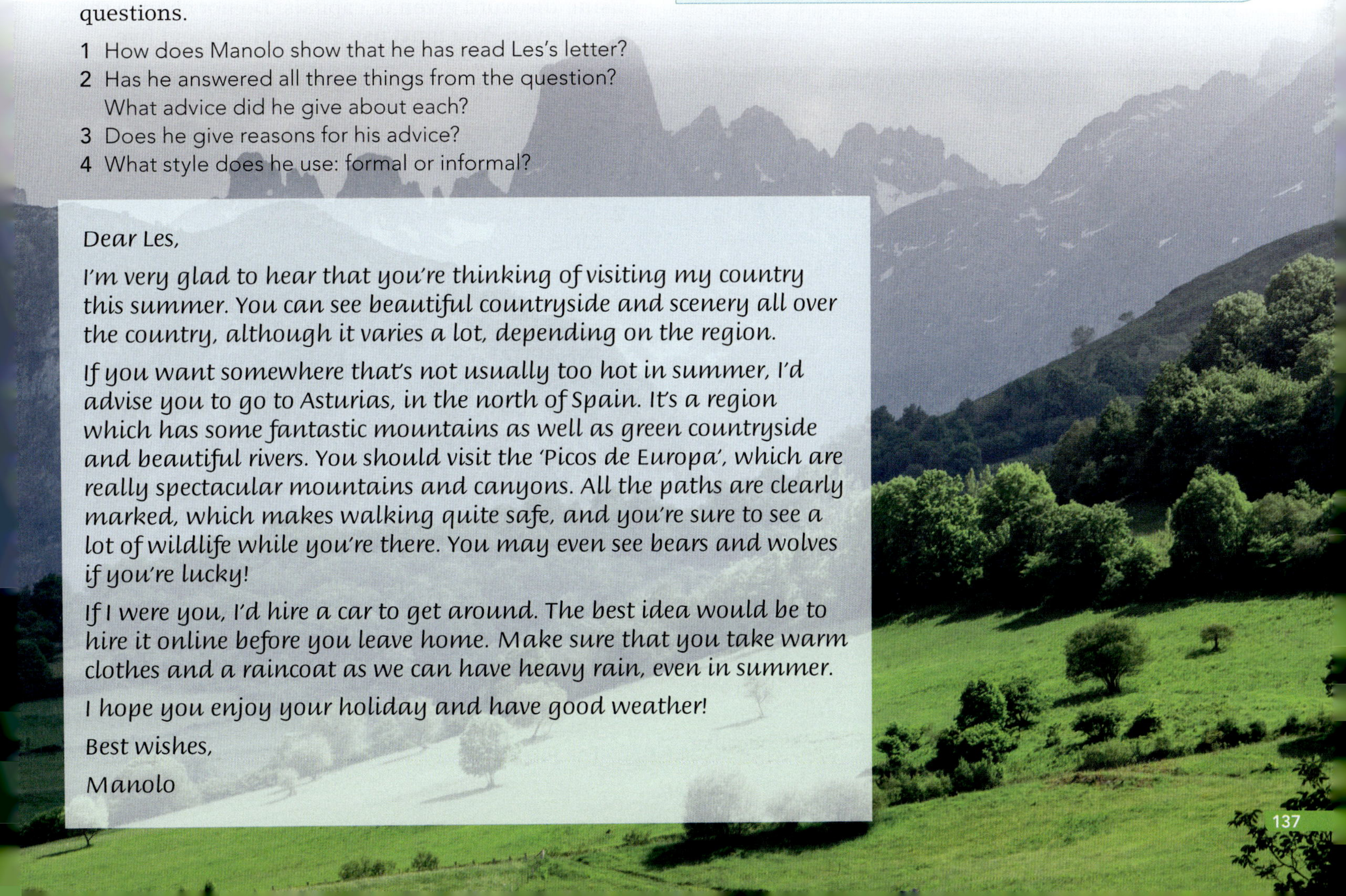

Dear Les,

I'm very glad to hear that you're thinking of visiting my country this summer. You can see beautiful countryside and scenery all over the country, although it varies a lot, depending on the region.

If you want somewhere that's not usually too hot in summer, I'd advise you to go to Asturias, in the north of Spain. It's a region which has some fantastic mountains as well as green countryside and beautiful rivers. You should visit the 'Picos de Europa', which are really spectacular mountains and canyons. All the paths are clearly marked, which makes walking quite safe, and you're sure to see a lot of wildlife while you're there. You may even see bears and wolves if you're lucky!

If I were you, I'd hire a car to get around. The best idea would be to hire it online before you leave home. Make sure that you take warm clothes and a raincoat as we can have heavy rain, even in summer.

I hope you enjoy your holiday and have good weather!

Best wishes,

Manolo

4 Find and underline these ways of giving advice in Manolo's letter.

1 *I'd advise you* + infinitive
2 *You should* + infinitive (without *to*)
3 *If I were you, I'd / I would ...*
4 *The best idea would be* + infinitive
5 *Make sure that ...*

5 Write five similar sentences using each of the five phrases in Exercise 4 once to give advice to Les for visiting your country.

6 Write your own answer to the question.

- Use Manolo's letter as a model.
- Write between 140 and 190 words.

Exam advice

- If you're writing a letter/email to a friend, use an informal style with contractions.
- Start in a friendly way with a phrase like *It's good to hear from you* or *I'm glad you're thinking of coming*, etc.
- Finish with something friendly like *I hope you enjoy yourself* or *Looking forward to seeing you.*

Vocabulary and grammar review Unit 11

Vocabulary

1 Complete sentences 1–10 below with a word from the box in the correct form in the gaps.

check-up cure diagnose fit get over heal infection prescription put on treatment

1 After a brief examination, my doctor .... that I was suffering from a slight infection.
2 As long as you keep the cut clean, it should .... on its own quite soon.
3 Farouk has been having .... in hospital following an accident he had last month.
4 She's spent the last two or three days in bed because of a minor .... she picked up at school.
5 I have to be quite careful what I eat so that I don't .... too much weight.
6 It's a good idea to keep .... by doing regular exercise – at least 40 minutes a day.
7 Rana's doctor has given her a .... for antibiotics to treat her illness.
8 Take this medicine. It should .... you in a couple of days.
9 You may not be very ill, but it's still worth going to the doctor for a .... to make sure it's nothing serious.
10 It took her several weeks to .... her illness, and she missed a lot of classes in that time.

Word formation

2 EP Complete each of these sentences by using the word given in capitals at the end of the sentences to form a word that fits in the gap.

1 I'm sorry about the mistake. The trouble is I .... the instructions. **UNDERSTAND**
2 My mum and dad .... of my friends because they make a lot of noise and don't study much. **APPROVE**
3 I felt very .... with the quality of the food at that restaurant and I'm thinking of complaining. **SATISFY**
4 Although she's a little .... , she's very keen and she tries hard. **EXPERIENCE**
5 Luis goes to school even when he's feeling ill because he .... missing lessons. **LIKE**
6 Even though Sandra offered to invite Toni to lunch, he was .... to help her with her essay. **WILL**
7 It feels strange and .... to be chatting with my teachers on Facebook. **NATURE**
8 We got the answers wrong because we were given .... information by the teacher. **LEAD**
9 I don't like to wear .... clothes even when I'm at school. **FASHION**
10 My aunt sent me home because she said my behaviour was .... in her home. **ACCEPT**
11 Teresa is quite .... , so I'm not sure if she'll turn up. **RELY**
12 I want to know the truth, so don't be .... with me. **HONEST**

Grammar

3 Complete the second sentence in each question so that it has a similar meaning to the first sentence, using the word given in capitals. Do not change the word given. You must use between two and five words, including the word given.

1 The boy with the broken arm is still in hospital.
IS
The boy .... not left hospital yet.
2 Did the doctor treat this injury?
ONE
Is this .... doctor treated?
3 Everyone who lives in the town Paola comes from is very friendly.
INHABITANTS
Paola comes from a town .... very friendly.
4 The teacher liked how Jan had answered the questions.
WAY
Jan answered the questions .... the teacher liked.
5 His email left us in no doubt about his opinion.
WHAT
It was clear to us .... his opinion was.
6 No one finds Chiaro's jokes amusing.
TELLS
The jokes .... amuse anyone.

Vocabulary and grammar review Unit 12

Vocabulary

1 For questions 1–6, read this text and decide which answer (A, B, C, or D) best fits each gap.

Due to the destruction of their natural habitats, more and more animals need to be **(1)** .... by creating nature reserves and passing laws. The laws are often designed to **(2)** .... farmers from using land where rare species live. The idea is that humans and animals **(3)** .... coming into conflict by not competing for the same land. Sometimes local people complain about losing farm land to nature reserves. However, jobs are often created for game wardens, whose job is to **(4)** .... the nature reserves to make sure everything functions correctly. Other people get jobs selling tickets to visitors, and there are also jobs for people to **(5)** .... the tickets as the visitors pass the entrance. In nature reserves containing dangerous animals, it may only be possible to visit them by car, and wardens need to **(6)** .... the number of cars entering the reserve to make sure they keep within reasonable limits.

1	A prevented	B protected	C avoided	D defended
2	A avoid	B cease	C prevent	D disallow
3	A avoid	B prevent	C miss	D fail
4	A check	B control	C prevent	D supervise
5	A check	B control	C look	D supervise
6	A check	B control	C prevent	D supervise

Grammar

2 Complete these sentences with the correct form of the verb in brackets. In some sentences more than one answer is possible.

1 The lions wouldn't have attacked us if they .... (*not be*) so hungry.
2 I wish it .... (*be*) summer – then we could go to the beach!
3 If my maths teacher .... (*be*) ill at the moment, we .... (*have*) a maths test yesterday.
4 If only you .... (*not make*) so much noise! I can't concentrate on my studies, and it's really annoying me!
5 I wish I .... (*live*) near the city centre. It's such a long bus ride from here.
6 Where's Candice? I hope she .... (*not miss*) the train.
7 I wish you .... (*speak*) more clearly so I could understand you better.
8 I think this soup .... (*be*) nicer if I'd used a bit less salt, don't you?
9 I hope you .... (*change*) your shirt before we go out to the restaurant.
10 I know my mother wishes she .... (*study*) harder when she was my age.
11 We .... (*get*) to the cinema in time if there hadn't been so much traffic.
12 If you .... (*eat*) more breakfast this morning, you wouldn't be feeling hungry now.

3 Complete the second sentence in each question so that it has a similar meaning to the first sentence, using the word given in capitals. Do not change the word given. You must use between two and five words, including the word given.

1 We are lost because we did not bring the map with us.
LEFT
If we .... the map behind, we would not be lost now.

2 Magda only did the work because we gave her the money beforehand.
PAID
Magda would not have done the work unless we .... advance.

3 Even if he had worked harder, the result would have been the same.
DIFFERENCE
It would not .... if he had worked harder.

4 It is a pity I do not get on better with my brother.
RELATIONSHIP
I wish I .... my brother.

5 Sasha would like Irina to help him from time to time.
ONCE
Sasha wishes Irina .... a while.

6 Sergei is disappointed because the university rejected him.
TURNED
If the university ...., Sergei would not be disappointed.

13 House space

Starting off

1 Work in pairs. Match each of these types of place to live with the photos.

a a villa
b a chalet in the mountains
c a block of flats with several storeys
d a house in a village
e a housing estate
f a mobile home

2 Which of these things do you think are important when choosing somewhere to live? Why? / Why not?

a quiet neighbourhood   a good view
shops within walking distance   a garden
parking space   public parks or gardens
good public transport   a good local school

3 Work in groups. Imagine you are going to live together for a year. Decide which type of place shown in the photos would be best for all of you.

Reading and Use of English | Part 5

1 Work in pairs. You are going to read an extract from a historical novel about a house in Venice. Before you read, look at the painting. Do you think you would have enjoyed life in 18th-century Venice? Why? / Why not?

2 Before doing Reading and Use of English Part 5, answer the questions in the Exam round-up box.

Exam round-up

How much do you remember about Reading and Use of English Part 5? Circle the correct option in *italics* in each of these sentences.

In Reading and Use of English Part 5:

1 there are *six / eight* questions; you must choose the best option: A, B, C or D.
2 you should read *the text quickly before reading the questions / the questions quickly before reading the text.*
3 you should read the options *before / after* reading the section of text where a question is answered.

3 Read the extract quite quickly to find out why the writer thinks the house is in a good location.

My new home in Venice, 1733

Uncle Leo gives me a suspicious look when I call this place the 'Scacchi Palace'. It is really a house, called Ca'Scacchi in Venetian. Anywhere else in the world, this would surely be regarded as a palace, although it is one in need of a little care and attention.

Our house is by the side of the little San Cassian canal and a small square of the same name. We have a door which leads onto the street and two entrances from the water. One runs under a grand, rounded arch into the ground floor of the house, which, as is customary in the city, is used instead of a cellar for storing things. The second is used for our commercial activities and it is situated in another building, which is three storeys high, attached to the north side, towards the Grand Canal.

Finally, there is yet another exit: a wooden bridge, with handrails, runs from the first floor of the house between the two river entrances straight over the canal and into the square itself. Consequently I can wander over it in the morning and find fresh water from the well in the centre of the square while still rubbing the sleep from my eyes. Or I may call a gondola from my bedroom window, find it waiting for me by the time I get downstairs and, just one minute later, be in the middle of the greatest waterway on Earth: the Grand Canal of Venice.

The house is almost 200 years old, I am told, and built of bricks of a rich dark brown colour. It has elegant arched windows and green-painted shutters to keep out the cruel summer heat. I live on the third floor in the third room on the right with a view over the canal and the square. When I lie in bed at night, I can hear the chatter and songs of the passing gondoliers and the conversations in the square nearby. I understand why Uncle runs his business here. The prices are not too steep. The location of the house is near the city centre and easy for our clients to find. Furthermore, the printing trade has many roots in this area of Venice, even if some of the old publishers from the area no longer exist.

Oh sister! I long for the day when I can show you these things instead of struggling to describe them in a letter which may take a long time to reach you in Spain! Venice is like a vast imitation of our old library at home, full of dark corners and unexpected surprises, some very close to me. Last night, while searching in the jumbled corners of the warehouse cellar, I found a single copy of *Aristotle's Poetics*, published in the city in 1502. I raced to Uncle Leo with my discovery and – now here's a victory – a smile almost appeared on his face. 'A find, boy! This'll fetch good money when I sell it down in the market.'

'May I read a little first, sir?' I asked, and felt some anxiety when I made the request. Leo has a frightening manner at times.

'Books are for selling, not reading,' he replied immediately. But at least I had it for the night, since the dealers were by that time closed.

Adapted from *The Cemetery of Secrets* by David Hewson

4 For questions 1–8, choose the answer (A, B, C or D) which you think fits best according to the text.

1 In what way is the house typical of Venice, according to the writer?
- A There are several ways of entering it.
- B People live and work in the same building.
- C The storage area is not below ground.
- D It consists of two separate buildings.

2 What does *it* refer to in line 10?
- A the family business
- B an entrance
- C a floor
- D a building

3 What does the writer say about his uncle's printing business in the fourth paragraph?
- A His printing business is less expensive than others.
- B The business has plenty of customers.
- C There are other similar businesses in the district.
- D It's the only printing business left in the district.

4 What do we understand about the writer and his sister in the fifth paragraph?
- A They both enjoy reading.
- B They both used to live in Venice.
- C They write to each other often.
- D They don't expect to see each other soon.

5 What does the incident with the book show about Uncle Leo?
- A He dislikes having the writer in his house.
- B He has a good sense of humour.
- C He has problems with money.
- D His main interest is making money.

6 In the text as a whole, the writer regards Venice as
- A a strange and special place to live in.
- B somewhere that could never be home.
- C a city it's easy to get lost in.
- D a place dominated by money.

5 Work in pairs. Take turns to describe a house which you have really enjoyed living in or visiting. You should each speak for about one minute.

- Before you speak, spend a few minutes planning what you are going to say.
- When your partner speaks, listen and think of one or two questions to ask at the end.

Vocabulary

space, place, room, area, location and *square*

1 Candidates often confuse the following words: *space, place, room, area, location* and *square*. Circle the correct word in *italics* in these sentences from Reading and Use of English Part 5.

1 Uncle Leo gives me a suspicious look when I call this *place / area* the 'Scacchi Palace'.
2 When I lie in bed at night, I can hear the chatter and songs of the passing gondoliers and the conversations in the *square / place* nearby.
3 The *place / location* of the house is near the city centre and easy for our clients to find.
4 Furthermore, the printing trade has many roots in this *area / place* of Venice.

2 Look at the definitions on page 185. Then circle the correct word in *italics* in these sentences.

1 We don't have enough *area / space* in our garden to hold the party.
2 I hope I will have enough *place / room* for all the things I am bringing.
3 Sorry I'm late. I just couldn't find a parking *place / space* anywhere.
4 I'm enclosing a map which shows the *location / place* of my school.
5 It's dangerous to go walking in a mountainous *area / place* without the correct equipment.
6 The animals in this zoo have a lot of *area / space* to move around.
7 The concert will take place in the main *square / place* in front of the cathedral.
8 The *area / space* of forest where they're going to build a new shopping centre is over 500 years old.
9 There isn't enough *place / space* to build more houses in this neighbourhood.
10 It's fine for you to stay at our place, as we've got loads of *room / place*.

3 Work in pairs. Write *area, place, room* or *space* in the gaps to form collocations, e.g. *hiding place*. Then discuss what each of them means, e.g. *A hiding place is a place to hide or to hide something.*

1 *hiding / market / meeting* ....
2 *floor / green / office / parking / personal / public* ....
3 *head / leg / standing* ....
4 *dining / penalty / picnic / play / reception* ....

4 Complete these sentences by writing one of the collocations from Exercise 3 in the gaps.

1 Teachers get angry when students leave their cars in their personal ....
2 If someone makes you feel uncomfortable by standing too close to you, we say that they have entered your ....
3 I love my school. It's surrounded by .... with lots of trees and lawns.
4 I'm tall, and the seats on the plane didn't have enough ....
5 There are lots of stalls in the .... selling fresh fruit and vegetables.
6 When you go to the country, it's good to find a .... where you can sit and eat a sandwich.

Listening | Part 2

1 Work in pairs. You are going to hear a student giving a talk to his classmates about his house, which he claims is haunted. Before you listen, do you think it's possible for houses to be haunted? Why? / Why not?

2 Answer the questions in the Exam round-up box.

Exam round-up

How much do you remember about Listening Part 2? Say whether these statements are true (T) or false (F). If a statement is false, correct it.

1 In Listening Part 2, you hear a conversation.
2 There are eight questions.
3 You will need just one or two words for each gap.
4 You hear the actual words you need to write.
5 You must spell your answers correctly.
6 Before you listen, read the questions as quickly as possible.
7 When you finish, make sure your answers form grammatical sentences.

3 Now read these sentences and predict what type of information or what type of words you need for each gap, e.g. question 1 is probably *a length of time*.

Jeff has lived in the house for **(1)** ....
He thinks his house is haunted because of the **(2)** .... which people have had there.
His **(3)** .... saw medieval soldiers.
Another guest saw furniture moving in the **(4)** ....
When doing homework, Jeff has felt a person **(5)** .... him .
His mother decided to convert the **(6)** .... into a study.
An expert told them the house was built on the site of a **(7)** ....
His father recently had a **(8)** .... installed.
One of the workers saw a man with **(9)** .... on his clothes.
His father is normally at home **(10)** ....

4 31 For questions 1–10, listen and complete the sentences with a word or short phrase.

5 Work in groups. Would you be happy to live in a house with a reputation for being haunted? Do you know of any haunted houses?

Grammar

Causative *have* and *get*

1 In Listening Part 2, Jeff describes two changes to the house. What were they? Listen again if necessary.

2 Look at these sentences and answer the questions in the next column.

1 a She turned the old garage at the back of the house into a study.
  b She had the old garage at the back of the house turned into a study.

2 a Then my dad checked the whole house.
  b Then my dad got the whole house checked by a specialist.

1 Which sentences (a or b) did you hear in Listening Part 2?
2 Which sentences (a or b) mean ...?
- he/she did it himself/herself?
- he/she asked someone else to do it for them?
3 In the b sentences, who do you think did these things?

page 164 Language reference: Causative *have* and *get*

3 Complete the sentences below by writing the correct form of *have* or *get* and the correct form of one of the verbs in the box in the gaps.

cut down	deliver	pull out	extend	paint	renew

1 You'll need .... your passport .... before you go to America next autumn.
2 She went to the dentist yesterday and .... a tooth .... , so she's not feeling too well today.
3 We're thinking of .... the house .... blue. What do you think?
4 There's a tree hanging dangerously over the house, and I think we ought to .... it ....
5 Our house is too small. If we could afford it, we'd .... it ....
6 He hates cooking and .... all his meals .... from the restaurant opposite.

4 For questions 1–4, complete the second sentence so that it has a similar meaning to the first sentence, using the word given. Do not change the word given. You must use between two and five words, including the word given.

1 Someone stole my bag during the bus journey.
HAD
I .... I was on the bus.
2 A professional photographer is taking a photo of Stephan.
PICTURE
Stephan .... by a professional photographer.
3 Marianne wants the hairdresser to change the colour of her hair.
DYED
Marianne wants to .... at the hairdresser's.
4 The college rejected Pascual's application.
TURNED
Pascual had .... by the college.

Reading and Use of English | Part 2

1 Work in pairs. Look at the photo. Would you like to live here? Why? / Why not?

2 Before doing Reading and Use of English Part 2, answer the questions in the Exam round-up box.

Exam round-up

How much do you remember about Reading and Use of English Part 2? Complete the following sentences with the words and phrases in *italics*.

eight before and after one word ONLY general idea grammar the completed text

1 There are .... questions in this part.
2 The words you need are .... words: articles, pronouns, auxiliary verbs, etc. and parts of fixed phrases (e.g. *take part in*) or phrasal verbs (e.g. *make up*).
3 First, read the text quickly to get a .... of what it's about.
4 Read .... the gaps to decide what type of word you need.
5 Answer every question with .... , and check your spelling.
6 When you have finished, quickly read .... to check.

3 Read this article quickly, ignoring the gaps. Do you think you'd enjoy living on a houseboat?

Living on a houseboat

When we first moved onto our houseboat on the River Crouch, there **(0)** ...was... a big storm. The lights swung backwards and forwards **(1)** .... though we were at sea, but in **(2)** .... of the bad weather, not a single cup fell off the shelves. In fact, in the four years **(3)** .... we moved from our small house in the town nearby, **(4)** .... anything has been broken.

The boat is huge: 20 metres long and 4 metres wide. **(5)** .... to my dad, it is about four times the size of the house we had before. The kitchen **(6)** .... up about half of the main living space and it is not separated from the rest of it, so that whoever is cooking doesn't feel left **(7)** .... Our friends often **(8)** .... round to see us after we have been to school. In the living area, there is even room for a ping-pong table.

Adapted from *The Observer*

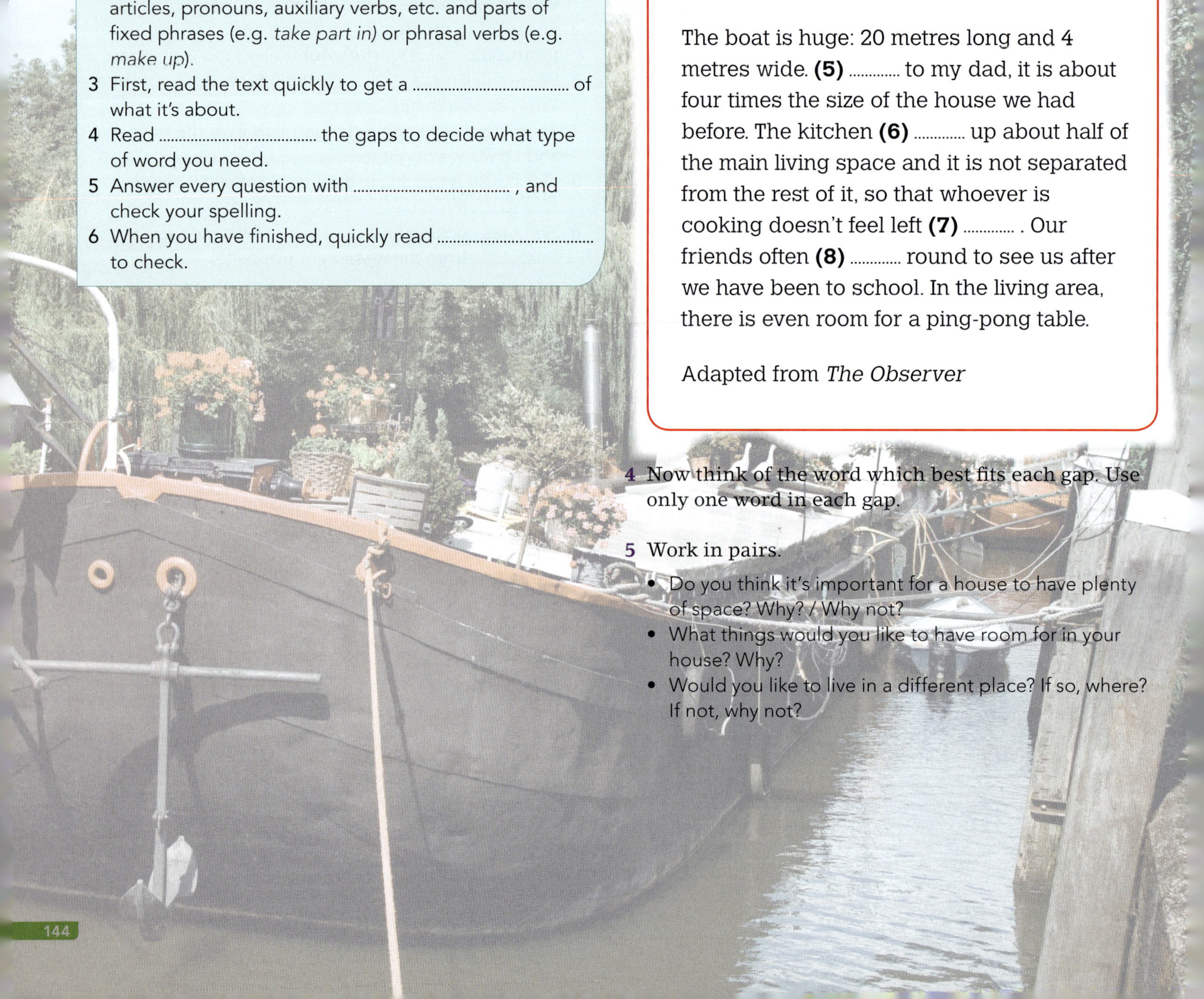

4 Now think of the word which best fits each gap. Use only one word in each gap.

5 Work in pairs.

- Do you think it's important for a house to have plenty of space? Why? / Why not?
- What things would you like to have room for in your house? Why?
- Would you like to live in a different place? If so, where? If not, why not?

Speaking | Part 2

1 Work in pairs. Before doing Speaking Part 2, answer the questions in the Exam round-up box.

Exam round-up

How much do you remember about Speaking Part 2? Say whether the following statements are true (T) or false (F). If a statement is false, correct it.

1 Each candidate must speak alone for about one minute.
2 You have to compare four photos and answer a more general question about them.
3 You should compare the photos in detail.
4 You should spend about half the time on the photos and half the time on the printed question.
5 After your partner has spoken, you will be asked a question about the same photos.

2 Work in pairs. Look at the speaking task on the right and the examiner's instructions. Then brainstorm words and phrases you could use to talk about each photo.

"Here are your photographs. They show two different places to live. I'd like you to compare the photographs and say what you think it is like for the people to live in each of these places."

3 Look at these words and phrases. Which could you use with the first photo (1), which with the second photo (2) and which with both (B)?

close to nature .... environment .... fresh air ....
hi-tech .... maintain a lifestyle .... occupants ....
organic food .... a rural setting ....
spend quality time .... social life ....
sophisticated entertainment .... pollution ....

4 Work in pairs. Take turns to speak for a minute about the photographs following the examiner's instructions.

What is it like for the people to live in each of these places?

5 32 Work in pairs. Listen to Peter and Martyna doing the task, then say whether the statements on this checklist are true (T) or false (F).

	Checklist	T	F
1	Peter spends a lot of time describing what he sees in each photo.		
2	He outlines the main idea of each photo.		
3	He concentrates on answering the question more than comparing the details of the photos.		
4	He compares what it would be like to live in each place.		
5	He mentions things which he thinks are similar about the people in both photos.		
6	He uses language which shows he is imagining the lifestyle in each photo.		
7	He uses a good range of vocabulary to express his ideas.		
8	He uses short, simple sentences.		
9	Martyna gives a long, detailed answer to her question.		

6 Pronunciation: linking (2)

In order to speak more fluently, you sometimes put a consonant between the first and the second word when the second word begins with a vowel.

1 ▶33 Listen to these extracts from Peter's answer. In the highlighted phrases, what consonant is used in the extracts to link:

a the yellow highlighted words?
- with the occupants, a family standing in the garden
- On the other hand, living in the city flat might be quite exciting

b the green highlighted words?
- where they grow their own vegetables
- Money and success in your career are not so important as being close to nature and the countryside
- which is probably busier and more stressful

c the blue highlighted words?
- Money and success in your career are not so important
- The family in the second photo must need to earn quite a lot of money

2 Work in pairs. Take turns to read Peter's phrases in Exercise 1 aloud.

3 ▶34 In the gaps in these sentences, write the consonant which you think can link the two words. Then listen to check your answers.

1 We live further........away from the........old town.
2 Does he........ever........answer your questions?
3 Our........aunt comes to stay........at our house just now........and then.
4 Fewer........and fewer shops in our........area are........open at weekends.
5 Many........of you are busy........and in a hurry.
6 The........end of the story is more........exciting than the beginning.

4 Work in pairs. Take turns to read sentences 1–6 in Exercise 3 aloud.

5 Write three or four sentences as part of your answer to the task in (Speaking) Exercise 2.
- Think about how you can link words in the sentences using consonants.
- Then work with a partner and take turns to read your sentences aloud.

7 Work in pairs. Choose either Task A or Task B. Then discuss what you can say to do the task in a similar way to Peter (see questions 2–7 from the checklist in (Speaking) Exercise 5).

8 Change partners and work with someone who chose the other task.
- Take turns to do your tasks.
- While you are listening to your partner, use questions 2–7 from the checklist in (Speaking) Exercise 5 as a checklist.
- When your partner has finished, use all the questions from the checklist in Exercise 5 to give him/her feedback.

Task A

"Here are your photographs. They show people on holiday in different places. I'd like you to compare the photographs and say what you think the people are enjoying about having a holiday in these places."

What are the people enjoying about having a holiday in these places?

Task B

"Here are your photographs. They show old people living in two different types of place. I'd like you to compare the photographs and say which place you think is better for old people to live."

Which place is better for old people to live?

Grammar

Expressing obligation and permission

1 Work in pairs. You will hear five students who are staying with host families while studying in Britain. Before you listen, make a list of things students who stay with a host family in your country should and shouldn't do, e.g. *You should keep your room tidy. You shouldn't come home too late.*

2 Look at these sentences and then answer the questions below.

A *I can* invite my friends to dinner sometimes.
B *I have to* help with the housework.
C *I can't* take food from the fridge.
D *I'm supposed to* be back home early.
E *They let me* borrow their car.
F *They won't let me* do any cooking.

1 Which phrases in *italics* have a similar meaning to:
  a I must? ....
  b I'm not allowed to? ....
  c I'm allowed to? ....
2 Which phrase (a or b) has a similar meaning to *I'm supposed to* in D?
  a I must be
  b I should be, but sometimes I'm not

3 35 Listen and, for questions 1–5, choose which sentence in Exercise 2 (A–F) best summarises what each student says. There is one extra letter which you do not need to use.

1 Miguel ☐
2 Irene ☐
3 Martyna ☐
4 Nikolai ☐
5 Antonia ☐

4 Which speaker said each of these sentences? If necessary, listen again to check.

1 *I don't have to* do anything around the house.
2 I *had to* buy the food and cook it.
3 *They don't allow me to* have big parties.
4 Apparently, *I was supposed to* phone to say I wasn't coming.
5 *They didn't let me* invite a couple of friends to dinner the other day.
6 *I needn't* clean the bathroom or do any shopping.

5 Work in pairs. Copy this table into your notebook. Complete it using the phrases from Exercises 2 and 4.

	obligation	prohibition	permission	no obligation
present				
past				

page 171 Language reference: Modal verbs – expressing obligation, prohibition and permission

6 Complete the second sentence so that it has a similar meaning to the first sentence, using the word given. Do not change the word given. You must use between two and five words.

1 'You can't go to the club,' Steve's father told him.
ALLOW
Steve's father did .... to go to the club.
2 When you do the exam, it's not necessary to copy out the question.
HAVE
You .... copy out the question when you do the exam.
3 I shouldn't wear shoes inside the house.
SUPPOSED
I .... off my shoes before I enter the house.
4 You can't enter the room marked 'Private'.
ALLOWED
You .... into the room marked 'Private'.
5 Diane wouldn't lend Celia her car.
LET
Diane refused .... her car.
6 We were not allowed to use dictionaries during the exam.
LET
They did .... dictionaries during the exam.

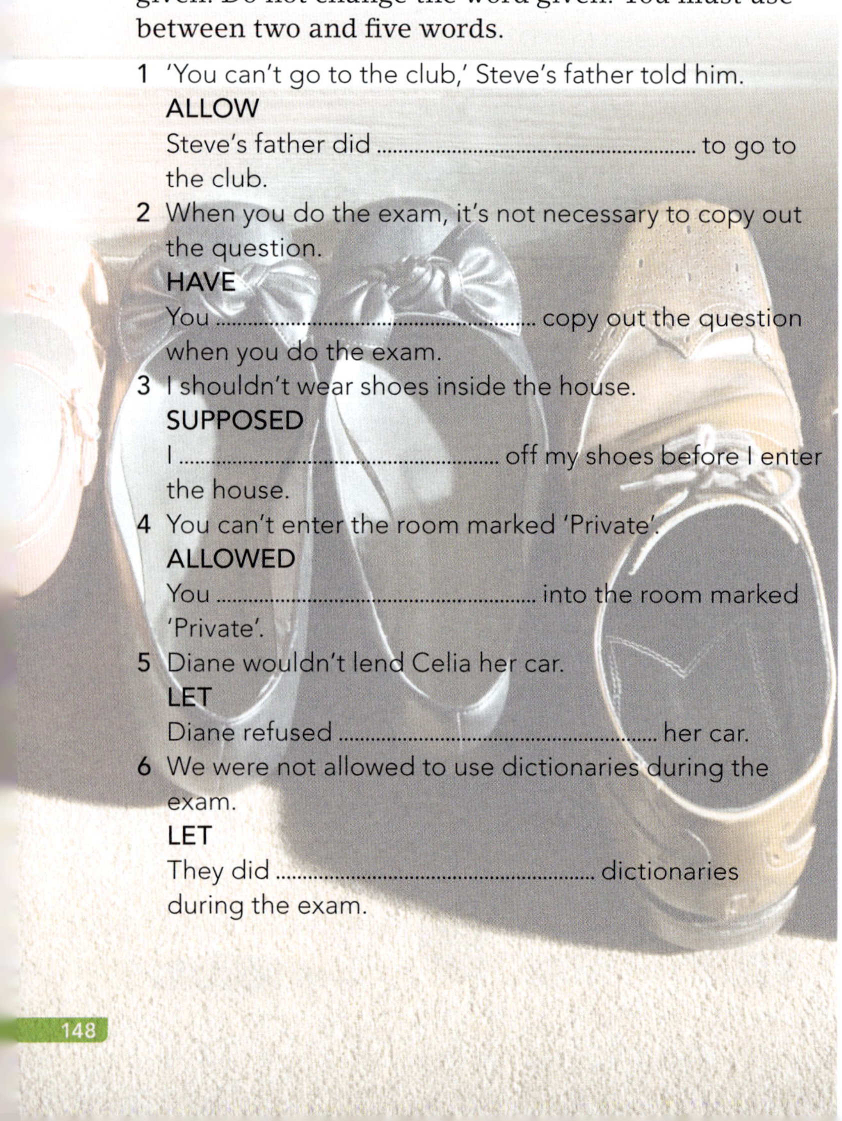

Writing | Part 2 An article

1 Work in pairs. Before working on Writing Part 2, answer the questions in the Exam round-up box.

Exam round-up

How much do you remember about how to do Writing Part 2? Put these tasks in the correct order by writing a number 1–6 by each.

a Check what you have written, looking for specific mistakes you know you make. ☐
b Organise your notes into a plan. ☐
c Read all the questions and quickly choose the one you think you will find easiest. ☐
d Think and make notes. ☐
e Underline the things you must deal with in your answer. ☐
f Write your answer (140–190 words) following your plan. ☐

2 Work in groups of three. Read this writing task and discuss the questions below.

You see this announcement in your college magazine.

My ideal home

If you could choose the type of house you would like to live in and its location, where would you live, what sort of house would it be and what features would it have?

The best articles will be published in the next issue of our magazine.

Write your **article**.

1 What would be the ideal location for your house?
2 What sort of house would you choose?
3 What features would your ideal house have?

3 Work in pairs with someone from another group.

- Take turns to give a short talk describing your ideal house.
- When your partner finishes speaking, ask a few questions to find out more details.

4 Look at the writing task again and discuss these questions.

1 Who will read your article?
2 What style would be suitable for this article?
3 Which of these should your article particularly use: present simple, *going to*/*will*, conditional? Why?
4 What information must it contain?
5 How can you make the article interesting for your readers?

5 Read the sample answer below to the writing task, ignoring the gaps.

1 How does this ideal home compare with your own?
2 Has the writer answered the question completely?

My space, my place

I dream of living in a small, stylish modern flat in a historic old building near the centre of a large city **(0)** ..*such*.. as Barcelona or Bologna. What a change that would be **(1)** .... the ordinary suburban house **(2)** .... I'm living now! I could live like a sophisticated girl-about-town, dropping into art galleries, smart boutiques and street cafés with all my glamorous friends who live nearby popping in from time to time.

What would the flat be like? Well, for a start, I'd live on my **(3)** .... , so I'd be able to do **(4)** .... I wanted whenever I wanted. The flat would be hi-tech, with the heating and lighting controlled automatically, a cosy bedroom, a light, airy sitting room, and a handy little kitchen. Ideally, it would **(5)** .... a small balcony with a **(6)** .... plants where I could sit out in the sun.

I wouldn't need much space, as **(7)** .... as I had room to keep my books and clothes. **(8)** .... I had all these things, I'd be happy for years.

6 Complete this plan for the sample answer in Exercise 5 by writing the notes in *italics* below beside the correct paragraphs.

Para. 1: ....
Para. 2: ....
Para. 3: ....

Advantages of ideal flat
Characteristics of flat
Conclusion: room for my things
My present accommodation
Type of flat and location

7 Complete the sample answer by writing one word in each of the gaps.

8 Work in pairs. Discuss whether these statements are true (T) or false (F).

		T	F
1	The article uses plenty of adjectives.		
2	It uses conditional tenses.		
3	The writer mentions the furniture she would need.		
4	You can tell something about the writer's personality and tastes from the article.		
5	There are plenty of relative clauses.		
6	The writer doesn't say where she lives now.		

9 Write your own article.

- Before you write, decide what features of the sample answer on the left you could also use. Then think and write a plan.
- When you write, follow your plan.
- Write 140–190 words.

14 Fiesta!

Starting off

1 Work in pairs. Write one of the verbs from the box in the correct form in each of the gaps below to complete the descriptions of festivals and celebrations. Use each verb once only.

celebrate	commemorate	dress up	gather round
hold	let off	march	perform
play	wearing		

1 We hold a festival every March to .... the arrival of spring.
2 People in our region .... in **traditional costumes** and then they .... one of our **traditional dances.**
3 People .... through the town in a spectacular **parade** to .... a famous battle.
4 In many parts of the town, residents .... **street parties**.
5 **Bands** .... dance music all night long.
6 Crowds .... **street performers**.
7 During the festival, we .... **fireworks**.
8 People from the town go out in the streets .... **disguises**.

2 Find the words and phrases in bold in Exercise 1 illustrated in the photos on this page and the next.

3 Look at the photos again. They show different events which take place during festivals.

1 Why do people do these different things at festivals?
2 Which type of activity is most enjoyable for people to watch?
3 Which country do you think each of the photos was taken in?

4 Take turns to talk about a festival in your town or country.

- What does the festival celebrate?
- What happens during the festival?
- Do you participate? Why? / Why not?

Listening | Part 4

1 Work in pairs. You are going to hear an interview with a street performer at festivals, including one called the Hat Fair. Before you listen discuss these questions.

- What sort of things do street performers do?
- Do you enjoy watching street theatre? Why? / Why not?

2 Answer the questions in the Exam round-up box.

Exam round-up

How much do you remember about Listening Part 4? Complete the following sentences with the words and phrases in *italics*.

seven *general ideas* *an interview* *underline* *different words*

1 Listening Part 4 is .... or a conversation between two or more speakers.
2 There are .... questions; you must choose A, B or C.
3 Read the questions carefully and .... the main ideas. These will be expressed using .... from the question.
4 Listen for .... as well as specific information.

3 36 Now listen, and for questions 1–7, choose the best answer (A, B or C).

1 Why is the festival called the Hat Fair?
A It was started by local hat-makers.
B Many participants wear hats.
C Street performers collect money in hats.

2 What does Max most enjoy about the Hat Fair?
A the type of audiences he gets
B the other street performers he meets
C the shows he can do

3 How did Max start in street theatre?
A He lost his job in a circus.
B He did it while he was at university.
C He learned it from his father.

4 What do audiences enjoy most about Max's act?
A the jokes
B the acrobatics
C the danger

5 According to Max, what makes street performers perform well?
A They earn a lot of money.
B They are paid by results.
C They enjoy their work.

6 What does he say is usually the main problem with street theatre?
A the weather
B the location
C the police

7 According to Max, how does the Hat Fair help the city?
A It attracts visitors to the town.
B It encourages people to work together.
C It helps people to relax together.

4 Work in pairs. Sometimes towns and cities discourage street theatre. Why do you think this is?

Grammar
The passive

1 The passive is formed by the verbs *be* or *get* + a past participle (*eaten, done, played,* etc.). Read the following extracts from the recording script and underline the verbs in the passive.

a I've been told the fair was only started in 1974, as a way of encouraging street performers like myself.
b A hat's passed around so that the performers can earn a living.
c They really seem to love it when they're being made a fool of by other people in the crowd.
d I actually went to quite a famous circus school in Canada as a teenager where I was taught juggling and acrobatics.
e Here we're given the main shopping street, which is fine. In other places, if you haven't got permission, you'll get moved on by the police.

2 Work in pairs. In which extracts (a–e) does the speaker do the following? (You can use the extracts for more than one answer.)

1 He tells us who or what does/did the action.
In extract c and part of extract e (the police)
2 He uses the passive because he doesn't know who or what does/did something.
3 He uses the passive because he doesn't need to say who or what does/did something because it's obvious from the situation or context.
4 He uses the passive because what happens is more important than who does it.

➔ page 177 Language reference: The passive

3 Rewrite these sentences in the passive, starting with the words given.

1 They founded our school in 1904.
Our school ....
2 Someone has stolen my wallet!
My wallet .... !
3 You won't be able to email me while they are repairing my laptop.
You won't be able to email me while my laptop ....
4 Have you heard? They've given me a place on the course!
Have you heard? I ....
5 If you hadn't done the work, your teacher would have told you off.
If you hadn't done the work, you ....

4 Candidates often make mistakes when they use the passive. Correct one mistake in each of these sentences.

1 First of all, I'd like to show you a castle, which ~~might be built~~ in the 16th century. might have been built
2 I was expecting the performer to be Danny Brook, but you didn't even mention that he was going to replace by someone else.
3 I'm writing to you now because I've been told that is going to be read on the radio a short story by Agatha Christie.
4 Moreover, how could we acquire a knowledge of the universe if the computer weren't invented?
5 Ekaterina's story, which has already published in the school magazine, is really fun to read.
6 Also, museums display many old things which have been using in the past.
7 To sum up, nobody wants to be revealed their private life in public.

5 Read this text quickly to find out what happens at the Egyptian festival of Sham el Nessim.

Sham el Nessím

A large number of contemporary Egyptian traditions (1) .... said to have their origins in very ancient times. These include the holiday which is known (2) .... Sham el Nessim. This holiday may have (3) .... celebrated as early as 4,500 years ago. It is thought (4) .... have been the first festival to celebrate the beginning of the spring.

Nowadays, in the early morning of Sham el Nessim millions of Egyptians come out to crowded public parks and other open areas. Young men swim in the Nile and families generally enjoy the cool breeze of spring.

Sham el Nessim (5) .... also celebrated by eating traditional foods and these include salted fish, coloured eggs, sunflower seeds and raw onions. The reason for each of these foods (6) .... eaten is supported (7) .... a different myth. For example, offerings of fish are believed to (8) .... been made to the ancient gods and by (9) .... this a good harvest was ensured. Salted fish symbolised welfare to the ancient Egyptians and in ancient times fish (10) .... easily caught by being trapped in natural pools created by the movement of the Nile.

6 For questions 1–10, read the text again and think of the word which best fits each gap. Use only one word in each gap.

7 Look at this sentence from the text about Sham el Nessim and answer the questions below.

It is thought to have been the first festival to celebrate the beginning of spring.

1 What does the sentence mean?
   a People think that this was the first festival that celebrated the beginning of spring.
   b It used to be the first festival to celebrate spring.
2 It follows the pattern 'subject + passive verb + infinitive'. Other verbs which can be used in this way include: believe, report, say, consider, expect. Which other two sentences in the text follow the same pattern?
3 The sentence could also be expressed as follows: It is thought that this was the first festival to celebrate the beginning of spring. How would the other two sentences be expressed using this pattern instead?

page 177 Language reference: The passive – the passive with reporting verbs

8 Rewrite the following sentences beginning with the words given.

1 Sham el Nessím is thought to have marked the start of the spring festival in ancient Egypt.
   It is thought …
2 Eating salted fish is known to have been a custom of the ancient Egyptians.
   It is known …
3 It is reported that five thousand people joined in the festivities.
   Five thousand people are reported …
4 It is said that our festival has the best fireworks in the world.
   Our festival is said …

9 For questions 1–6, complete the second sentence so that it has a similar meaning to the first sentence, using the word given. Do not change the word given. You must use between two and five words, including the word given.

1 People believe that the festival originated in the 18th century.
   HAVE
   The festival .... in the 18th century.
2 People expect that she will be chosen as carnival queen.
   BE
   She is .... as carnival queen.
3 The festival is said to be more popular than ever.
   THAT
   It is .... more popular than ever.
4 They think Channel 4 is the only channel which will broadcast the opening ceremony.
   THOUGHT
   Channel 4 .... the only channel which will broadcast the opening ceremony.
5 People think that Carnival is the best festival of the year.
   CONSIDERED
   Carnival .... the best festival of the year.
6 We know the festival started more than three thousand years ago.
   BACK
   The festival is known .... three thousand years.

Reading and Use of English | Part 6

1 Answer the questions in the Exam round-up box.

Exam round-up

How much do you remember about Reading and Use of English Part 6?

Say whether the following statements are true (T) or false (F). If a statement is false, correct it.

1 This part of the exam will contain eight questions, including the example.
2 You should first read the whole text carefully to form an idea of how it develops.
3 Underline clues in the text while you read such as pronouns (e.g. *this, he*, etc.), adverbs which suggest something mentioned before (e.g. *the second point, however*, etc.), relationships of meaning, (e.g. *it was* ***expected*** *to be* ***huge*** *... in* ***fact*** *it was* ***tiny*** *...*, etc.).
4 Read each sentence carefully, thinking about where it could fit and looking for clues.
5 When you've finished, quickly go to the next part of the paper.

2 Work in groups. You will read an article about a Peruvian festival. Before you read, look at the festival in the photos.

- What do you think is happening?
- Would you enjoy a festival like this? Why? / Why not?

3 Six sentences have been removed from the article. Read the article (but not the missing sentences) quite carefully. As you read:

- think about and perhaps quickly note down the subject of each paragraph.
- underline any words and phrases before and after the gaps which may refer to the missing sentences (one has been done for you as an example).

The world's highest festival?

Where the writer was going

It felt as if we had been climbing for hours. I stopped to catch my breath as a wave of dizziness swept over me in the thin mountain air. I stood to one side of the path to let the mass of travellers with us pass. I was trekking with Marco, my guide to experience the festival of Qoyllur Rit'i which takes place at 4,300 metres in the southern Andes of Peru, a festival which few foreign tourists see.

As I looked back down the trail we had climbed and up towards where we had to go, I marvelled at the colourful sight. Entire families wearing local costumes were travelling to this unique festival from all over Peru. Among them there were old men, mothers with small babies and children all following the same route. Many of them had horses and donkeys to carry their food, blankets, cooking pots and tents. **1** ☐ Others had made their way on foot through the mountains for days to attend this remarkable event.

We continued our upward ascent for another hour and a half before reaching the Sinakara valley. There we looked down on a flat plain of open grassland crossed with streams from the glaciers and overlooked by snow-topped mountain peaks. Right across this flat piece of ground people were putting up shelters and tents of blue plastic to protect themselves from the freezing mist and rain. **2** ☐ The air of excitement, even from our vantage point more than a mile away, was palpable.

We chose a spot between two icy streams to put up our tent. While thus occupied, one of the many women dressed in the traditional costume of a wide-brimmed hat, woolly jacket, skirt and stockings came to sell us some very welcome hot soup and fish. **3** ☐

Not far away in another open market, people were buying tiny houses, cars or small pictures showing a baby or a wedding. Marco explained that these represented something the pilgrims desired. **4** ☐ This, they believed, would ensure that what they wished for would come true in the year ahead.

After dining in a makeshift restaurant and sampling the dancing and partying, we went to bed fully clothed inside our sleeping bags. **5** ☐ The ukukus, men wearing black masks and costumes, had left the encampment in the early hours to climb the nearest mountain by the light of the full moon. **6** ☐ In the dawn light, we watched them winding their way back down like a great black serpent. As they descended, they were joined by groups of dancers in bright traditional costumes. They performed wherever there was a space. Although there did not seem to be anyone organising them or any timetable, the whole festival had become a huge harmonious celebration.

4 Now choose from the sentences A–G the one which fits each gap (1–6) in the text. There is one extra sentence which you do not need to use. As you do this,

- think about how the sentence matches the subject of the paragraph
- underline words in the sentences which refer to things in the paragraph.

A From time to time during the procession, they stopped to dance on the glaciers, believing this would bring luck to their villages for the year to come.

B We were up early the next morning, the main day of the festival, despite having slept badly on the frozen ground.

C It was clear, however, from the sound of drums and singing rising from this improvised camp that the weather was not going to dampen the festival spirit.

D But just as the celebrations were reaching their climax, it began to rain and everyone ran for shelter.

E Others, meanwhile, were offering goods for purchase such as warm clothes, food, torches and trinkets by spreading them on blankets on the ground.

F Some, like me, had come by bus to Mahuayani, the nearest town, and were walking up from there.

G They would take them and bury them in the mountain.

5 Quickly read the article again with your answers to check that it makes sense.

6 Work in pairs.

- Would you be interested in visiting this festival?Why? / Why not?
- Do you think festivals in your country are more for tourists or more for local people?

Reading and Use of English | Part 3

1 Look at these extracts from Reading and Use of English Part 6 and use the word given in capitals at the end to form a word that fits in the gap. Then check your answer by looking at the text again.

1 … a festival which few .... see. TOUR
2 They were joined by groups of .... in bright traditional costumes. DANCE

page 181 Language reference: Word formation – forming personal nouns

2 EP Form personal nouns from the noun or verb given.

noun/verb	person	noun/verb	person
1 design		7 motor	
2 novel		8 comedy	
3 research		9 sales	
4 collect		10 special	
5 survive		11 refuge	
6 consult			

3 Answer the questions in the Exam round-up box.

Exam round-up

How much do you remember about Reading and Use of English Part 3?

Circle the correct option in *italics* in these sentences.

1 This part contains *eight / ten* questions.
2 *Write an answer as soon as you see a gap / Read the whole text quickly before answering the questions.*
3 If you can't think what to write, *leave the gap blank / think what type of word you need.*
4 *Make sure you have spelled the word correctly (look at the base word you have been given) / Correct spelling is not important in this part.*
5 When you have finished, *go to Part 4 / read the completed text again.*

4 EP For questions 1–8, read this text. Use the word given in capitals at the end of some of the lines to form a word that fits in the gap in the same line. There is an example at the beginning (0).

My local festival

The **(0)** ....preparations......... for the	**PREPARE**
festival in my town are an extremely exciting time. Months before, the	
(1) .... who work together	**ORGANISE**
on the committee start making all the	
necessary **(2)** .... and	**ARRANGE**
finalising the details of the processions	
and other **(3)** .... that	**ACT**
are going to take place. They also keep	
the main **(4)** .... up	**PARTICIPATE**
to date with what is going on so that everyone knows when and where things will happen. When the festival finally arrives, it becomes virtually impossible to drive around the town because the streets are full of local people, visitors	
from **(5)** .... towns, and	**SURROUND**
tourists. Everyone in the town seems to	
become more **(6)** .... as	**ENERGY**
the excitement grows. They dress up in traditional costumes, stay out all night with their friends and behave in an	
(7) .... noisy way for our	**USUAL**
normally quiet, respectable town. For me,	
however, the most **(8)**	**IMPRESS**
part of the town's festivities is the firework display.	

Speaking | Parts 3 and 4

1 Before doing Speaking Parts 3 and 4, answer the questions in the Exam round-up box.

Exam round-up

How much do you remember about Speaking Parts 3 and 4?

Say whether the following statements are true (T) or false (F). If a statement is false, correct it.

Speaking Part 3

1 There are two parts: the first part takes two minutes and the second part one minute.
2 In the first part, you needn't discuss all five prompts – it's better to discuss a few in more detail.
3 You should ask your partner to express his/her ideas.
4 In the second part, you must reach a decision together.

Speaking Part 4

5 You are asked your opinions on a new subject.
6 You and your partner may be asked the same questions or different questions.
7 You should try to give your opinion plus an explanation, reason or example.
8 In both Speaking Parts 3 and 4, you should listen carefully to what your partner says and be ready to say something about it or comment on it.

2 37 Work in pairs. Listen to the examiner's instructions and then spend two minutes doing the first part of this Part 3 task.

3 38 Listen to the examiner's next instruction and spend a minute doing the second part of the Speaking Part 3 task.

4 ▶39 Now listen to Antonia and Nikolai doing the first part of Speaking Part 3. Were their ideas different from yours?

5 Listen again. Antonia and Nikolai help each other to do this part of the exam.

1 How is it clear that they are listening carefully to each other, and why is this important?
2 What phrases do they use to:
  a encourage each other?
  b help their partner to express an idea?
  c take over when their partner gets into trouble?

6 ▶40 Work in pairs. Listen to the examiner's instructions and do the first part of this Part 3 task. Try to use phrases you noted down in Exercise 5 to help the discussion along.

7 ▶41 Listen to the examiner's instructions and do the second part of the Part 3 task.

8 ▶42 Work in pairs. Listen to Antonia and Nikolai answering this Part 4 question. Who do you agree with more? Why?

> How do towns and cities benefit from having festivals and other celebrations?

9 **Pronunciation:** improving fluency

1 ▶43 Work in pairs. Read and listen to Antonia's answer and underline the words she stresses

> Hmm, ↗that's a good ↘question. / Some people say that it's good for, what's it called, community spirit, but I think the main benefit is for local businesses because tourists and visitors are attracted to the town to spend their money in shops and restaurants.

2 Listen again and mark with a ↗ or a ↘ to show where her voice rises or falls on stressed words.

3 Use a (/) to mark where you think she pauses. Then listen again to check your answers.

4 ▶44 Now read and listen to Nikolai's answer and follow steps 1–3 above.

> Yes, I partly agree with her. I think in many places people spend a lot of time during the year preparing for their festival and I think it really encourages a feeling of cooperation and a community feeling.

5 Take turns to read both answers aloud.

6 Think for a moment how you will answer this question. Then take turns to answer the question using stress, intonation and pauses suitably.

> Do you think festivals should be organised more for tourists or more for local people?

10 Work in groups of three. One student should take the role of the examiner and ask these questions to the others. When you have finished, change roles and ask and answer the questions again.

1 What can tourists learn from visiting a festival in another country?
2 Do you think that some towns and cities spend too much time and money on organising festivals?
3 How important is it for people to remember their traditions?
4 Do you think there should be a limit to noise at festivals or other celebrations?

Writing | Part 1 An essay

1 Before doing Writing Part 1, answer the questions in the Exam round-up box.

Exam round-up

How much do you remember about Writing Part 1? Choose the best option in *italics* in these sentences.

In Writing Part 1:

1 you must write an essay of between *120–180 words / 140—190 words* in *40 / 60* minutes.
2 you *can write whatever you want / must deal with three points, one of which is your own idea.*
3 you should *write a plan first / just start writing your answer.*
4 *you should check your answer carefully when you finish / you won't have time to check your answer.*

2 Work in pairs. Read the writing task below.

- Underline the key points in the task.
- Make a list of the advantages and disadvantages of going to music festivals and concerts to listen to live music instead of listening to recorded music.
- Discuss: Which do you prefer? Why?

In your English class, you have been talking about the advantages and disadvantages of going to music festivals and concerts to listen to live music instead of recorded music.

Now your English teacher has asked you to write an essay.

Write an essay using **all** your notes and give reasons for your point of view.

Essay question
Is it better to listen to live music or recorded music?

Notes
Write about:

1. quality
2. convenience
3. .... (your own idea)

Write your **essay**.

3 Decide which of the ideas you discussed you can use in this essay and write a brief plan.

When you have finished, work in pairs and compare your plans.

4 Read Ulli's essay and answer these questions.

1 Which of her ideas are the same as yours?
2 Which is her own idea?
3 Do you agree with her opinion?

Although people can listen to recorded music on their music players when they[1] are travelling working or studying music festivals and concerts are becoming more and more popular. This[2] is because I believe they[3] offer two main advantages.

The first advantage is that the quality of the sound is much better at live concerts where the music and voices come directly from the performers. This[4] makes it[5] a much more emotional experience because you have direct contact with the musicians and you react to them[6] and they react to you.

The second advantage is the atmosphere. Instead of listening to a recording alone on your personal music player you are listening with a huge crowd of people and enjoying the music together. This[7] means it is a social as well as an artistic experience.

The main disadvantage is that you cannot listen to live music whenever you want like you can on a personal device. Apart from that[8], the noise from the audience sometimes spoils the quality of the sound.

In my opinion however the best way to enjoy music is the spontaneous atmosphere of a live concert. It[9] is more exciting because you are surrounded by other enthusiastic fans who are dancing with you.

5 Candidates often make mistakes with punctuation. Ulli's answer in Exercise 4 is missing ten commas. Punctuate it correctly by placing the ten commas.

page 177 Language reference: Using commas

6 Work in pairs. Ulli connects her ideas by using words which refer to other parts of her essay. What does each of the underlined words in her essay refer to?

1 'they' refers to people.

page 178 Language reference: Using *it, this, that* or *they*

7 Candidates often make mistakes with *it, this, that* and *they* when referring to other parts of their writing. Complete these sentences by writing *it, this, that* or *they* in the gaps. In some cases, more than one answer may be possible.

1 In my opinion, going to live concerts is better. .... gives you the chance to really connect with the band.
2 Listening to live music is better, but on the other hand .... is more expensive.
3 A further disadvantage is that when young people want to go to a concert, ... cannot always afford the ticket price.
4 During the tour, the band performed in Paris and Berlin, but .... had played in Amsterdam before ....
5 The band's tour had various problems: the bus broke down and some of their equipment was stolen. On top of all .... , there was a storm on the night of the concert.
6 Many live concerts are held late at night. .... leads to complaints from people living nearby who cannot sleep.
7 The sound quality of the recording is not very good, and in addition to .... , it is quite expensive.
8 I am not very keen on being in large crowds. In spite of .... , I would never miss a concert by my favourite band.

8 Work alone. Do this writing task.

In your English class, you have been talking about the advantages and disadvantages of going to the cinema rather than watching films on DVD or television.

Now your English teacher has asked you to write an essay.

Write an essay using **all** your notes and give reasons for your point of view.

Essay question

Is it better to watch films at the cinema or at home?

Notes

Write about:

1. quality
2. cost
3. .... (your own idea)

Write your **essay**.

Vocabulary and grammar review Unit 13

Vocabulary

1 Circle the correct word in *italics* in these sentences.

1 You can leave your car in the parking *space / place* just outside my house.
2 Bring your family to stay with us! We've got plenty of *room / place* for all of you.
3 He loves travelling and the first thing he does when he arrives in a new *location / place* is take a photo.
4 The university campus is in an excellent *location / space* surrounded by countryside, but within easy reach of the city centre.
5 The schools are excellent in this *area / location*, so it might be a good place to buy a house.
6 There's an empty *place / room* at that table if you want to sit there.
7 We may have to take two taxis because I don't think there's *space / place* in one for all of us.
8 You can buy international newspapers at the newsagent's in the main *square / place*, just behind the station.
9 I found the flight uncomfortable because there wasn't enough leg *place / room*.
10 She's got a good hiding *place / room* for the money she keeps in her bedroom.

Grammar

2 For questions 1–8, read this text and think of the word which best fits each gap. Use only one word in each gap.

3 For questions 1–6, complete the second sentence so that it has a similar meaning to the first sentence, using the word given. Do not change the word given. You must use between two and five words.

1 We're hoping to employ someone to build a tennis court for us in the garden.
HAVE
We're hoping to .... for us in the garden.
2 Make sure that someone checks the car before you buy it.
HAVE
Make sure that .... before you buy it.
3 Magda must tidy her room each morning.
CLEAR
Magda has .... her room each morning
4 They make us do three hours of homework a day in this school.
HAVE
We .... three hours of homework a day in this school.
5 In this restaurant, you should pay for your food when you order it.
SUPPOSED
In this restaurant, you .... for your food when you order it.
6 Speaking is forbidden during the exam.
ALLOWED
You .... during the exam.

home | news | search | living green | stories | advice | contact

LIVING IN CAVES

Wherever people live, they need to protect themselves (0) ......from...... the weather, and ever (1) .... humans started to walk the Earth, they have lived in caves. To start with, they (2) .... use of natural caves, but they soon ran (3) .... of these. It then became simpler for them to create their own caves (4) .... to build shelters using other materials or techniques. On volcanic islands, for example, people found the rock was soft (5) .... to dig into, and (6) .... are places in the world where these artificial caves are still inhabited.

Modern-day caves have some unexpected advantages. For anyone who has ever visited (7) .... , the benefits are immediately apparent: they will have found that the cave is isolated from noise and has a generally pleasant temperature. It is not too hot in the summer, while it stays warm in the winter. (8) .... is more, a modern cave is likely to contain all the modern household gadgets that make life comfortable.

Vocabulary and grammar review Unit 14

Word formation

1 EP Read this text. Use the word given in capitals at the end of the lines to form a word that fits in the gap in the same line.

Getting work experience is a good way for young people who are still at school to see whether they will enjoy a particular career. Future **(0)** ...employers...	EMPLOY
like to see work experience on CVs and it can be a good way to see whether, for example, someone will enjoy being a **(1)** .... before they start on a law	LAW
degree. They get the chance to consider various **(2)** .... for a future career	POSSIBLE
with working professionals whose advice they will find **(3)** .... helpful when	SPECIAL
thinking about the different choices they will have to make. Work experience often involves uncomfortable situations but people who do it learn how to behave **(4)** .... in front of clients and	SUIT
how to take **(5)** .... for things in	RESPOND
the workplace. Appearance is important and they need to dress **(6)**	APPROPRIATE
whether they are going for a job as an air-traffic controller or an IT specialist or a job which is perhaps less technical but equally **(7)** .... such as a sales	DEMAND
(8) .... or teacher.	REPRESENT

2 Complete each of the following sentences by using the word given in capitals at the end of each question to form a word that fits in the gap.

1 Tanya has a .... as a very hard-working student. **REPUTE**
2 In this airline, we make sure that we follow all the .... procedures in order to avoid accidents. **SAFE**
3 My teacher just looked at me in .... when I answered all the questions perfectly. **AMAZE**
4 We have expressed our .... with the work, which was very badly done. **SATISFY**
5 Visitors are often confused to find the .... of two streets with similar names in the town. **EXIST**
6 If only Maria would tell us the .... instead of trying to deceive us with obvious lies! **TRUE**
7 Pierre swam the .... of the river in five minutes. **WIDE**
8 The .... of a swimming pool has made the hotel much more popular. **ADD**
9 Can you tell the .... between this fake Rolex and the original one made in Switzerland? **DIFFER**
10 I have several other .... in July, so I won't be able to go on holiday then. **OBLIGE**

Grammar

3 For questions 1–6, complete the second sentence so that it has a similar meaning to the first sentence, using the word given. Do not change the word given. You must use between two and five words, including the word given.

1 It is almost certain that the flight will arrive on time.
EXPECTED
The flight .... on time.
2 Thieves entered my house last night.
BROKEN
My house .... thieves last night.
3 According to reports, seven firefighters were injured in the fire.
REPORTED
Seven firefighters .... been injured in the fire.
4 It's five months since my car was serviced.
BEEN
My car .... five months.
5 According to many people, she's living in Mexico.
SAID
She .... in Mexico.
6 There were very few cakes left by the end of yesterday's party.
EATEN
Almost every .... by the end of yesterday's party.

Language reference

Contents

Non-defining relative clauses

Relative clauses which give us extra information are called non-defining relative clauses:

My doctor, **who belongs to the same tennis club as you,** *vaccinated me yesterday.*

We already know which doctor (it's my doctor); *who belongs to the same tennis club as you* does not tell us which doctor we are talking about; it just adds extra information.

There are differences in grammar:

defining relative clauses	non-defining relative clauses
• Don't have commas. • Use the following relative pronouns: *who, which, whose, where, when* and *why*. • Can use *that* instead of *who* or *which*. • *who, which* or *that* can be omitted when they are the object of the clause: *The medicine* (*–* / ***which*** / ***that***) *the doctor gave me should be taken twice a day* (the doctor is the subject and *– / which / that* the object of the clause).	• Use commas (or pauses in spoken English). • Use the following relative pronouns: *who, which, whose, where* and *when*. • Don't use *that*. • The relative pronoun cannot be omitted.

Reported speech

Tense changes in reported speech

If the reporting verb (*said, told, admitted, warned,* etc.) is in the past, we tend to change the original verb to a past form as well. Here are some changes we make:

present simple ➔ past simple	*'I* ***live*** *in Berlin.'*	*She said she* ***lived*** *in Berlin.*
present continuous ➔ past continuous	*'I'****m watching*** *TV.'*	*He said he* ***was watching*** *TV.*
present perfect ➔ past perfect	*'I'****ve seen*** *the film already.'*	*She said she* ***had seen*** *the film already.*
past simple ➔ past perfect	*'I* ***missed*** *the concert.'*	*He told me he* ***had missed*** *the concert.*
will ➔ *would*	*'I****'ll phone*** *you soon.'*	*She promised she* ***would phone*** *me soon.*

We also change these modal verbs:

can ➔ *could*	*'I* ***can understand*** *German, but I* ***can't speak*** *it.'*	*She said she* ***could understand*** *German but she* ***couldn't speak*** *it.*
may ➔ *might*	*'I* ***may give*** *the book to John.'*	*Sam suggested he* ***might give*** *the book to John.*
must ➔ *had to*	*'I* ***must cook*** *dinner.'*	*Tanya said she* ***had to*** *cook dinner.*

We do not change these modal verbs in reported speech: *could, would, should, might, ought to* and *used to*:
'I ***would prefer to study*** *in London.'* ➔ *She said that she* ***would prefer to study*** *in London.*

must can change to *had to*:
'You ***must read*** *this text for the next lesson.'* ➔ *My teacher told me I* ***had to read*** *the text for the following lesson.*

But we don't change *must* when:

- it's negative:
  'You ***mustn't tell*** *Katya our secret.'*
  ➔ *Ana told Stefan he* ***mustn't tell*** *Katya their secret.*
- it expresses a deduction:
  'Arturo ***must*** *still* ***be*** *asleep.'*
  ➔ *She said that Arturo* ***must*** *still* ***be*** *asleep.*

Note: If the reporting verb is in a present tense, no tense changes are necessary: *'I****'ll help*** *you with your homework.'* ➔ *She* ***says*** *she****'ll help*** *me with my homework.*

Questions in reported speech

To report a question, we make the following changes.

- We change the word order in the question to the same as a normal sentence.
- We make the same tense changes as in reported speech (see above).
- We use the same question words (*when, how,* etc.).
- We use a full stop (.), not a question mark (?):
  'How long have you been living in London?' ➔ *She asked me how long I had been living in London.*
  'When can I phone you?' ➔ *Abdullah asked Magdi when he could phone him.*
- We do not use the auxiliary verbs *do, does* and *did*; the question has the same form as a normal sentence:
  *'****What time does the lesson start****?'* ➔ *Ludmila asked what time* ***the lesson started****.*
- We use *if* or *whether* with Yes/No questions:
  'Can I come to your party?' ➔ *Aniela wanted to know* ***whether*** *she could come to our party.*

We often use these verbs and phrases to introduce reported questions: *ask, wonder, want to know, enquire.*

Pronoun, adjective and adverb changes in reported speech

We usually make the following changes:

you ➔ *he/she/they*	*'I spoke to **you** earlier.'*	*He said he had spoken to **her** earlier.*
• *your* ➔ *his/her/their* • *our* ➔ *their*	*'I saw **your** brother earlier.'*	*He mentioned that he had seen **her** brother earlier.*
this/that (as pronouns) ➔ *it*	*'You should give **this** to Joan.'*	*She told him he should give **it** to Joan.*
this/that/these/those + noun ➔ *the* + noun	*'**This work** is very good.'*	*She told him **the work was** very good.*

Remember that references to times also need to change in reported speech:
*'I saw Adam **this morning**.'* ➔ *She said she had seen Adam **that morning**.*

Other changes include:

present reference	• ***today*** • ***this** week / **this** month / **this** year*	• ***that day*** • ***that** week / **that** month / **that** year*
future reference	• ***tomorrow*** • ***next** month/ **next** year*	• ***the next / the following** day* • ***the next / the following** month/year*
past reference	• ***yesterday*** • ***last** week/ month/year*	• ***the day before** OR **the previous day*** • ***the previous** week/month/ year OR the week/month/ year **before***

Descriptions of place also frequently change: *'Did I leave my book **here**?' He asked if he'd left his book **there**.*

Imperatives in reported speech

We use verb + infinitive to report orders and commands:
*'**Fetch** that book!'* ➔ *She asked him **to fetch** the book.*
*'**Don't look** out of the window!'* ➔ *She told him **not to look** out of the window.*

Reporting verbs

There are many verbs which we can use to introduce reported speech, each followed by different grammatical patterns. You will see that most verbs can be followed by more than one grammatical pattern.

verb + infinitive

- agree: *Magda **agreed to look after** the children.*
- offer: *She **offered to take** the children to the zoo.*
- promise: *She's **promised to phone** me later.*

verb + object + infinitive

- advise: *The doctor **advised Mrs Carter to take** a long holiday.*
- ask: *The neighbours **asked us to turn** our music down.*
- invite: *Patsy **has invited me to go** to the party with her.*
- order: *The police **ordered everyone to leave** the building.*
- persuade: *I **persuaded my mother to take** a holiday.*
- remind: *Can you **remind me to phone** Stephen?*
- tell: *Carl **told Jane to close** all the windows.*
- warn: *They **warned us not to walk** on the ice.*

verb + preposition + noun or verb + *-ing*

- accuse of: *Sophie **accused Marcel of stealing** her books.*
- admit to: *Bill **admitted to the mistake**.*
  *Sally **admitted to taking** the money.*
- apologise for: *Tommy **apologised for the accident**.*
  *Mandy **apologised for being** late.*
- complain about: *The neighbours **have been complaining about the noise**.*
  *We **complained about being** given too much homework to do.*

verb + noun or verb + *-ing*

- admit: *Danny **admitted the theft**.*
  *Sue **admitted stealing** the money.*
- deny: *Silvia **denied the crime**.*
  *Sean **denied causing** the accident.*
- recommend: *I can really **recommend this book**.*
  *I **recommend cycling** as a way of getting fit.*
- suggest*: *Jasmine **suggested the solution** to the problem.*
  *Mike **suggested going** climbing at the weekend.*

verb + *(that)* + sentence

- admit: *Sally **admitted (that)** she had taken the money.*
- agree: *The headteacher **agreed (that)** the exam had been too difficult.*
- complain: *We **complained that** we had been given too much homework to do.*
- deny: *Pablo **denied that** he had caused the accident.*
- explain: *She **explained that** she wasn't feeling very well.*
- promise: *Mandy **promised (that)** she would phone later.*
- recommend: *The doctor **recommended (that)** I take more exercise.*
- say: *Robin **said (that)** he was going swimming later.*
- suggest*: *Liz **suggested (that)** I should try the shopping centre on the edge of town.*

verb + object + *(that)* + sentence

- persuade: *I* ***persuaded my mother that*** *she should take a holiday.*
- promise: *Lynn* ***promised Charlie (that)*** *she would phone him later.*
- remind: ***Can I remind you (that)*** *you've got to phone Stephen?*
- tell: *The school* ***told the students (that)*** *they had the rest of the day free.*
- warn: *Nobody* ***warned me (that)*** *my grandmother was visiting us today.*

***Note:** *suggest* is never followed by the infinitive. The following patterns are possible:

- *suggest* + verb + *-ing*:
  Maria ***suggested buying*** *a new computer.*
- *suggest* + noun:
  Phil ***suggested the idea****.*
- *suggest* + *(that)* + sentence:
  Tony ***suggested that*** *they played football that afternoon.*
- *suggest* + *(that)* + *should*:
  Chantal ***suggested (that)*** *I* ***should*** *write a letter.*

Other common patterns are:

- *ask* + *if/what*, etc. + sentence:
  She ***asked*** *me* ***what*** *I was doing.*
  He ***asked*** *me if I was free.*
- *invite* + object + *to* + noun:
  Patsy ***has invited me to the party.***

See also page 166: Infinitive and verb + *-ing* forms

See also page 177: The passive – the passive with reporting verbs

so and *such*, *too* and *enough*

so and *such*

so and *such (a/an)* mean 'very', 'extremely':
That was ***so*** *kind of you!*
I've had ***such a*** *nice time.*
We use *so* and *such (a/an)* to talk about cause and effect:
He was ***so*** *late that he missed the beginning of the exam.*
She gave ***such a*** *good performance that she won an Oscar.*

so + adjective or adverb (+ *that*):	*such* + adjective + uncountable noun / plural noun (+ *that*)
• *He was* ***so nervous*** *before the exam* ***that*** *he couldn't sleep at all.* • *That remark was just* ***so silly****!* • *He cooks* ***so well that*** *I think he'll win the competition.*	• *She tells* ***such good jokes****.* • *Switzerland has* ***such spectacular scenery that*** *we always choose it for our holidays.*

so + *much/many/few/little* + noun (+ *that*)	*such a/an* + adjective + singular countable noun (+ *that*); *such a lot of …*
• *We had* ***so little money*** *left at the end of our holiday that we had to sleep on a bench in the station.* • *Marta makes* ***so many mistakes*** *when she's speaking!*	• *Why did you come in* ***such an old pair of jeans****?* • *It was* ***such a beautiful day*** *that we decided to go for a picnic.* • *Elena's got* ***such a lot of friends*** *that the telephone never stops ringing.*

We also use *such* (+ noun) to mean 'of a similar type':
When children commit crimes, adults are often shocked. Fortunately ***such behaviour*** *is not as common as newspapers make us believe.*

too and *enough*

- *too* means 'more than is needed or wanted': *She's **too old** to join the police.*
- *enough* means 'as much as is necessary or needed': *Have we got **enough eggs** to make a cake?*

too + adjective (+ noun) + (for somebody) (+ infinitive)	adjective/adverb + *enough* + (for somebody) (+ infinitive)
*He's **too young to drive**.* *That suitcase is **too heavy for me to lift**.*	*This coffee is **not warm enough**! Please heat it up again.* *Franz didn't answer the questions **convincingly enough to get** the job.* *That hotel is **not smart enough for her**.*

too + adverb + (for somebody) (+ infinitive); *too much / too many* + noun + (for somebody) (+ infinitive)	*enough* + noun + (for somebody) (+ infinitive)
*You're driving **too dangerously**. Please slow down.* *They brought **too much food for us to eat**.* *I've received **too many emails to answer**.*	*Have you got **enough money to get** to London?* *There is**n't enough cake** in the cupboard **for me to give** some to everyone.*

Spelling

Spelling changes when adding *-ed, -ing, -er* and *-est* to words

We double the final consonant when we add *-ed, -ing, -er* or *-est* to words:

- which are one syllable and end in a consonant-vowel-consonant: *stop – stopped, hit – hitting, flat – flatter*
- which have two or more syllables which end in consonant-vowel-consonant and the final syllable is stressed: *admit – admitted, occur – occurring*

Note: In British English, we always double a final 'l' after a single vowel: *travel – travelling, cancel – cancelled*

We don't double the final consonant when:

- there are two final consonants: *send – sending, hard – hardest*
- there are two vowels before the final consonant: *appeal – appealed, mean – meanest*
- the word ends in a vowel: *strike – striking, safe – safest*
- for a verb, the stress is not on the final syllable: *open – opening*
- the word ends in *-w, -x* or *-y*: *slow – slower, relax – relaxing, display – displayed*

When adding *-ed*, a final 'y' after a consonant becomes 'i': *study – studied, lovely – loveliest*
When adding *-ing*, a final 'y' after a consonant does not change: *study – studying*

Note: Notice how the spelling of these words changes: *lie – lying – lied; die – dying – died; lay – laying – laid; try – trying – tried*

Spelling changes when adding prefixes and other suffixes

We normally do not change the spelling of the base word when we add a prefix or a suffix: *need – unneeded, arrange – arrangement*

However:

- we drop the final 'e' when there is a consonant before it and the suffix begins with a vowel (*-er, -ed, -ing, -ance, -ation*, etc.): *irritate – irritating, fame – famous*
- we do not drop the final 'e' when the suffix begins with a consonant: *safe – safety, manage – management*
- a final 'y' becomes 'i': *industry – industrial*

Adding prefixes

When we add a syllable like *un-, dis-*, or *in-* before the word to make it negative, we do not change the spelling, e.g. with *dis-* and *un-*: *appoint – **dis**appoint, satisfied – **dis**satisfied, like – **un**like, necessary – **un**necessary*

Note: Before words beginning with 'r', we use *ir-*: *irrelevant*; before words beginning with 'm' or 'p', we use *im-*: *immature, impatient*; before words beginning with 'l', we use *il-*: *illogical, illiterate*.

These words are frequently misspelled by exam candidates:

The most common spelling errors by candidates

accommodation advertisement beautiful because beginning believe between children comfortable communicate convenient country/countries course different embarrassed/embarrassing environment excellent experience government loose lose necessary nowadays opinion opportunity/opportunities prefer receive recommend restaurant society their until wealthy which

The passive

The passive is formed by the verb *to be* + past participle (*done/eaten/cleaned*, etc.).

active	passive
• ***They ate** all the food very quickly.* • ***We've sold** the car.* • *It's nice when **people invite** me to dinner.* • *On a clear day, **you can see** Ibiza from the mainland.*	• *All the food **was eaten** very quickly.* • *The car **has been sold**.* • *It's nice when **I'm invited** to dinner.* • *On a clear day, Ibiza **can be seen** from the mainland.*

We use the passive when:
- what happens is more important than who does it:
  *The car **has been repaired**, so we can go away this weekend.*
- we don't know who or what does/did something:
  *My mobile phone **has been stolen**!*
- we don't need to say who or what does/did something because it's obvious from the situation or context:
  *The law **was passed** earlier this year* (obviously by a government).
- when writing in an official style:
  *Your ticket has **been booked** and can be collected from our office.*

The passive with *get*

- We can use *get* instead of *be* to form the passive, especially when we want to say that something happened to someone or something:
  *He **got hurt** playing football yesterday.* (He was hurt.)
  *I'm afraid we were playing football and one of your windows **got broken**.* (One of your windows was broken.)
- *get* is used mainly in informal spoken English.
- We only use *get* when something happens or changes:
  *He **got arrested** by the police.*
- It is not possible with state verbs:
  ~~*The car got owned by a film star*~~. *The car **was owned** by a film star.*

The passive with reporting verbs

We often use the passive to report what people say, think, etc., especially when we don't know who said it or thought it, or it's not important:
*The Queen **is thought to be suffering** from a heavy cold.*
*Fernando Alonso **is considered to be** the best Spanish Formula One driver of all time.*
This use of the passive is common in news reports.

We use three possible forms:
- *He/She is said/thought/considered*, etc. + infinitive:
  *Lions **are known to hunt** in this area.*
  *Elena is **thought to be** highly intelligent.*
- Verbs that we can use with this pattern are:

consider expect feel know say suppose think understand

- To talk about the past, we can use: *She is said to have played/eaten/been*, etc.:
  *The Prime Minister **is understood to have spoken** to the rebels on the phone.*
- *It is said/thought/considered*, etc. + *that* + a sentence:
  ***It is thought that** Elena is highly intelligent.*
  ***It is known that** lions hunt in this area.*
- Verbs that we can use with this pattern are:

agree announce consider decide expect feel find know propose recommend say suggest suppose think understand

- *It is agreed/planned*, etc. + infinitive:
  ***It has been agreed to change** the dates of the meeting.*
- Verbs that we can use with this pattern are:

agree decide forbid hope plan propose

Using commas

We use commas (,):
- when we make lists:
  *I like playing tennis, listening to music, chatting with friends **and** watching TV.*

Note: We don't use a comma with the final item on the list; we use *and*.

- to separate adjectives when there are a number of adjectives before the noun:
  He's an enthusiastic, hard-working student.

Note: With short common adjectives, commas are not necessary:
My village is quite a friendly little place.

- after an adverb or a short introductory phrase at the beginning of a sentence such as *first, as a result, consequently, for this reason, all in all, generally, finally, however, in my opinion*, etc.:
  ***Generally**, people in my country start university aged 19.*
  ***In my opinion**, young people should help their parents to do the housework.*

- after a time phrase at the beginning of a sentence:
  ***In 2014,** he left school and went to university.*
- after clauses at the beginning of sentences starting with *if, unless, when, while, after, before, although, even though, whereas, as,* etc.:
  ***When** everyone in a family helps with the housework, they have a better relationship.*
- when we join two sentences with *but*, we often put a comma before *but*:
  *He got quite good marks in his exams**, but** he wasn't happy with his results.*

Using *it, this, that* or *they*

We use *it, this* and *that* (in the plural *they, these* and *those*) to refer to something we have already mentioned. Often more than one of them is correct in the context. However:

- we use *it* when we are not making any emphasis:
  *I prefer listening to live music. **It**'s more spontaneous.*
- *this* and *that* are more emphatic in drawing attention to the thing just mentioned:
  *People usually **listen to music through headphones**. There's some evidence that **this** damages their hearing.*
- we often use *this* when:
  - we still have something more to say about the thing we are referring to:
    ***File sharing** has become a common activity. **This** is having serious effects on the music industry.*
  - we refer to the second of two things mentioned in the previous sentence. Compare:
    1. *While many festivals are welcomed by local people, they are usually very **noisy. This** means that people living in the district find it hard to sleep.* (*This* = the noise)
    2. *While many **festivals** are welcomed by local people, **they** are usually very noisy. Also, they are normally held in the summer.* (*they* = the festivals)
- we often use *that* in conditional sentences:
  *I think that every town and village should have a festival if **that** is what local people want.*

Verb tenses

Simple and continuous forms

- Present simple describes a situation which is permanent, or happens regularly:
  *Paul **lives** in London.*
  *He **catches** the bus at eight every morning.*
- Present continuous describes a temporary situation or one in progress:
  ***I'm staying** with my aunt while Mum and Dad are away.*
  ***He's playing** tennis at the moment.*

State verbs

We do not usually use verbs which describe states, not actions, in the continuous. These verbs describe:

- thoughts: *believe, know, remember, think* (meaning 'believe'), *feel* (meaning 'believe'), *suppose*, etc.
- feelings: *love, like, hate, want, prefer*, etc.
- senses: *smell, hear, taste, see, feel, touch*
- possession: *have, belong, own*, etc.
- the verb *to be*

Note:

- When *think* means 'to use your brain to plan something, solve a problem, make a decision', etc., it can be used in the continuous:
  ***I'm thinking** about what to do today.* (I'm planning.)
- When *feel* means 'to experience something physical or emotional', it can be used in the continuous:
  *I don't want to come to the party because **I'm feeling** tired.*

Candidates often spell these words wrong:

~~writting~~ writing ~~studing~~ studying ~~comming~~ coming

See also page 176: Spelling

Present perfect simple and continuous

Both the present perfect simple and present perfect continuous talk about something which started in the past and:

- either has a result in the present:
  ***He's twisted** his ankle, so he can't play football with us this afternoon.*
  ***I've been partying** all weekend, so I'm feeling tired now.*
- or is still happening now:
  ***We've been building** an extension to our house* (and we haven't finished yet).

Often they are interchangeable. However:

The present perfect simple	The present perfect continuous
emphasises the **result**: ***I've phoned** all my friends and they're coming to the party.*	emphasises the **action**: ***I've been phoning** my friends* (and that's why I haven't done my homework).
says how much of an activity is **complete**: *I've written two essays.*	says how long the activity has been **in progress**: ***I've been studying** all afternoon.*

Words which are often confused

These words are often confused by candidates at Cambridge English: First.

Unit 4, Vocabulary, Exercise 1 (page 42)

food *noun* [U] something that people and animals eat, or plants absorb, to keep them alive: *baby food. There was lots of food and drink at the party.*

dish FOOD *noun* [C] food prepared in a particular way as part of a meal: *a chicken/vegetarian dish*

meal FOOD *noun* [C] an occasion when food is eaten, or the food which is eaten on such an occasion: I have my main meal at midday. *You must come round for a meal sometime.*

Unit 6, Vocabulary, Exercise 1 (page 63)

fun or **funny**?

If something is **fun**, you enjoy doing it.
I really liked the skating – it was such fun.

1 If something is **funny**, it makes you laugh.
It's a very funny film.

2 If something is **funny**, it is strange, surprising, unexpected or difficult to explain or understand.
The washing machine is making a funny noise again.

possibility, occasion or **opportunity**?

A **possibility** is a chance that something may happen or be true. **Possibility** cannot be followed by an infinitive.
Is there a possibility of getting a job in your organisation?

An **occasion** is an event, or a time when something happens. Occasion does not mean 'chance' or 'opportunity'.
Birthdays are always special occasions.

An **opportunity** is a possibility of doing something, or a situation which gives you the possibility of doing something.
The trip to Paris gave me an opportunity to speak French.
I have more opportunity to travel than my parents did.

work or **job**?

Work is something you do to earn money. This noun is uncountable.
She enjoys her work in the hospital.

Job is used to talk about the particular type of work activity which you do. This noun is countable.
He's looking for a job in computer programming.

Unit 5, Vocabulary, Exercise 3 (page 54)

assist *verb* [I or T] *formal*: to help: *You will be expected to assist the editor with the selection of illustrations for the book.*

attend BE PRESENT *verb* [I or T] *slightly formal*: to go to an event, place, etc.: *The meeting is on the fifth and we're hoping everyone will attend.*

get to know sb/sth: to spend time with somebody or something so that you gradually learn more about them: *The first couple of meetings are for the doctor and patient to get to know each other.*

join BECOME A MEMBER *verb* [I or T]: to become a member of an organisation: *I felt so unfit after Christmas that I decided to join a gym.*

take part: to be involved in an activity with other people: *She doesn't usually take part in any of the class activities.*

know or **find out**?

If you **know** something, you already have the information.
Andy knows what time the train leaves.

If you **find** something **out**, you learn new information for the first time.
I'll ring the station to find out what time the train leaves.

learn, teach or **study**?

To **learn** is to get new knowledge or skills.
I want to learn how to drive.

When you **teach** someone, you give them new knowledge or skills.
My dad taught me how to drive.

When you **study**, you go to classes, read books, etc. to try to understand new ideas and facts.
He is studying biology at university.

Unit 7, Vocabulary, Exercise 2 (page 80)

look, see or **watch**?

See means to notice people and things with your eyes.
She saw a big spider and screamed.

Look (**at**) is used when you are trying to see something or someone. If **look** is followed by an object, you must use a preposition. The usual preposition is **at**.
I've looked everywhere, but can't find my keys.
I looked at the map to find the road.

Watch means to look at something for a period of time, usually something which moves or changes.
He watched television all evening.

listen, listen to or **hear**?
Use **hear** when you want to say that sounds, music, etc. come to your ears. You can hear something without wanting to.
I could hear his music through the wall.

Use **listen** to say that you pay attention to sounds or try to hear something.
The audience listened carefully.

Use **listen to** when you want to say what it is that you are trying to hear.
The audience listened to the speaker.

Unit 8, Vocabulary, Exercise 6 (page 87)

acting *noun* [U] the job of performing in films or plays:
He wants to get into acting.

audience *group noun* [C] the group of people gathered in one place to watch or listen to a play, film, someone speaking, etc., or the (number of) people watching or listening to a particular television or radio programme, or reading a particular book

performance *noun* [C] the action of entertaining other people by dancing, singing, acting or playing music

play *noun* [C] a piece of writing that is intended to be acted in a theatre or on radio or television

(the) public *noun* [U + singular or plural verb] all ordinary people

scene *noun* [C] a part of a play or film in which the action stays in one place for a continuous period of time

spectator *noun* [C] a person who watches an activity, especially a sports event, without taking part

stage *noun* [C] the area in a theatre which is often raised above ground level and on which actors or entertainers perform

Unit 9, Vocabulary, Exercise 1 (page 98)

stay *verb* to continue doing something, or to continue to be in a particular state:
He's decided not to stay in teaching.
The shops stay open until nine o'clock.

spend *verb* to use time doing something or being somewhere:
My sister always spends ages in the bathroom.

pass *verb* If you **pass** time, you do something to stop yourself being bored during that period:
The visitors pass their days swimming, windsurfing and playing volleyball.

make *verb (+ noun/adjective)* to cause to be, to become or to appear as:
It's the good weather that makes Spain such a popular tourist destination.
Don't stand over me all the time – it makes me nervous.

cause *verb* to make something happen, especially something bad:
The difficult driving conditions caused several accidents.

Some common collocations with **cause**: *cause trouble, cause problems, cause damage, cause traffic jams, cause stress, cause pollution.*

Note, however, these collocations:
have an effect (on): *The good weather has had a beneficial effect on his health and happiness.*
have/make an impact (on): *The anti-smoking campaign had/made quite an impact on young people.*

Part 3

In Part 3, you work with the other candidate.

This part of the Speaking paper is divided into two parts.

In the first part, which takes two minutes:

- The examiner gives you a page with a question and five prompts.
- You have 15 seconds to consider the options before you start speaking.
- You should discuss each of the options in turn.

In the second part, the examiner asks you to summarise your thoughts, for example by choosing the option that is best and saying why. You have one minute for this.

You studied and practised Part 3 in Units 3, 7, 12 and 14.

How to do Part 3

For the first part:

1 Listen carefully to the question, which is also printed next to the options to help you. It will be in a mind map with the question in the middle of the page and the prompts around it.

2 You have 15 seconds to think about the task before you start speaking:
   Think about:
   - the options and how you can express them in your own words and discuss their relative merits in relation to the question
   - how you can start the discussion, perhaps with a suggestion and a reason for your idea.

3 To start the conversation, you can give a brief opinion about one of the options or make a suggestion and ask your partner what he/she thinks.

4 When you discuss, deal with each option in turn.

5 When your partner says something, react to his/her ideas. Listen carefully to what he/she is saying. Try to make the discussion like a natural conversation. Don't try to dominate the conversation.

6 Keep the discussion moving by saying things like *What about this option? What do you think?* or *Shall we move on to the next option?*.

7 Don't spend too long talking about one particular option.

8 Continue your discussion until the examiner says 'Thank you'.

For the second part:

1 Don't discuss each option again, but discuss the options which seem most reasonable to you.

2 Try to reach a decision, but remember that it's not essential to agree.

3 Remember you should discuss the question for a minute, so if you agree with your partner's first idea, say so, but suggest discussing other options (see Unit 3).

4 Continue your discussion until the examiner says 'Thank you'.

Example task: First part

I'd like you to imagine that a town wants to attract more visitors and tourists. Here are some of the ideas they are considering. Talk to each other about how effective these different ideas might be. You now have some time to look at the task. Then decide which two would attract the most tourists.

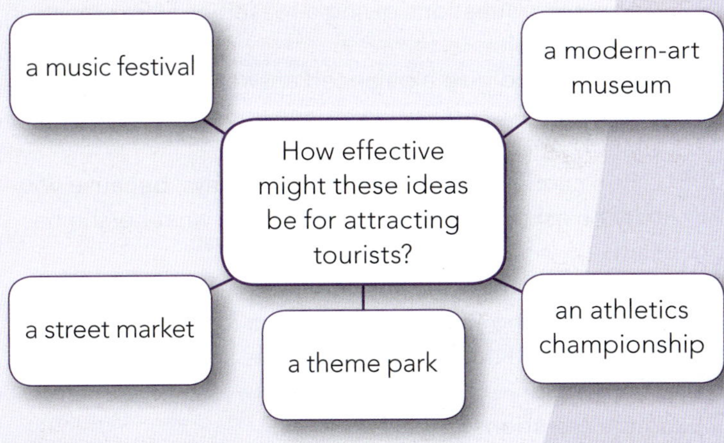

Example task : Second part

Now you have a minute to decide which two ideas would be best for attracting tourists.

Involving your partner

- What do you think?
- Do you agree?
- What about (a music festival)?
- I think … What about you?

Keeping the discussion moving

- What about (a theme park)? What do you think?
- Let's move on to the next option.
- Shall we move on to the next option?

Part 4

In Part 4, you continue to work together.

- The examiner asks both of you questions about your opinions connected with the topic you discussed in Part 3.
- You may be asked the same question as your partner, if you agree with your partner's answer, or a completely different question.

Part 4 lasts about four minutes.

You studied and practised Part 4 in Units 4, 8, 12 and 14.

How to do Part 4

1 Listen carefully to the questions. If you don't understand a question, don't feel afraid to ask the examiner to repeat (*Sorry could you say that again, please?*). You won't lose any marks asking them to repeat.
2 Give general answers to questions.
3 Answer the questions giving a reason or an explanation or an example.
4 You can try to give a balanced answer, i.e. express two points of view and say which one you agree with (see Units 12 and 14).
5 Listen carefully to what your partner says, because you may be asked to give your opinion on what he/she has said.
6 If you don't know the answer to a question, don't just say *I don't know*. Say *I don't know a lot about this subject, but I think* … and then give some ideas.

Example questions

- Some places attract large numbers of tourists. What problems are caused by having too many tourists?
- What can people learn by going as tourists to other places?
- Do you think it's better for people to spend their holidays in their own country or travel to other countries? Why?
- What are the advantages of living in another country instead of just going as a tourist? What's the main advantage?
- What things should people try to find out before visiting a country? (Why?)
- How important is it for tourists to respect the culture of the country they are visiting?

Introducing an opinion and giving a reason

- I think …
- Well, in my opinion, … because …
- I feel …
- I'm not sure. I think …
- No, I don't think so …

Introducing an explanation

- I mean …
- You see …

Giving an example

- For example …
- For instance …
- … such as …

Speaking in general

- In general, …
- Generally, …
- As a rule, …
- … tend to …

Grammar

Past simple, past continuous and *used to*

1 **1** used to go **2** used to be **3** was **4** were going **5** got **6** dumped **7** went **8** had **9** stayed **10** were doing

2 **1** was walking **2** used to do **3** got; jumped; rode **4** used to spend **5** were walking; began **6** used to visit; was

3 developed, enjoyed, happened, mentioned, occurred, opened, planned, preferred, stopped, studied, travelled (BrE) / traveled (AmE), tried

Vocabulary

travel, journey, trip and *way*

1 **1** trip **2** Way **3** travel **4** journey

2 **1** trip **2** way **3** trip **4** trip **5** travel **6** journey **7** trip **8** journey **9** way

3 **1** pleasant/safe/successful **2** overnight **3** outward **4** shopping **5** forthcoming **6** safe/pleasant

Reading and Use of English | Part 3

1 **2** adventurous **3** friendly **4** memorable **5** mysterious **6** risky **7** crowded **8** thrilled/thrilling **9** doubtful **10** successful **11** remarkable **12** accessible

2 artist – artistic; caution – cautious; colour – colourful, colourless; educate – educational, educated; emotion – emotional; energy – energetic; mass – massive; predict – predictable; reason – reasonable; respond – responsible; storm – stormy; thought – thoughtful, thoughtless; wealth – wealthy

3 **1** uncomfortable **2** thoughtful **3** colourful **4** unforgettable **5** optimistic **6** considerable **7** anxious **8** sympathetic

Grammar

at, in or *on* in time phrases

1 **1** in, in **2** on **3** at, at **4** in

2 **1** ~~on July~~ in July **2** ~~In the weekends~~ At the weekends*, ~~on the afternoon~~ in the afternoon **3** ~~in 11.00~~ at 11.00 **4** correct **5** ~~at 2008~~ in 2008 **6** correct **7** ~~in certain times~~ at certain times **8** ~~at the morning in a normal day~~ in the morning on a normal day

*Note: *on the weekends* is correct in American English.

Reading and Use of English | Part 7

2 *Suggested underlining*
1 hide from danger **2** employee intimidating **3** not pleased, spend so long **4** visited, previous occasion **5** worried, strong **6** missed speaking, people **7** painful experience **8** travelled with, ex-criminal **9** unaware, danger **10** holiday, mistake, before arriving

3 **1** B **2** C **3** C **4** D **5** B **6** D **7** A **8** C **9** A **10** D

Grammar

Past perfect simple and continuous

1 **1** A **2** had organised (past perfect) **3** In the first sentence, her father organised the trip before they arrived; in the second sentence, he organised it when they were already in the country.

2 **A** Pauline Vernon: *until that point, no one* ***had bothered*** *to mention the sea-snakes – The sting, on both legs, was agony, …*
B Sandy Henderson: *we'****d passed*** *a small cabin a little way back on the trail – we made a dash for that*
C Cat O'Donovan: *what I* ***had let*** *myself in for – Twenty-three hours into an epic bus trip across the States, I began to wonder; I* ***had been filled*** *with romantic ideas – Before boarding the first bus in LA; After the guy next to me* ***had finished*** *talking about his time in jail – I realised my expectations were a bit off; she* ***had eaten*** *several passengers – One unfriendly staff member was so large I feared*

3 **1** had eaten **2** had never been **3** organised / had organised **4** arrived; had lost **5** recognised; had never spoken **6** had damaged

4 **1** A
2 A past perfect continuous **B** past perfect simple

5 **1** had been living **2** had been walking; began **3** had already finished; offered **4** had only been speaking **5** got; had been walking

6 **1** ~~have done~~ had done **2** ~~didn't have~~ hadn't had **3** ~~didn't go~~ hadn't been **4** ~~had bought~~ bought; ~~always wanted~~ had always wanted **5** ~~she just finished~~ she had just finished **6** ~~I have been cleaning~~ I had been cleaning

Speaking | Part 3

2 A city sightseeing tour: you learn about architecture and history, other cultures and visit somewhere different. A weekend camping trip in the mountains: you have exciting experiences and adventures, and learn to be independent, learn to work together to solve problems, learn teamwork, educational. A beach activity day: learn something from doing different sports and activities.

CD 1 Track 10

Miguel: Shall we start with this one?

Antonia: OK.

Miguel: How do you think doing a sightseeing tour of a city might be good for students?

Antonia: I think you can learn a lot about architecture and history and things like that.

Miguel: Yes, and also you can visit somewhere very different and learn about other cultures.

Antonia: Right. What about this sort of activity holiday in the mountains? I think it can give young people exciting experiences and adventures, things they don't get in their everyday lives.

Miguel: Yes, and they learn to be more independent because they're away from home and their families, don't you think?

Antonia: I think that's right. Also, they learn to work together to solve problems, so it's good for learning teamwork.

Miguel: That's an important point, because if the school's organising the trip, it should be educational, shouldn't it? I mean, students have got to be learning something. And the beach activity day: what about that?

Antonia: It sounds great, doesn't it? And I think just by doing sports and activities they don't normally do at school, students learn something.

Miguel: I agree.

3 **1** Shall; this one **2** think **3** What about **4** don't you **5** about that

Pronunciation: intonation (1)

4.1 **1** good for students ↘
2 architecture ↗, history ↗, things like that ↘
3 different ↘, cultures ↘
4 activity ↗, mountains ↘
5 experiences ↗, adventures ↗, lives ↘

CD 1 Track 11 See page 38.

6 *Suggested answers*
1 N, there isn't time – you need to reach a decision in one minute.
2 Y, it gets the discussion started and your partner involved.
3 N, it prevents further discussion.
4 Y, this is a possible way of creating more discussion
5 Y, it creates further discussion.
6 N, you only have a minute and you'll get higher marks if you can have a natural conversation.

7 Miguel does 2; Antonia does 4; Irene and Nikolai both do 5

CD 1 Track 12

Miguel and Antonia

Miguel: Well, Antonia, in my opinion, the best choice for the trip is the camping and walking activity in the mountains, because it'll be an adventure for everyone, and if it goes well, everyone will enjoy it. What do you think?

Antonia: Hmm, I think your suggestion would be fine if the weather is good, but no one will enjoy it if it rains all the time, and it's a lot of responsibility for the teachers who're supervising the trip. I think the beach-activities trip is a better option because at least the kids'll be staying in a hostel if the weather turns bad.

Irene and Nikolai

Irene: OK, I think we should choose the theme park because all teenagers enjoy the thrill of a theme park, and it gives everyone plenty to talk about and discuss before and after they go.

Nikolai: Yes, I think you're right, but I think we should also consider the visit to the museum because that might be more popular with the teachers, and we have to take their preferences into consideration as well.

Irene: Hmm, you might be right, but I think we should put the students' tastes first because it is their trip.

Nikolai: Maybe, but they can go to a theme park in their own time.

Irene: Yes, of course they can, but sometimes it's important to do these activities as a school group.

8 **1** a **2** a **3** b **4** e **5** e **6** d **7** c

Writing | Part 2
A report

1 *Suggested underlining*
one-day excursion, local place of interest, what you did, why, the day, a success

3 **1** took **2** went **3** was **4** had been **5** rode **6** were **7** took **8** had operated **9** was **10** were **11** enjoyed **12** learned **13** had **14** found

4 **1** yes, *Excursion to London*
2 three, each has a heading: *Purpose of trip, What we did, Comments*
3 three: a break from normal lessons, to see the London Eye and do a tour of the Globe Theatre
4 The activities were interesting, different, everyone enjoyed something, plenty of opportunities to practise English, motivating.

4 Food, glorious food

Starting off

1 See page 42.

2 **1** Photo 5 **2** Photo 1 **3** Photo 2 **4** Photo 3 **5** Photo 4

Reading and Use of English | Part 6

2 *Suggested answers*
Para. 2: the campaign and the reasons for it; Para. 3: the food and where it comes from; Para. 4: classroom activities in the garden; Para. 5: classroom activities in the kitchen; Para. 6: Teo's opinion; Para. 7: The general aim of the garden

3 *Suggested underlining*
C One lesson **D** The problem, these projects
E These two projects **F** We, in this small space
G Lessons like this one

4 **1** G **2** E **3** F **4** B **5** C **6** A

Vocabulary
food, dish and *meal*

1 **1** food, meals **2** food, dishes **3** meal

2 **2** ~~meals~~ dishes **3** ~~food~~ dish **4** ~~meal~~ food
5 ~~meals~~ food **6** ~~food~~ dish **7** ~~dishes~~ meals

3 **1** food **2** food **3** meal; dish **4** meal

4 **2** food shortages **3** heavy/filling meal
4 food source **5** convenience food **6** balanced meals **7** food supply **8** organic food

Grammar
so and *such*

1 **1** such a; So **2** such a; so **3** such

2 **1** such **2** so **3** such a **4** so **5** so **6** such a

3 **1** ~~such~~ so **2** ~~a so much~~ such **3** correct **4** ~~so~~ such
5 ~~so~~ such a **6** ~~such~~ so **7** correct **8** ~~so~~ such

4 **1** never eaten such a good **2** so quickly that we
3 answered the question so well/excellently **4** with so little food **5** had so much fun at **6** make so much noise

Listening | Part 4

2 *Suggested underlining*
1 started, because
2 most important, chose the site **3** décor **4** How, behave with, customers **5** purpose, back room
6 food, should be **7** What, parents like

3 **1** B **2** C **3** C **4** A **5** B **6** B **7** A

CD 1 Track 13

Interviewer: Hi! Today I'm talking to Cherry Smith, owner of Cherry's Café, a well-known spot for youngsters in our town. Cherry – can you tell us a little bit about your café and why you started it?

Cherry: Sure. I was working in one of the local supermarkets – it was always my ambition from when I was quite little to be working with people and I noticed that there were lots of secondary school kids coming in to buy snacks and soft drinks and things and just hanging around and I thought, 'Poor things, they've got too much free time and they're not eating well enough and they need somewhere they can hang out.' So I came up with this idea of a café where kids could just spend their free time and I could make a living out of it as well.

Interviewer: Great! So did you choose this site for your café because it's between the two local schools?

Cherry: Well, that was one consideration, but I thought it was essential to have a place which was just that bit bigger than the other cafés in the area and I found this place with an extra room at the back where customers can go and not be seen from the street by passers-by and you know everyone from the two schools does go past.

Interviewer: And, Cherry, did you need to put much thought into the interior decoration?

Cherry: Yeah, lots. I was really wanting a place where kids can come at lunchtime or after school and feel comfortable, so comfy chairs, warm colours, things that make them feel at home. Nothing fragile because we don't want to be replacing furniture every five minutes. I get them to help out a bit too, so, you know, they help wipe tables and sweep up from time to time, otherwise we wouldn't manage.

Interviewer: So, your customers are mainly young people from the local schools. Do they give you any problems?

Cherry: They're almost all from the local schools and not really. They behave quite well really, and I say 'quite' because they are young, so they're going to be noisy and want to play around a bit, but they're never rude to me or rough. I just like people and young people especially. I think everyone's interesting so I try to find out things about them and I pull their legs sometimes – we have a good laugh – like they're friends. And they react to that. I don't impose discipline or anything 'cos it's not like lessons. And that doesn't mean I'm always going to look happy – I have my 'off' days, just like anyone else.

Interviewer: You mentioned a room at the back as being important. Why's that?

Cherry: Well, I want kids to come here and feel that it's like another home. Somewhere they can just be themselves, so the back room is the sort of quiet room where they can just sit down and read, or do their internet stuff, or finish their homework, or have a quiet chat. You know, young people need these sorts of places where they can be quiet if they want to be, but have company if they want it too.

Interviewer: Fantastic. How about food? Do you just give your customers whatever they want?

Cherry: Well, I think it's important to offer young people food they can afford. I mean, I don't worry about if it's good for them or not. We do serve things like, hamburgers and chips, but we also offer salads and fresh vegetables. You'd be surprised how popular they are. I don't do the cooking – Mikey does that 'cos I don't have enough time. They're all simple dishes but they can be quite filling.

Interviewer: Great! And finally, Cherry, what do parents think of your café? Do you get any comments?

Cherry: Actually, I don't see too many parents, but the odd comment comes back. I think what they really appreciate is that, you know, their kids are in a friendly place where they feel happy. Parents sometimes sort of jokingly complain when their kids tell them they don't cook as well as Mikey. And you know, in the end, this café is a cost for the parents, but I think they think it's worth it.

Interviewer: Cherry, thanks.

Cherry: Thank you.

Grammar

too and *enough*

1 **1** too much; enough **2** too **3** enough **4** enough **5** too many

2 **1** too many; enough **2** enough **3** too **4** too **5** enough

3 **1** ~~the food wasn't enough~~ there wasn't enough food **2** ~~not too much good~~ not very good **3** ~~money enough~~ enough money **4** ~~enough comfortable~~ comfortable enough **5** ~~too much long~~ (much) too long **6** ~~doing too hard work~~ working too hard / doing too much hard work **7** ~~too much tasty~~ very tasty **8** ~~too much expensive~~ (much) too expensive

4 **1** is too expensive for **2** enough petrol to get **3** was too astonished by **4** was not / wasn't warm enough for

Speaking | Part 4

1 **b** balanced diet **c** cut down **d** junk food **e** dairy products **f** live on **g** lifestyle

2 **1** in other words **2** because **3** On the other hand **4** then **5** but **6** which **7** what

CD 1 Track 14

Examiner: Do you think fast food is bad for you?

Martyna: I think it depends. I think the most important thing / is to have a balanced diet, / in other words, you eat a variety of / vegetables, / meat, /cereals and so on. I'm not sure it matters so much / how long it takes to prepare, / because I think fast food is / just / food which is prepared quickly. On the other hand, / if you just live on / what's it called / junk food, / for instance hamburgers and pizzas and things like that, / then you probably need to cut down / and have a more balanced diet.

Examiner: And Miguel, what do you think?

Miguel: I agree with Martyna. / I think it's fine to eat fast food occasionally, / but you have to balance it with other things like / fresh fruit and / vegetables which are in season and / cut down on dairy products and fat. / Also I think that what you eat is only one part of a / healthy lifestyle.

Martyna: I agree.

3 **1** in other words **2** because **3** for instance, like **4** but, on the other hand

Pronunciation: grouping words and pausing (1)

4.1

CD 1 Track 15

Examiner: How can families benefit from eating together?

Miguel: Well, / the important thing is not eating, / it's spending time together / so that they can talk about / what they have been doing during the day. / They get the chance to / exchange opinions / and make plans as well, / because everyone can contribute and / that's what makes a / rich, / meaningful family life. / Children learn ideas and attitudes from their parents, / while parents keep up to date with their children / and what they are thinking and doing.

Examiner: And Martyna, do you agree?

Martyna: Yes, I do. / And also I think people cook better / when they are cooking for several people / than when they are just cooking for themselves, / so that as a result, / people who eat together / eat more healthily.

4.3 See recording script for Track 15 above.

Reading and Use of English | Part 1

1 The surroundings, the service, the food, the price

2 **1** C **2** B **3** C **4** B **5** A **6** D **7** C **8** A

Writing | Part 2

A review

1 *Suggested underlining*
local English-language newspaper, recommend, local restaurant, café or snack bar, review, what, place, food, like, why, family, enjoy eating there

2 **2** a, b, c, d, f, h, i

3 and **4** *Suggested answers*
the waiters / the service: rushed, welcoming, informative, cheerful, exceptional, satisfactory, superb
the interior: airy, cosy, modern, attractive, cheerful, colourful, elegant, exclusive, original, welcoming
the food and menu: delicious, fresh, satisfying, tasty, wonderful, attractive, colourful, delightful, elegant, exceptional, original, raw, satisfactory, superb, well-balanced
the price: reasonable, competitive
the restaurant in general: modern, attractive, colourful, delightful, exceptional, elegant, exclusive, original, superb, welcoming

5 *Suggested underlining*
college magazine, favourite restaurant, café or snack bar, review, 'Free Time' section, what, place, like, why, recommend it

Vocabulary and grammar review Unit 3

1 **1** journey **2** trip **3** travel **4** way **5** journey **6** way **7** trip **8** journey

2 **1** while I was visiting **2** I had lost **3** used to go to school **4** she was still going to **5** had never met **6** used to be more

3 **1** considerable **2** exclusive **3** dramatic **4** unacceptable **5** disorganised **6** unhelpful **7** remaining **8** preferable

Vocabulary and grammar review Unit 4

1 **1** meal **2** food **3** dish **4** food **5** dish **6** food/meal **7** meal **8** food

2 **1** too hot (for us) to **2** slowly enough (for us) to **3** was so full (that) **4** such delicious food that **5** cook well enough **6** such a long time / so much time

3 **1** filling **2** convenience **3** increasingly **4** organisations **5** discourage **6** balanced **7** disappearance **8** choice

5 Study time

Listening | Part 1

1 **1** h **2** d **3** b **4** a **5** i **6** e **7** f **8** c **9** g

2 *Suggested underlining*
1 How does he feel, now **2** What, problem **3** What, like most **4** What, main benefit **5** Why, talking **6** What surprised her, school **7** think about, lesson **8** What, advice about

3 **1** C **2** B **3** B **4** A **5** A **6** C **7** C **8** B

CD 1 Track 16

Presenter: One. You overhear a student talking about a course he has been doing.

Will: Actually, at the beginning of term, I was a bit lost. You know, my family has only just moved to this country, so I was new in this school, and I felt that everyone else knew more about the subject than I did. Listening to them, I got the impression that some of them felt this particular course was a bit of a waste of time. In my case, I was having problems not just with the language but also with the ideas. But I managed to get over all that and, in fact, the course has lived up to my original expectations, so I feel all the hard work's been worth it. I mean, we've got an exam next week, which I expected to feel a bit anxious about, but in fact I'm feeling fine about it.

Presenter: Two. You hear a student complaining about a problem she has had.

Mike: Oh, Helena! What's up?

Helena: Do you know what just happened? I was given an essay to write at the beginning of the month and I spent lots of time researching it. Anyway, Valerie – you know her – she came round to my place and while she was there she must have copied all my notes! All my research! I only found out in my tutorial just now when the tutor handed my essay back to me. He said he couldn't mark it because my essay repeated all the same key points that Valerie had made in hers. I'm absolutely furious, and she's going to get away with it, too!

Presenter: Three. You hear a student at a language school in Japan.

Boy: So, what are you doing here in Japan?

Girl: I'm learning Japanese at a language school. I go to classes for just two hours a day, which is good because I learn Japanese from Japanese teachers, and then I'm free to practise it during the rest of the day.

Boy: That sounds a good idea.

Girl: It is. You see, it's not all academic work. They also organise lots of other things for us learners to take part in after school. There are clubs we can join if we're interested, and they really are the best part. For example, I'm also doing a karate course taught in Japanese, which is great fun. I'm learning something completely different in the language I'm studying and I'm getting to know lots of local people.

Boy: Fantastic!

Girl: Yes, if you speak a bit of the language, it's much easier to make friends.

Presenter: Four. You hear an interview with a student who is thinking of studying abroad.

Sandra: I'm not sure whether I'll study abroad. I've been thinking of going to an Italian university and studying international business for a year – that's if I get through the admission process. The trouble is partly that if I went, it might make it more difficult for me to get a good pass in my exams back home. On the other hand, I think the opportunity to live abroad for a year would be extremely educational, because I'd learn about the Italian way of life and way of thinking. Trouble is, I'd have to leave all my friends and probably live on my own, and I'm not sure if I'm ready for that.